CUCKFIELD REMEMBERED

Cuckfield Remembered

A catalogue record of this book is available from the British Library

To order copies of this book please visit: www.ypd-books.com

ISBN: 978-0-9558911-0-6

Printed and distributed by:
York Publishing Services Ltd
64 Hallfield Road,
Layerthorpe,
York YO31 7ZQ
www.yps-publishing.co.uk

Published by:
Woodlands Publishing
15 Woodlands Drive,
Yarm,
North Yorkshire TS15 9NU
UK

info@woodlandspublishing.co.uk
www.woodlandspublishing.co.uk

First Edition: September 2007
Second Edition: 2008

CUCKFIELD REMEMBERED

by

Shirley Bond

'CUCKFIELD REMEMBERED'
IS
DEDICATED TO THE MEN
OF
CUCKFIELD
WHO GAVE THEIR LIVES
IN WORLD WAR I

CONTENTS

ACKNOWLEDGEMENTS

I am indebted to the following for their help, and where necessary, their permission to copy or quote from sources under their control.

The Reverend Nicholas Wetherall, the present Vicar of Holy Trinity Church, Cuckfield

Grahame Campbell, the present Editor of The Mid-Sussex Times Newspaper

The Commonwealth War Graves Commission

www.ancestry.co.uk website for census information

Frances Stenlake, former curator of Cuckfield Museum

Dr Brian Cutler, former Chairman of the Sussex Family History Group

It was the idea of Richard Bevan of 'Horsegate', Cuckfield to collect photographs of each soldier from the town who died during the war. Mr Bevan sadly died in 1918 before the collection was complete, but the relatives of seventy three of the eighty one soldiers who died had already sent him photographs. These were framed and hung in the Queen's Hall as Richard Bevan had planned. The originals are now preserved in the museum, and copies are in an album in the museum for all to see.

INTRODUCTION

Cuckfield is a small town in the Weald of Sussex, about thirty eight miles south of London and about twelve miles inland from the seaside resort of Brighton. Although a town, having been granted a Market Charter by King Charles 11 in 1670, it still retains its village-like rural character. It has a very interesting history dating back to Norman times and the name is said to derive from the Norman word kukefelde, meaning a clearing full of cuckoos, hence the illustration of a cuckoo on the town signpost.

It is difficult to imagine that the inhabitants of this small quiet town suffered such heart ache and sorrow during the First World War. Yet from this small area, eighty one soldiers, plus men from other services, gave their lives for their country at that time. Many men who returned from the war scenes were severely wounded and unable to resume their previous occupations.

I decided that a written history of each man from Cuckfield who died, would be a fitting memorial to his memory. I also considered that an account of many of the events which took place in Cuckfield during the war years would be of interest to their descendants, to those who once resided in the town and the more recent inhabitants.

Frances Stenlake, who was curator of the Cuckfield Museum, showed me photographs of some of the soldiers from Cuckfield who gave their lives, and the inclusion of these has added further interest to my research.

The names and year of death of those who gave their lives are listed on three memorials around the town, but no further information on the men is available from these sources. Who they were, their ages, their families, where they lived and went to school, the part they played in the social life of the town, where they worked, where they served during the war, how they were wounded or killed and where they were buried abroad or remembered on a foreign memorial, has never previously been fully researched, recorded, and gathered together in one place.

Articles and letters, written by the men and sent from the war scenes to the local newspaper, or to the families, include graphic accounts of conditions in war areas, in the trenches, the hospitals and so on. All make fascinating reading, so have been included along with the letters sent by the soldiers' military superiors or chaplains to the parents of each soldier killed. Each explains just how he died, where, and who was with him. These letters often explained the act of bravery in which the man was involved.

Sadly, most of those who lost their lives are buried in graves or remembered on memorials around the world. For those relatives or friends who may wish to visit these sites, reference details are given.

During the war, and when Peace was declared, the Churches played a very important role in the life of the community. Details of the many Church Services and celebrations are included.

Those left at home, especially the women, played a valuable part in the war effort. They are included in the long list of awards and promotions received by the residents of Cuckfield of whom the town should be proud.

There was of course great rejoicing when Peace was declared and the men returned home to attend the special events and welcome home parties described.

I hope this book will give an interesting glimpse into the lives of the families of Cuckfield during, and shortly after, the First World War, and that many family historians will be able to connect with the numerous names and places mentioned. I also hope that it will go some way towards ensuring that the men who gave their lives will never be forgotten.

Every attempt has been made to ensure that the information in this book is accurate. However, it must be realised that much of the information has been obtained from very old documents which have aged over time making them difficult to read, and some transcriptions from other documents such as the censuses may contain flaws from source. Quotations from newspapers, letters and Parish Magazines have not been altered and the photographs have not been enhanced.

If anyone has any further information which could be incorporated into further editions of this book I would be very pleased to hear from them. I may be contacted directly by email at info@woodlandspublishing.co.uk

CHAPTER 1

1914

WAR IS DECLARED

Mid-Sussex Times - Tuesday 4th August 1914

ENGLAND DECLARED WAR AGAINST GERMANY

WAR : EUROPE IN ARMS !

OUR FLEET MOBILISED AND OUR ARMY MOBILISING

ARMY RESERVES AND TERRITORIALS TO BE CALLED UP

WILL ENGLAND FIGHT?

Such a war as has never been known in history threatens to overwhelm the world. In fact, the conflict has begun, and death, devastation and ruin must follow in its train. What the outcome will be is beyond the range of human vision, but Europe is up in arms, nations are thirsting for and shedding each others' blood, prospect of awful carnage and calamitous consequences of several great powers endeavouring to wipe each other out by such death-dealing machines and devices as modern science and ingenuity have conceived is indeed staggering and appalling.

Yet we are proud to find that of all the nations concerned, England stands out pre-eminently the calmest and the most self possessed of the lot. It is not that we do not realise the immense gravity of the issues involved. We face it without demonstrative jingoism, but with teeth and purpose set, as a people with great traditions and widespread Imperial responsibilities. So far we have not been drawn into the vortex of battle, and our statesmen and our King have striven their utmost to maintain peace right to the very last.

We have much to lose and little, if anything to gain by the war, but if we have to enter into it in support of our allies, to maintain the balance of power in Europe, or for the protection of our vast interests we must once more show 'what Englishmen can do'.

We have confidence in our men and in our ships; we have the assurance of ready assistance from our Colonies, if necessary; we have sunk all our party and petty differences at home, and we present to the world a united front.

In Mid-Sussex and other churches and chapels on Sunday the war was mentioned in sermons and prayers. The local railway lines are being carefully guarded, particularly at tunnels, bridges and viaducts, by railway men and policemen, and yesterday Boy Scouts were called out for the purpose. It was a unique experience for the lads, who were very keen and alert. Signals by whistles had been arranged. Today the Military are guarding the railway. Though soldiers and sailors in uniform, on leave, are generally very conspicuous in the neighbourhood at holiday times, hardly one was to be seen here yesterday.

ROLL OF HONOUR

As soon as war was declared, a Roll of Honour was set up by the Vicar, the Reverend R. Fisher, in the porch of Holy Trinity Church, Cuckfield to list the local men who were already on active service. It reads:

The list of Cuckfield men who by August 1914 were on active service is given below.

ROYAL NAVY

Albert Barrow	H.M.S. Sutley
William Barrow	H.M.S. Southampton
Arthur Burgess	H.M.S. Southampton
Arthur Douglas	H.M.S. Iron Duke
H. Clarke	H.M.S. Falcon
F. Clarke	H.M.S. Irresistible
James Gordon	H.M.S Glory
William Brookshaw	H.M.S. Iron Duke
William Edward Hillman	H.M.S. Myrmidon
Albert Morgan	Torpedo Boat Zulu
Harry Smith	H.M.S. Glory
Samuel Whapham	Torpedo Boat Sparrow
Charles Webber	Royal Navy Reserve
Perry James Wood	H.M.S. Venus

ARMY - REGULAR FORCES

Cecil Bowell	Royal Engineers
Walter Barrow	Royal Engineers
A.E.Brookshaw	Yorkshire Garrison Artillery
Alfred Richard Burness	Seaforth Highlanders
Peter Gander	Royal Sussex
William Hards	Royal Horse Artillery
Frank Henley	9th Lancers
Eric James Hillman	19th Hussars
William Hornsby	Royal Field Artillery
Albert Jennings	Royal Sussex
A.A.Knight	1st Sussex
Herbert Knight	2nd Sussex
Charles Knight	2nd Sussex
Tom Mitchell	Coldstream Guards
Harry Mitchell	Royal Sussex
Leonard Palmer	Royal Field Artilery
Percy Lester Reid (Captain)	Irish Guards
Montagu Turner (Lieutenant)	Royal Sussex
Horace Upton	3rd Kings Royal Rifles
Robert Whapham	Highland Light Infantry
Edward Williams	Royal Sussex
Paynton Latham	

TERRITORIAL FORCE
'A' Company, 4th Battalion, Royal Sussex Regiment

Fred Anscombe
Frederick George Beard
George Bennett
Frank Berry
Norman Bowell
Sydney Burt
Frank Gander
Robert Gibson
Ernest Knight

Frank Leney
Wilfred Mitchell
Joseph Jenner
W. Norris
George Rapley (Colour Sergeant)
Stuart K. Reid (Lieutenant)
Henry Upton
James G. Webber
Richard Worsley (Lieutenant)
William Henry Burtenshaw
Joseph Markwick

A CALL TO ARMS !!
KITCHENER'S ARMY.
Your King and Country need you urgently.
ANOTHER NEW REGULAR BATTALION
is being added to your County Regiment,
CALLED THE
10TH SPECIAL SERVICE
BATTALION
ROYAL SUSSEX REGIMENT.
It is being raised at Dover, where the 3rd Battalion is now stationed.
Will you Come Forward
We are confident you will help to uphold
the honor of the County of Sussex.
Men between ages of 19 & 35 can enlist for 3 years or duration of war.
Men must be medically fit: be 5ft. 5in. high and upwards; have chest measurement of 34¼ inches.
Ex N.C. Officers ages up to 45; Specially Selected up to 50 years.
Married men or Widowers with children will be accepted, and will
draw separation allowances.
APPLY AT ONCE TO THE NEAREST RECRUITING OFFICE.
Owners of cars will greatly assist by driving intending recruits direct to the nearest recruiting office or to the Barracks at Chichester.
RECRUITING OFFICES: God Save the King.

CHICHESTER—The Barracks.	HAYWARDS HEATH—Drill Hall.	NEWHAVEN—The Fort.
HORSHAM—Park St., opposite Drill Hall.	HURSTPIERPOINT—Drill Hall.	BRIGHTON—Town Hall, and 8, Coombe
WORTHING—Bank Buildings.	BEXHILL—Drill Hall.	Terrace, Lewes Road.
UCKFIELD—Drill Hall.	BATTLE—Drill Hall.	HOVE—20 Church Road.
		HASTINGS

Mid-Sussex Times - 8th September 1914

THE COUNTRY'S CALL

GOOD RESPONSE AT CUCKFIELD
FIGHTING THE STRONGEST MILITARY POWER
IN THE WORLD

At the suggestion of Colonel Stephenson R. Clarke. C.B., J.P., a meeting was held at the Queen's Hall, Cuckfield on Friday night, for the purpose of gathering in recruits for Lord Kitchener's Army. The spade work in connection with the meeting was evidently thoroughly done, for there was a very large attendance of persons in all stations of life, and there was no lack of enthusiasm.

The Chair was occupied by Colonel S. R. Clarke and he was supported by the Rev. Robert Fisher, Major Kenney-Herbert, Major Talbot, Mr R. A. Bevan, J.P., Mr B. Y. Bevan, J.P., Mr A. Beeching J.P., Mr W. Stevens, J.P., Mr A. V. Courage and Mr C. H. Waugh.

In his introductory remarks the Chairman said that during the previous weeks he had had one or two casual conversations with friends as to the advisability of holding a meeting at Cuckfield to promote recruiting.

On the previous Saturday some of his family went to a meeting at Cowfold, and they told him there was a splendid response to the appeal for recruits. Forty five men came forward and offered their services to their country, and seventeen more, he believed, had since enrolled themselves as recruits in Lord Kitchener's Army.

In view of that he felt a meeting at Cuckfield should be held without delay. He greatly appreciated the large number of Cuckfield lads who had joined the Army at this momentous crisis in England's history. We were fighting the strongest military power in the world, but we were fighting in a good and righteous cause and he felt that a further opportunity should be given to Cuckfield lads, if any remained of a military age, to show their true mettle and come forward and join the Army.

It was wonderful the number of men coming forward and enlisting voluntarily. When they considered that practically every nation except the Anglo-Saxon speaking nations had adopted conscription, it was a proud thing that we as Englishmen had so far managed to defend our country and take care of ourselves without conscription.

The war had been foreseen by farsighted men for some years. Their good neighbour, the late Captain Sergison, frequently spoke to him as to the inevitable character of the war and what a dreadful affair it would be. At that time Captain Sergison was advocating that we should have national service, and perhaps if we had had national service we should never have had this war. But we had got to face it, and to ask all who were of military age to come forward for service. He did not think there were any 'doubting Thomasses' at Cuckfield, but he assured all men joining that they would be well trained before being sent on active service. Lord Kitchener was not the man to risk making a failure of the job by sending out inefficient men. A man could be made a very useful infantryman in six months if he put his heart into his work. He advised young soldiers to become good shots - the rifle was a man's best friend in action - also to see that they got a good fitting pair of boots - very useful things in a campaign.

Major Kenny-Herbert was the next speaker, and made as favourable an impression as he did at Haywards Heath and Lindfield. He pointed out that about a month ago Lord Kitchener took charge of the War Office and the first thing he did was to ask the nation for 500,000 recruits. Up to yesterday he had barely received 200,000 ! And yet Great Britain had eight million men capable of bearing arms. The voluntary service system was being weighed in the balance. Was it going to be found wanting? Englishmen had the greatest confidence in Lord Kitchener. His administrative abilities could not be excelled. The way to show their appreciation of him, and that they were conscious of the necessities of Great Britain today, was to give him the 500,000 men he asked for. That was the reason for holding these recruiting meetings, and the country should not rest until Lord Kitchener obtained the number of men he required. There were those who said that the Englishman of today was not as good as the Englishman of the past; that he was a slacker, liked comfort and a steady job and was not prepared for discomforts. But he (the speaker) held the opinion that the Englishman of today was as good as his father or grandfather. Look what their tiny army had done in France. It had held its own and had only given ground as a strategical necessity and advantage. He was afraid there were many who did not realise how serious the war was and was going to be to all of them. No matter what their rank or profession might be, they would all suffer - and suffer long after the war had finished. God help England if Prussia were victorious! Soldiering was a profession to be studied and worked at. A great deal had to be borne and learned before a man was fit to be a soldier. They had a choice Army which could face any foe, but it was not an army from a European point of view. Were it not for their Navy they would have no value in the Councils of Europe. Had the country listened to Lord Roberts it was questionable whether the war would have taken place. Owing to their internal dissensions, the German Emperor no doubt thought England would not enter the conflict. He was mistaken. The war was a just one. They were fighting as Britain always had done - for religious and individual liberty.

Having referred to the atrocities which the German Army had been guilty of, the speaker asked how Englishmen would like to be under the heels of such a people? Were they going to allow themselves to be crushed by German autocracy, or would they spread the love of liberty which they possessed to the rest of Europe? The war would not be carried on to a successful finish unless every British man threw his heart and soul into it. The War Office was working '25 hours to the 24' and doing its very utmost to fit England to carry on the war. Lord Kitchener said it might last three years. They all hoped it wouldn't. Owing to teeth or some other cause men might be rejected today, but the speaker believed in six months time the men who were now rebuffed would have their chance for service. In closing, Major Kenny-Herbert made a stirring appeal for recruits and subsequently it was ascertained that 26 came forward. The Rev. R. Fisher proposed a vote of thanks to Major Kenny-Herbert for a speech which had done them all good to listen to and to Colonel S. R. Clarke for having got the meeting up. They were all very glad to see so many volunteering for service. It showed that Cuckfield was not going to be behind in doing its duty for the welfare of the nation.

There were a number of others belonging to Cuckfield, apart from those who had come forward that evening, who had volunteered for service. The country was face to face with a great big job, and much patience was required. If England put its whole shoulder to the wheel, and the whole strength of the manhood of England came forward to do its duty, we should win in the long run. The war might last a very long time. But no matter how long it lasted, they would never give up, they would go through to the very end, putting their trust in God, Who worked all things together for good.

The young men who went from Cuckfield to serve their country looked to those who remained behind to care for their dependents. And he felt sure that Cuckfield would do so. Daily at twelve o'clock the church bell rang, and those who heard it should pause for a moment and say a prayer on behalf of our soldiers and sailors. The parish was a wide one, and some might not hear the bell. But they had watches and clocks, and he knew the hour that the bell rang, and he asked them all to let a prayer go like an arrow from their hearts to the throne of God Let them put their trust in Him, hoping that in His own good time He would give them a true, lasting and honourable peace.

Mr Beeching in seconding the proposition, said it behoved them all to try and do what they could for their young men who answered their country's call and also their dependents. He himself meant to do all he could to help them.

The vote of thanks was carried with acclamation, and the meeting was brought to a close with the National Anthem. The recruits sworn in were kindly entertained to supper at the King's Head Hotel by Colonel Clarke.

YOU ARE WANTED

By your Chums in the Trenches, to fill the gaps in the ranks of the

4th BATT. ROYAL SUSSEX REGT.

Read this Extract from a letter written by Major BEALE, who is with the 4th Royal Sussex in Gallipoli :—

"It is more and more impressed on me here that one battalion at home is not enough to keep one battalion on this sort of service up to strength unless the home unit is constantly and steadily filled up with men as the drafts are sent. Our real need, therefore, is for more men, and it will be the same for some time to come. I am quite sure that the news that the battalion had been in action brought some recruits. Please try to make East Grinstead undertsand that the news of more recruits will be the signal for the battalion to be sent into action again. In our attack the men were splendid, a fact which, I am glad to say, is likely to be recognised in a public way soon. On two occasions parties of the enemy have tried to find our men asleep in the trenches, and both attacks were handsomely repulsed. In fact, on the last occasion we not only had dead Turks to show, but a patrol followed them up and brought in some more rifles and ammunition. The casualties, I am glad to say, have not been severe, considering the conditions of the fighting, but the wastage generally has been rather heavy and should be replaced without delay."

JOIN AT ONCE !

Printed, by permission of the Censor, by Henry W. Cullen, East Grinstead.

The 2/8th Battalion of the Post Office Rifles trained at Cuckfield before leaving for France in 1917

Don't be Alarmed,
the Post Office Rifles
are on guard at Cuckfield.

Cuckfield Parish Magazine - December 1914

POST OFFICE RIFLES

The 8th (Reserve) Battalion of the City of London Regiment, called the P.O.Rifles, is quartered amongst us and Cuckfield has maintained its character for hospitality. The Church Room, next to the Clergy House, not being taken for billeting, has been thrown open as a reading and writing room for the troops. Newspapers and stationery are provided and the use of the room has been much appreciated. The members of the Church of England Men's Society have undertaken the charge of the room. Other rooms also have been kindly offered and are in use.

We are glad that the Rev. E.H. Pearce, Canon of Westminster, has come to act as their Chaplain. Two houses have been taken as Clubs - the one 'Landcroft', in Broad Street, the other in High Street, which has been placed under the charge of Mr Pulley, of the Y.M.C.A. Both Clubs are much appreciated.

MESSAGE FROM THE KING.

BUCKINGHAM PALACE.

You are leaving home to fight for the safety and honour of my Empire.

Belgium, whose country we are pledged to defend, has been attacked and France is about to be invaded by the same powerful foe.

I have implicit confidence in you my soldiers. Duty is your watchword, and I know your duty will be nobly done.

I shall follow your every movement with deepest interest and mark with eager satisfaction your daily progress; indeed your welfare will never be absent from my thoughts.

I pray God to bless you and guard you and bring you back victorious.

GEORGE, R.I.

9th August, 1914.

CHAPTER 2

1915

THE WAR CONTINUES

THE FIRST ANNIVERSARY OF THE DECLARATION OF WAR

Intercession services at Cuckfield Parish Church on Wednesday were largely attended by parishioners, many of whom have relatives fighting for their country, whilst a few in the congregations wearing black denoted that their sons or brothers had made the supreme sacrifice.

The service in the evening enabled many to be present who could not attend the earlier ones, and at this time the Vicar (The Rev. C. W. G. Wilson) gave a short address. The choir was present, and the hymns sung were 'God moves in a mysterious way', 'O God of Love', 'O King of Peace' and the supplication for absent friends 'Holy Father in Thy mercy'. Psalms 46, 'God is our Hope and Strength', and 90, 'Lord Thou hast been our refuge', were chanted, and the latter part of the service took an appointed form of intercession. The Vicar took his text from 1st Kings viii, 44 and 45, 'If Thy people go out to battle against their enemy, whithersoever Thou shalt send them, and shall pray unto the Lord toward the city which Thou has chosen, and toward the house that I have built for Thy name: then hear Thou in heaven their prayer and their supplication, and maintain their cause'.

Those, said the preacher, were noble and remarkable words which formed the prayer of Solomon at the dedication of the Temple, that in time of war as in time of peace, in time of adversity as in time of prosperity, God would be mindful of His people who were mindful of Him, that when they cried He would hear, and hearing He would help.

A RENEWED CALL

On that day, the anniversary of the declaration of war, they were turning to God, instinctively asking Him to help them in their trouble and time of need. In looking back on the last twelve months they recalled the thrill which went through the country when they were aroused to the realisation that they were in danger of war. They remembered how the nation faced the crisis and bore itself bravely, how the manhood of the nation answered to the call, and how the country recognised in the war a distinct call to faith, earnestness and prayer. Reference was made to the great day of intercession last August and repeated on the first Sunday of the New Year. They had passed through a very trying period, and they commenced the second year of this terrible war with renewed enthusiasm, renewed determination and renewed hope. On that day there was a renewed call to dedicate themselves to the service of God and to promote the cause of righteousness, justice and truth for which they and their Allies were fighting in the titanic struggle which had been forced upon them. The end to which they looked forward was the destruction of that great Germanic military power, and they would carry the struggle through to a successful conclusion.

At the close of the service a verse of the National Anthem was sung.

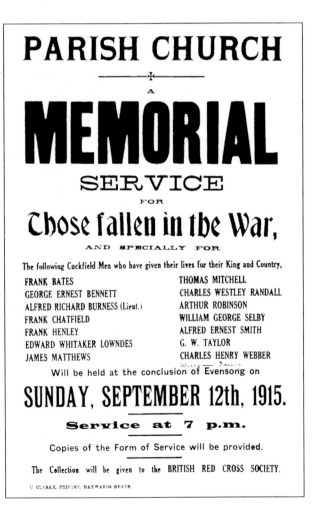

PARISH CHURCH

A

MEMORIAL

SERVICE

FOR

Those fallen in the War,

AND SPECIALLY FOR

The following Cuckfield Men who have given their lives for their King and Country,

FRANK BATES	THOMAS MITCHELL
GEORGE ERNEST BENNETT	CHARLES WESTLEY RANDALL
ALFRED RICHARD BURNESS (Lieut.)	ARTHUR ROBINSON
FRANK CHATFIELD	WILLIAM GEORGE SELBY
FRANK HENLEY	ALFRED ERNEST SMITH
EDWARD WHITAKER LOWNDES	G. W. TAYLOR
JAMES MATTHEWS	CHARLES HENRY WEBBER

Will be held at the conclusion of Evensong on

SUNDAY, SEPTEMBER 12th, 1915.

Service at 7 p.m.

Copies of the Form of Service will be provided.

The Collection will be given to the BRITISH RED CROSS SOCIETY.

C. CLARKE, PRINTER, HAYWARDS HEATH

Mid-Sussex Times - 14th September 1915

MEMORIAL SERVICE FOR CUCKFIELD'S HEROES

A Tribute to the Gallant Dead - The Vicar's address

A memorial service is always impressive to the mind, even though one may not be immediately interested in the person or persons so commemorated. But in these days of war, when each week brings its local casualties, one especially likes to attend at church and remember in the presence of God, those who have given themselves - their greatest gift - for the sake of all that is good and true. Be they known or unknown, it is the last service we can do for them when their souls have returned to the God who gave them.

Fifteen Cuckfieldians have already made the supreme sacrifice, and in their memory a service was held on Sunday evening at the Parish Church. The bells were muffled for the occasion, and rang out in quiet melody. Some time before seven o'clock and right up till the service actually began, a steady stream of the general public poured into the sacred edifice, Mr. T. E. P. Attewell playing soft music on the organ meanwhile. In seats immediately facing the pulpit were accommodated the Staplefield Company of the Volunteer Training Corps, under the command of Major J. J. Lister J. P. the local men being led by Platoon Commander C. H. Waugh. Seats were also reserved for members of the bereaved families.

The service began with the hymn, 'Brief Life is Here Our Portion'.

The choristers and the Vicar came from the tower vestry preceded by the processional cross born by Mr. W. Herrington, immediately followed by a large Union Jack, surmounted by a crepe knot, carried by one of the choir boys. The sight of the great flag, preceded by the silver cross, held on the steps of the violet-frontalled altar, brought home the truth that symbolism is indeed a very real help in things spiritual, and the words sung brought hope in the great crisis.

Evensong was based on a note of assurance. Special lessons were read by Mr. B. Y. Bevan, J.P. who wore the V.T.C.uniform. The selected passages were 1.Kings viii, 54-62 (Solomon's prayer at the dedication of the Temple) and 1. Corinthians xv., from the 50th verse (the conclusion of the lessons in the Burial Office).

At the end of the second lesson began the memorial service, prepared by the Bishop of Stepney. The Vicar of Cuckfield (the Rev. C. W. G. Wilson) wearing a violet stole, addressed to the chancel step, accompanied by the flag bearer, and read the names of Cuckfieldians who have given their lives, adding the name of one who, though not born in the parish, was well known to many - Lewis Frederick Bartlett, of the London Rifle Brigade - and also speaking of the circumstances under which notice had been received that morning of the death of Private William Henry Dancy.

The Vicar then recited the opening sentence of the Burial Service, and these were succeeded by Psalms 23 ('The Lord is my Shepherd') and 46 ('God is our hope and strength') The lesson, also read by the Vicar from the chancel step, was that magnificent passage of consolation, Revelation xxi, 1-5.

The Nunc Dimittis was sung, and Evensong continued to the third collect, at which point was sung the hymn, 'O God of love, O King of peace'. Whilst this was in progress the Vicar went into the pulpit. His sermon was based on the text from St John xv. 13 ('Greater Love hath no man than this, that a man lay down his life for his friends'). It was prefaced by a bidding prayer, in which the congregation was exhorted to pray 'for God's help and guidance in this time of trouble and particularly those who have gone from Cuckfield, for whom we are specially bound to pray'. One looked with pride upon that long Cuckfield Roll of Honour and saw how the parish, with its traditions of patriotism, had responded to the call.

Never had England called upon her sons and called in vain. Throughout the ages, men had been ready to give up the comforts and pleasures of home; ready even to sacrifice their lives for the sake of the Motherland which gave them birth.

Never before in history had such a demand been made upon the manhood of England as had been made since that day in August 1914, when England declared war on Germany; never before had war been waged with such ferocity; never before had the inventions of man's brain been used so entirely for the destruction - sometimes in most terrible and cruel forms - of human life.

The offertory hymn was Bishop Bickersteth's well known 'Peace, perfect peace'. The offertory that night, Mr Wilson said, would be devoted to the funds of the British Red Cross Society which was doing such a splendid service in the present war, and the expenditure of which was estimated at £3,000 per day, or £2.00 a minute.

The Vicar pronounced the Blessing, and then from the organ sounded forth the strains of the Dead March in Saul, with its triumphant crashes succeeding mournful airs. When the last note had died away there was a silence, broken by the notes of the Last Post, sounded by ex-Sergeant Bugler Hounsell outside the open west door, the national flag being dipped in salute.

Thus ended one of the most solemn services ever held in Cuckfield Parish Church.

CUCKFIELD PARISH CHURCH.

A

MEMORIAL

SERVICE

FOR

Those fallen in the War,

AND SPECIALLY FOR

The following Cuckfield Men who have recently given their lives for their King and Country,

WILLIAM BOWLEY,
HARRY SMITH,
NATHAN UPTON,
EDWARD WILLIAMS,

Will be held at Evensong on

SUNDAY, NOVEMBER 7th, 1915.

Service at 7 p.m.

Copies of the Form of Service will be provided.

The Collection will be given to the BRITISH RED SOCIETY Local Branch.

Shirley Bond

Mid-Sussex Times - 9th November 1915

OUR FALLEN SOLDIERS
MEMORIAL SERVICE AT CUCKFIELD

Cuckfield Parish Church was crowded on Sunday night on the occasion of a memorial service for those who have fallen in the war, and specially for the four Cuckfield men who have recently given their lives for their King and Country: –

Able-Seaman Harry Smith
Private William Bowley
Private Nathan Upton
Private Edward Williams

It was the second memorial service held by the newly appointed vicar, the first for 15 men having been held on September 12th.

Previous to the service a muffled peal was rung on the church bells, a striking effect being produced by the tenor being half muffled, and so striking clear every alternate round.

The service, which was conducted by the vicar (the Rev. C.W.G Wilson) commenced with a processional hymn, 'Through the night of Doubt and Sorrow'.

At the head of the procession the silver cross (one of the memorials of the late revered vicar, Canon Cooper), was carried by Mr W. Herrington and that was followed by a large Union Jack draped in crepe, which was carried by E. Mays the senior choir boy.

Among the congregation were the widow and daughter of Mr Harry Smith, Mr and Mrs Bowley, Mr Upton and Mr and Mrs Williams and other friends of the deceased soldiers. There was also a strong detachment of the V.T.C. under the command of Major J. J. Lister, J.P and Platoon Commander Darroch, and a number of wounded soldiers from the local Red Cross Hospital.

The service was the usual evensong, and it was noticed that the Psalm and the Lessons were particularly appropriate to the occasion, the latter being read by Major Lister. At the close of the second lesson the vicar came to the chancel step accompanied by the standard bearer with the flag and made a solemn commemoration of the dead soldiers, which was followed by a very impressive rendering of the requiescant, 'Father, we bring our dead to Thee'.

The memorial service then proceeded according to the set form and special prayers of thanksgiving, commendation of the fallen, prayers also for the comfort of friends of the fallen, and for the strengthening of their comrades.

In his sermon the Vicar spoke of the mingled feelings of pride and sorrow with which they were animated. They were proud of the great empire of which they were citizens, of their country, and of their county, fair 'Sussex by the Sea'. They were proud of the spirit of their countrymen, their restraint and dignity, the absence of arrogant boasting and bitter clamour, the generous out pouring of money from all classes to alleviate the sufferings of the wounded and sick and the need and distress not only in our own country, but in Belgium, Serbia and Poland. They were proud of the willingness to serve, and if necessary to lay down their lives, shown by our fellow countrymen and fellow citizens throughout the Empire. They were proud of the magnificent courage and splendid endurance shown by our forces on the sea and on land and in the air. Then there came the feeling of intense sadness. The Empire was in mourning for the gallant dead. As in their procession, the Cross of Christ, the symbol of their salvation, had been borne, it had been followed by the flag, the symbol of their Empire, bearing the signs of grief.

The preacher spoke of the long casualty lists which are daily being published, and made special reference to the losses of Cuckfield, with personal details of the four men whom they were specially remembering. We owe it to their memory that whatever the cost may be, whatever the suffering and the sorrow may be, that we shall carry on the war and bring it to a successful conclusion, to a victorious peace, the terms of which shall make another such war impossible, so that they shall not have given their lives in vain. We owe it to their memory that the call to a nobler life which comes from their graves shall not be unheeded. He spoke of the way in which England had been drifting to degeneracy and of some of the changes which would take place after the war, but he pointed out that there is one change which must begin now - a moral and spiritual uplifting of our country, so that when our men, who have been solemnised and led to higher things by the terrible sights and lessons of the war, return home again they may come to a regenerate England, to a nation nobler, purer, more spiritual, closer to God than it had been before.

After the address, the Vicar went to the fald stool and offered special intercession for the sailors and soldiers of the King, for the wounded and the sick, for those who are prisoners in the hands of the enemy, specially mentioning Thomas Batchelor and Fred Simmonds and finally for victory and peace.

The hymn 'Abide with Me' was then sung and a collection was made for the Red Cross Society, the proceeds of which amounted to £5.8s.1d.

After the blessing the National Anthem was sung in full and the congregation remained standing while Mr T. E. P.Attewell, the organist, played the Dead March in 'Saul'. Then out of the darkness came the sounds of the 'Last Post', sounded by ex-Bugler-Sergeant F.Hounsell, and the flag was dipped in salute and a most impressive service came to an end.

CHAPTER 3

1916

SPECIAL DAY OF INTERCESSION

A notice issued by the Archbishops of Canterbury and York asks that -

The first Sunday in the New Year, January 2nd, is to be set apart in our Churches and all Places of Worship throughout the Empire for Solemn Intercession to Almighty God, and for thankful recognition of the devotion which has been forthcoming in the manhood and womanhood of our country. With a view to a really thoughtful use of so solemn an occasion it is proposed that the observance shall begin on the two preceding days - that Friday, December 31st, the closing day of the year, shall be kept as a day of Self Denial and Prayer and also of sorrow for all our sins and shortcomings as a people, and that on Saturday there shall be Special Services of Preparation for the Holy Communion and other Services of the Sunday.

We earnestly hope that every parishioner will, without fail, attend some of the Services specially arranged. A list of the services to be held at the Parish Church on Friday a chain of intercession from 8.00 a.m. to 8.p.m. each link to be of 15 minutes duration, and we shall be glad to receive the names of those who are willing to take part in this work. The Special Services specified above were held at the Parish church and at the Mission Churches.

CUCKFIELD PARISH CHURCH.

A

MEMORIAL

SERVICE

FOR

Those fallen in the War,

AND SPECIALLY FOR

The following Cuckfield Men who have recently given their lives for their
King and Country,

JESSE GANDER, *Thos: Charles Bourne*
DAVID H. C. MONRO (LIEUT.),
STANLEY QUAIFE (SERGT.),
G. ERIC STEVENS, *Cyril Ralph Smith*
HORACE W. UPTON,
GEORGE W. VICKERS,

Will be held at Morning Prayer

ON SUNDAY, MAY 28th, 1916.

Service at 11 a.m.

Copies of the Form of Service will be provided.

The Collection will be given to the BRITISH RED CROSS SOCIETY.

C. Clarke, Printer, &c., Haywards Heath.

Mid-Sussex Times - 30th May 1916

CUCKFIELD'S SOLDIER SONS

MEMORIAL SERVICE FOR THOSE WHO HAVE PASSED TO THE GREAT BEYOND

After an interval of six months, a third memorial service for soldiers fallen in the war was held at Cuckfield Parish Church on Sunday morning, and the sacred edifice was crowded almost to overflowing by an interested and sympathetic congregation.

Previous to the service a muffled peal was rung on the bells. The service commenced with the impressive hymn, 'Brief life is here our portion', and was sung by the choir in procession. In front was Mr Herrington with the silver Processional cross. Next was the Union Jack, carried by E. Mays and the Cross of St George carried by E. Malins.

Each flag was surmounted by a large bow of crepe. Among the congregation were a number of relatives of the deceased soldiers and a large detachment of the V.T.C. under the command of Major J. J. Lister with Mr Darroch (second in command), Mr C.H. Waugh (Platoon Sergeant). There were also several of the wounded soldiers from the V.A.D. Red Cross Hospital at the Queen's Hall, they being accompanied by Mrs Bannister, the Matron.

CUCKFIELD PARISH CHURCH.

Second Anniversary of the Outbreak of the Great War.

4th AUGUST, 1916.

SPECIAL INTERCESSIONS on behalf of our Country and our Forces on Sea and on Land.

SERVICES :

8 a.m.—Celebration of Holy Communion with Memorial for those who have Fallen in the War.

10.30 a.m.—Morning Prayer and Litany.

Noon.—THE PEACE BELL. Prayers for Victory and Peace.

4.30 p.m.—Evensong and Intercession.

7.30 p.m.—Service of Intercession, with Sermon.

Preacher :

REV. C. E. WILSON, B.D.,

Vicar of St. Margaret's, Brighton.

The Offerings throughout the day will be given to St. Dunstan's Hostel for Blinded Sailors and Soldiers.

C. CLARKE, PRINTER, "MID SUSSEX TIMES" OFFICES, HAYWARDS HEATH.

Mid-Sussex Times - 8th August 1916

CUCKFIELD AND THE WAR

IMPRESSIVE SERVICES AT THE PARISH CHURCH

There have been many soul-stirring services held at Cuckfield Parish Church during the past twelve months, but we feel justified in saying that the service on Friday evening in connection with the second anniversary of the declaration of war against Germany was about the most impressive and will long linger in the memory.

The day's services began with a celebration of the Holy Communion at 8.00a.m. at which the vicar, the Rev. Cannon Wilson was the celebrant, assisted by the Rev J. H. Layton and there was a good number of communicants. At this service there was solemn memorial of those who have fallen, and the roll, containing 30 names of the Cuckfield men who have died for King and Country was read.

Morning Prayer, with a special Litany, was said at half-past ten.

At noon, when there was a large congregation, the Peace bell was rung and prayers were offered for victory and peace.

At 4.30p.m. there were Evensong and Intercessions.

A Special Service of Intercession followed at 7.30p.m. the congregation being very large and representing the whole of Cuckfield. The members of the Urban District Council were present with their Chairman, Mr Rubens Anscombe, J.P. and also the local Volunteers under Platoon Commander A. R. Darroch, Sergeant Major McKerno and Platoon Sergeants Adair and Leslie Askew. The Cuckfield Troop of Boy Scouts attended in a body in charge of Acting Scoutmaster A. T. Rapley, and a number of wounded soldiers from the V.A.D. Hospital at the Queen's Hall were also present.

The services commenced with the processional hymn, 'Onward Christian Soldiers', the procession being headed by the silver cross carried by Mr W. Herrington and the flag of St George and the Union Jack -

carried by H. Stoner and T. Malins respectively. As the procession marched up the aisle the tones of this grand old hymn grew stronger and stronger till the air vibrated from floor to roof with its soul-stirring harmonies.

The opening part of the service was taken by the Rev. J. H. Layton and this was followed by Psalm X1V1., chanted by the choir and a lesson read by Rev. C. L .Richards. Next came the hymn, 'To Thee, our God, we fly,' sung to an old melody arranged by Mr T. E. P Attewell, the organist and then followed the sermon, which was preached by the Rev C. E .Wilson, B.D., Vicar of St Margaret's Brighton.

It was an eloquent and powerful discourse, which deeply impressed all present. The preacher took as his text the words of the Prophet Jeremiah - 'Call unto Me and I will answer thee, and will shew thee great things and difficult which thou knowest not'.

At the close of the sermon the Vicar proceeded to the fald stool and said a special litany of intercession, which was joined in with great fervour by the congregation, and when finished, while all remained kneeling, the Choir sang with great feeling Edward German's intercessory prayer, 'Father Omnipotent! Protect us we Pray Thee'.

The concluding hymn was one of thanksgiving - 'Now thank we all our God'. After the Blessing, the Vicar mounted the pulpit and read Mr Asquith's resolution recording the inflexible determination of the people of England to contribute, under Divine Providence, to a victorious end the struggle in maintenance of those ideals of liberty and justice which are the common and sacred cause of the Allies. He then requested all those who endorsed that resolution to stand up. The whole congregation immediately rose, and the sight was thrilling.

With great heartiness was sung the National Anthem, and thus ended a service which will long be remembered for its deep sincerity of earnest purpose. As a concluding voluntary Mr Attewell played the Russian National Anthem.

The offerings during the day, which amounted to £15.12s. 5d. were given to St Dunstan's Hostel for Sailors and Soldiers Blinded in the War.

CUCKFIELD PARISH CHURCH.

✠

A

MEMORIAL

SERVICE

FOR

Those fallen in the War,

AND SPECIALLY FOR

The following Cuckfield Men who have recently given their lives
for their King and Country,

JOSEPH CARD,	GEORGE GIBSON,
ALBERT A. CROUCHER,	ARNOLD W. HUCKETT
CHARLES F. DOICK,	MARK LONGHURST, (Lieut.),

Will be held at Evensong on

SUNDAY, SEPT. 10th, 1916.

PREACHER:

REV. R. H. C. MERTENS, M.A.

Service at 6.30 p.m.

Copies of the Form of Service will be provided.

The Collection will be given to the Lord Kitchener National Memorial Fund for
Disabled Officers and Men of the Navy and Army.

Mid-Sussex Times - 12th September 1916

MEMORIAL SERVICE AT CUCKFIELD CHURCH

COMMEMORATION OF DEAD SOLDIERS

Seldom has the old Parish Church at Cuckfield been so crowded as on the occasion of the fourth memorial service held last Sunday evening.

The service was attended as before, by a strong detachment of the Volunteers under the command of Major J. J. Lister, V.D. with whom were Platoon Commander A. R. Darroch, Platoon Sergeant C. H. Waugh and Sergeant Major McKerno, and the Cuckfield Troop of Boy Scouts under the command of Acting Scoutmaster A. T. Rapley. Some of the wounded soldiers from the V.A.D. Hospital were also present.

The service commenced with the singing of the hymn, 'Brief life is here our Portion', the procession being headed by the silver cross, carried by Mr. W. Herrington and the National Flag and the Union Jack, which were draped in black and were carried by Tom and John Malins.

Evensong was taken by the Vicar, the Rev Canon Wilson, the special lessons being read by the Rev R. H. C. Mertens. After the second lesson the vicar proceeded to the chancel steps, attended by the two choristers bearing the flags and read the names of the dead soldiers from whom the memorial was made -

Joseph Card	Albert Arthur Croucher
Charles Doick	George Gibson
Arnold Walter Huckett	George Izzard
Mark Longhurst	

After this the 'Requiescant', 'Father we bring our dead to thee', was sung. Throughout the service there was a deep reverend sorrow for the bereaved, mingled with pride at the noble sacrifices made. The form of service used on previous occasions was adopted, the special lesson being read by Major Lister.

After the hymn, 'Jesus lives', the Vicar proceeded again to the chapel steps and said the Bidding Prayer, the Lord's Prayer being recited by the whole congregation.

THE SERMON

As was fitting, the sermon was preached by the Rev R. H. C Mertens, an old curate of Cuckfield who had been associated with every phase of Cuckfield life and knew personally several of the deceased soldiers commemorated. Taking as his text the words, 'The Master is Come and calleth for Thee', (St John X1., V.28) he preached a powerful and inspiring sermon, which was listened to with rapt attention by the large congregation. Beginning with an allegory of the garden of life, he showed how the Angel of Death as a gardener gathers the flowers. He referred to the men in the pride of health and strength and who are being taken - whether in the trenches, in 'No man's Land', in the air, and on the sea. He touched on the sentiment which was attached to such a service and the religious hope which was emphasised by it.

He spoke in moving terms of the patriotism and self sacrifice which had been shown. Mr Mertens made reference to the National Mission, and said that repentance was necessary in order that the nation should be ready to win the war. He concluded by reading a touching poem called, 'The Salute'. At the conclusion of the sermon the hymn, 'Abide with Me', was sung, during which a collection was made for the Lord Kitchener Memorial Fund, this amounting to £7.5s.10p and then, after a prayer for our sailors and soldiers now on service, and one for victory and peace, the Vicar pronounced the Blessing.

The congregation rose and sang the National Anthem in full and this was followed by the Dead march in 'Saul', played by Mr T. E. P. Attewell (the organist). The Last Post was sounded by an ex-bugler - Sergeant F. Hounsell, during which the two flags were lowered in salute, and so ended another memorial service, tense with religious fervour and hope through God for a better future.

As the congregation dispersed, Mr Attewell played Chopin's Funeral March.

Members of the Cuckfield and Bolney Branches of the Sussex County Association of Change Ringers rang a quarter peal of Grandsire Triples upon the muffled bells previous to the service, as a tribute to the memory of the deceased soldiers and more especially to one of their number - Private George Gibson, of the 8th Royal Sussex - whose father is also one of the oldest members of the local branch.

The striking of the bells was exceptionally good. The ringers were - F. R. Hounsell (treble) C. Stephenson (2) W. Wheeler (3) T. Gasson (4) A. Absalom (5) E. Davey (6) W. Vincent (conductor) (7) and G. Woods (tenor).

CHAPTER 4

1917

CUCKFIELD
PARISH CHURCH

✠

A

MEMORIAL

SERVICE

FOR

Those fallen in the War,

AND SPECIALLY FOR

The following Cuckfield Men who have given their lives for their King and Country,

HUBERT W. CARTNER, *Killed 4 Sept. 1916*

FREDERICK G. DIVALL,

ERNEST HENLEY, *Killed 25 Sept. 1916*

ALBERT KEEP, *Killed 23 July 1916*

EDWARD LYCETT LYON (MAJOR), *d. 17 Sept. 1916*

PERCIVAL E. MORFEE, *d. 25 Jan. 1917*

FRANK S. ROWLAND, *Killed 17 Jan. 1917*

Will be held on

SUNDAY, FEBRUARY 11th, 1917.

Service at 11 a.m.

Copies of the Form of Service will be provided.

Church Log Book - August 1917

The third Anniversary of the Outbreak of the Great War will again be observed by us as a day of special intercessions on behalf of our Country, and our Forces on Sea and on Land. This year it will fall on a Saturday, but we hope that in spite of that, very many will be able to come to one or more of the services. We wonder how far it would be possible to close all places of business at 7.00 p.m that evening?

The offerings throughout the day will be given to St Dunstan's Hostel for Blinded Sailors and Soldiers and the services will be as shown on the poster.

CUCKFIELD PARISH CHURCH.

Third Anniversary of the Outbreak of the Great War.

4th AUGUST, 1917.

SPECIAL INTERCESSIONS on behalf of our Country, and for our Forces on Sea, on Land, and in the Air.

SERVICES:

8 a.m.—Celebration of Holy Communion, with Memorial for those who have Fallen in the War.

10.30 a.m.—Morning Prayer and Intercessions.

Noon.—THE PEACE BELL. Special Prayers for Victory and Peace.

4.30 p.m.—Evensong and Intercessions.

7.30 p.m.—Service of Intercession, with Sermon.

Preacher:

REV. G. M. HUTTON, M.A.,

Vicar of St. Mary's, Brighton.

The Offerings throughout the day will be given to St. Dunstan's Hostel for Blinded Sailors and Soldiers.

CHARLES CLARKE (Haywards Heath) LTD.

CUCKFIELD PARISH CHURCH

✠

A

MEMORIAL

SERVICE

FOR

Those fallen in the War,

AND SPECIALLY FOR

The following Cuckfield Men who have recently given their lives for their King and Country:

JAMES ATTREE,	ARTHUR E. HOLDEN,
CECIL BOWELL,	W. HOLFORD MITCHELL (LIEUT)
ALBERT E. CHINNERY,	GEORGE MURRELL,
ELLIS ALBERT DANCY,	JAMES F. RIDLEY,
THOMAS HENLEY,	ALFRED U. PENNIFOLD,

Will be held at Evensong on

SUNDAY, SEPTEMBER 2nd, 1917.

PREACHER:

REV. R. H. C. MERTENS, M.A.

Service at 6.30 p.m.

Copies of the Form of Service will be provided.

The Collection will be given to the Church Army Fund for Recreation Huts and Tents for our Sailors and Soldiers.

CHAPTER 5

1918

NEW YEAR MESSAGE

THE NEW YEAR MESSAGE

The year which has just come to a close has been for many in Cuckfield a time of sorrow, and to all of us it has been a time of anxiety and strain. We have, however, much for which we may well be thankful, especially when we consider that we are nearly half way through the fourth year of this terrible war. We look forward to the brighter days which we hope are before us, and we must pray that before this year comes to an end we may have attained to that righteous and lasting peace which we all so much desire. It will be indeed a happy day for us all when the bells ring out for Peace, though we fear that for many it will be a sad reminder of the great loss which they have had to bear. Meanwhile we must hold on with a grim and stern determination to see it through, though it will entail still further sacrifices and lay upon our country a burden which will be very heavy.

DAY OF INTERCESSION

A day of intercession on behalf of the Nation and Empire in this time of war. In addition to the ordinary services on Sunday 6th January 1918 - the Feast of the Epiphany and being the day appointed for Intercession on behalf of the Nation and Empire in this time of War we had a special service in the afternoon at 3.30 p.m when the church was crowded to overflowing and many were unable to get seats and went away. It was attended by Volunteers, members of the Urban District Council, Nurses, wounded soldiers, Scouts and Girl Guides.

THE KING'S PROCLAMATION
TO MY PEOPLE –

The world-wide struggle for the triumph of right and liberty is entering upon its last and most difficult phase. The enemy is striving by desperate assault and subtle intrigue to perpetuate the wrongs already committed and stem the tide of a free civilization. We have yet to complete the great task to which, more than three years ago, we dedicated ourselves.

At such a time I would call upon you to devote a special day to prayer that we may have the clear-sightedness and strength necessary to the victory of our cause. This victory will be gained only if we steadfastly remember the responsibility which rests upon us, and in a spirit of reverent obedience ask the blessing of Almighty God upon our endeavours. With hearts grateful for the Divine Guidance which has led us so far towards our goal, let us seek to be enlightened in our understanding and fortified in our courage in facing the sacrifices we may yet have to make before our work is done.

I therefore hereby appoint **January 6th** - the first Sunday of the year - to be set aside as **a special day of prayer and thanksgiving** in all the Churches throughout my dominions, and require that this Proclamation be read at the services held on that day.

Mid-Sussex Times - January 15th 1918

CUCKFIELD PARISH CHURCH

The Day of National Prayer and Thanksgiving as appointed by the King was well observed at the Parish Church. The usual Sunday services were held, beginning with celebrations of Holy Communion at 7.00 a.m. and 8.00 a.m. and at all of them the authorised forms of service was used. In the afternoon there was a special service for which the Church was crowded to overflowing and even after extra seating accommodation had been procured many had to go away unable to get in.

There was a strong detachment of Sussex Volunteers under the command of Major J. J. Lister V.D. and Second Lieutenant B. Y. Bevan. The members of the Urban District Council were present with their Chairman, Mr Rubens Anscombe, J.P. and Mr C. H. Waugh (Clerk). Several of the nurses from the V.A.D. Hospital attended and with them were a large number of wounded soldiers from the hospital. The Cuckfield Boy Scouts were present in force, under the command of Scoutmaster A. T. Rapley and also the Girl Guides, in the charge of Captain Alice McConnel and Lieutenant Marjorie Huckett.

The service began with the hymn, 'Praise my Soul the King of Heaven', sung in procession - the long procession of the choir being headed by Mr W. Herrington carrying the Cross, and the banner of St

George and the Union Jack carried by two of the choir boys, C. Philpot and W. Clark.

The opening prayers were taken by the Rev C.J.B. Webb and after the chanting of Psalm X1V1 the Lesson was read by Major Lister. This was followed by the hymn, now known so well, 'O God of Love, O King of Peace', and then came the sermon - a telling one - which was preached by the Vicar, Canon Wilson who took as his text 1 Timothy,ii,1.

After the sermon came the hymn 'O God our Help in Ages Past', and then the cross was brought out before the altar, and the Vicar, attended by the two flag bearers stood on the chancel step and read the King's Proclamation, which was immediately followed by the singing of the National Anthem.

The vicar then went into the pulpit and proceeded with the service of prayers and thanksgiving, as set forth in the authorised form, the congregation joining in with great earnestness and reverence.

The service concluded with the hymn, 'Through the Night of Doubt and Sorrow', and the Blessing. The memory of the service, we have no hesitation in saying, will long remain with all who were present, it being a solemn and reverent act of intercession and thanksgiving on the part of the people of Cuckfield.

The collections throughout the day were given to the British Red Cross and amounted to the very satisfactory total of £26.00.

HOLY WEEK AND SERVICES OF INTERCESSION
MARCH 25th 1918

Holy Week was a time of terrible anxiety to us all because of the German push on to the Western Front. On the Monday in Holy Week we began to have a five minutes service of intercession every day when the Peace Bell was rung at noon. This service was continued practically every day until the end of the war. The usual service of intercession every Wednesday was also continued and was always well attended. At this time there was an internment camp at Lindfield for German prisoners of War and as they were employed on different farms in the neighbourhood we often saw them passing through the village.

CUCKFIELD PARISH CHURCH

✠

A

MEMORIAL

SERVICE

FOR

Those fallen in the War,

AND SPECIALLY FOR

The following Men who have recently given their lives for their King and Country :

FRED. C. ANSCOMBE,
ERNEST ATTWATER (2nd LIEUT.),
WILFRID F. FISHER (2nd LIEUT.),
GEORGE FRANKS,
LEONARD FUNNELL,
AMBROSE HENLEY,

CECIL JOHN HOWE,
JOSEPH MARKWICK,
JOHN LAMBERT ROBERTS (LIEUT.),
JAMES ROWLAND,
PERCY HAROLD SELBY,
LAURENCE UPTON,

Will be held at Evensong

On SUNDAY, MAY 5th, 1918.

PREACHER:

REV. C. W. G. WILSON, M.A.

(Vicar of Cuckfield, Canon and Prebendary of Chichester).

Service at 6.30 p.m.

Copies of the Form of Service will be provided.

THE COLLECTION WILL BE GIVEN TO THE MISSIONS TO SEAMEN.

MEMORIAL SERVICE IN CUCKFIELD CHURCH
SUNDAY 5th MAY 1918

OUR DEPARTED BOYS

The old-world town of Cuckfield, in common with other localities, has rendered King and Country no little service. It has sent its brightest and best to the war, and many of them are now taking their last long sleep. Those whom they have left behind honour them in their hearts, keep them in their minds, and salute them with a reverence and gratitude which words cannot adequately express.

Every now and then, Cannon Wilson holds a memorial service in Cuckfield Parish Church, and there is always a packed congregation, testifying to the eagerness of the people to pay tribute to the memory of the gallant boys who have passed beyond the veil.

Such a service was held last Sunday evening, and appended are the names of the men closely connected with the parish who were commemorated -

Fred. C. Anscombe	ErnestAttwater (2nd Lieut)
Wilfred F Fisher (2nd Lieut)	George Franks
Leonard Funnell	Ambrose Henley
Cecil John Howe	Joseph Markwick
John Lambert Roberts (Lieut)	James Rowland
Percy. H. Selby	Lawrence Upton

Prior to the service there was rung upon the bells a muffled peal in memory of Second Lieutenant Ernest Attwater (a former ringer) by the following -

Messrs. F.Hounsell, Senior	F. Hounsell, Junior
A. Wheale	W. Gibson
A. E. Mitchell	T. Gasson
Watson and Pix	Miss Mary Wilson
Miss Ellen Thorpe	Miss Roffey
Miss Portway	

Upwards of 80 Volunteers attended, under the command of Major J. J. Lister. The Boy Scouts were under the supervision of Acting Scoutmaster A. T. Rapley and Scout J. Etherton carried the Scout flag given in memory of Scout Joseph Markwick; while the Girl Guides were in the charge of Lieutenant Helen Wilson.

It was a stirring sight to see the throng of worshipers rise to their feet as the clergy and choir proceeded from the Choir Vestry to the Chancel singing, 'Brief Life is here our portion.' Mr W. Herrington bore the processional cross, and W. Clarke and Christopher Monks (choristers) carried the Union Jack and the Cross of St George.

The Rev. E. H. Blake read the opening prayers and the special Psalms chosen were the 46th and the 121st - 'God is our hope and strength' and 'I will lift up mine eyes unto the hills'.

Mr B. Y. Bevan with earnestness and feeling read the lessons, taken from Isaiah XXV and 1 Thessalonians 1V, verses 13 - 18. At the end of the second lesson the Vicar (Canon Wilson) came forward, and the flag bearers on either side of him, called out the names of the fallen recorded above and the congregation remembered them specially before the Throne of Grace.

Then followed John Arkwright's sweetly pathetic hymn, 'Father we bring our dead to thee'. When the last notes had died away there was started the memorial service prepared by the Bishop of Stepney for those fallen in the war. The prayers were very beautiful. They made one feel it was good to draw near to the warm heart of Christ.

For the bereaved there was said this prayer -

'Comfort, O Lord, we pray Thee, all who are mourning the loss of those who are near and dear to them. Be with them in their sorrow, Support them in Thy love. Teach them to rest and lean on Thee. Give them the faith to look beyond the troubles of this present time, and to know that neither life or death can separate us from the love of God which is in Christ Jesus our Lord'.

The consoling lesson from Revelation XX1 v. 1-5 was read by Major Lister. After the hymn, 'The Son of God goes forth to War', the Bidding Prayer was said, and Canon Wilson then proceeded with his sermon. It can well be described as a manly utterance and uplifting, and just the right note was struck to give hope and courage to those whose dear ones had been taken from them.

As the sermon ended, the congregation joined in singing, 'Abide with me'.

An offertory was taken during the singing of the hymn and it was given to the Missions to Seaman.

A prayer for victory having been offered, Canon Wilson pronounced the Benediction. For a few moments there was a great hush, and the stillness was broken by Mr Attewell playing the National Anthem. The first verse was sung by the congregation and at the close there came from the organ the solemn strains of the Dead March in Saul. Finally Sergeant-Bugler F. Hounsell sounded the Last Post, the flags were dipped and everybody felt this to be the saddest period of the whole service.

As the congregation left the sacred building C. H. Lloyd's 'Solemn March' was effectively played by the Organist.

Mid-Sussex Times - 23rd July 1918

MESSAGE FROM THE KING

We may cherish, I believe, well founded hopes that in the furnace of war new links of understanding and sympathy are being forged between man and man, between class and class; and that we are coming to recognise as never before that we are all members of one community and that the welfare of each is dependent upon, and inseparable from, the welfare of all.

BY THE KING.

A PROCLAMATION.

GEORGE R.I.

WHEREAS it has pleased Almighty God to bring to a close the late wide-spread and sanguinary War in which We were engaged against Germany and her Allies; We, therefore, adoring the Divine Goodness and duly considering that the great and general blessings of Peace do call for public and solemn acknowledgment, have thought fit, by and with the advice of our Privy Council, to issue this Our Royal Proclamation hereby appointing and commanding that a General Thanksgiving to Almighty God for these His manifold and great mercies be observed throughout Our Dominions on Sunday, the Sixth day of July instant: And for the better and more devout solemnization of the same We have given directions to the Most Reverend the Archbishops and the Right Reverend the Bishops of England to compose a Form of Prayer suitable to this occasion, to be used in all Churches and Chapels, and to take care for the timely dispersing of the same throughout their respective Dioceses and to the same end We do further advertise and exhort the General Assembly of the Church of Scotland and all Spiritual Authorities and ministers of religion in their respective churches and other places of public worship throughout Our United Kingdom of Great Britain and Ireland and in all quarters of Our Dominions beyond the Seas to take part as it may properly behove them to do in this great and common act of worship, and We do strictly charge and command that the said Public Day of Thanksgiving be religiously observed by all as they tender the favour of Almighty God and have the sense of His Benefits.

Given at Our Court at Buckingham Palace, this First day of July, in the year of our Lord One thousand nine hundred and nineteen, and in the Tenth year of Our Reign.

GOD SAVE THE KING.

CUCKFIELD PARISH CHURCH.

Fourth Anniversary of the Outbreak of the Great War.

A DAY OF REMEMBRANCE.

SUNDAY, 4th AUGUST, 1918.

✠

SPECIAL INTERCESSIONS on behalf of our Country, and for our Forces on Sea, on Land, and in the Air.

SERVICES:

7 a.m. & 8 a.m.—Celebration of Holy Communion, with Memorial for those who have Fallen in the War.

11 a.m.—Morning Prayer and Sermon. Special Prayers for Victory and Peace.

12.15 p.m.—Celebration of Holy Communion.

3.30 p.m.—SPECIAL SERVICE, INTERCESSIONS & SERMON

PREACHER:

Very Rev. J. J. HANNAH, D.D.

(Dean of Chichester).

Shirley Bond

Mid-Sussex Times - 6th August 1918

4th August 1918 - Remembrance Day

In each Church, of all denominations, special references to the war were heard at a National Day of Prayer.

The following is what the Rev. Canon Wilson said at the service in Holy Trinity Church, Cuckfield.

The entry of Great Britain into the Great War marks an epoch in the history of our country and of the civilised world, and now that we have come to the fourth anniversary of that event it is as well for us to stop for a moment and think what this day should mean to all of us.

In the first place it should be a day of thanksgiving. There is so much for which we ought to be thankful. We need not specify; surely we know. But besides being a day of Thanksgiving it should be a day of Remembrance. We can never forget the wonderful heroism of our brave men, nor the self-sacrifice of those who have died that we might live.

It should also be a day of renewed dedication of ourselves to so great a cause, so that with quiet confidence, and unshaken courage, we may bear ourselves bravely in the days to come, and help others to be brave, and also devote ourselves and all our powers to the winning of the war. And finally, it should be to us, as a Christian people, a day of earnest intercession for our Forces and those of our Allies, and of fervent prayer that God will speedily give us the Victory and Peace for which we all so greatly long.

CUCKFIELD PARISH CHURCH

✠

A

MEMORIAL

SERVICE

FOR

Those fallen in the War

The following Men who have recently given their lives for their King and Country:

JOHN M. ANSELL,	JESSE PELLING,
JACK BATES,	STUART K. REID (CAPTAIN, M.C.),
HARRY ETHERTON,	WILLIAM RHODES,
ALBERT H. HOLE,	ALBERT E. SELBY (SERGT., M.M.),
OLIVER S. HUCKETT,	CHARLES SELBY,
HENRY T. KNAPP,	A. FRANKLIN YOUNG,
ERNEST LANDER,	Gerald Edward Drake (Lieut.)

Will be held at Evensong

On SUNDAY, SEPT. 15th, 1918.

PREACHER:

REV. C. W. G. WILSON, M.A.

(Vicar of Cuckfield, Canon and Prebendary of Chichester).

Service at 6.30 p.m.

Copies of the Form of Service will be provided.

THE COLLECTION WILL BE GIVEN TO THE SUSSEX PRISONERS OF WAR FUND.

Shirley Bond

Mid-Sussex Times - 17th September 1918

THE MEN WHO FOUGHT AND DIED

ANOTHER MEMORIAL SERVICE AT
CUCKFIELD CHURCH

The mothers of Cuckfield who have lost sons, and the wives who have lost husbands, in the terrible war now being waged, do not mourn alone. Their neighbours and fellow residents feel for them deeply, and with them pray that God, in his great mercy, will number their dear ones with His Saints in Glory Everlasting.

Say what we will, death carried with it a sting for the living, but in the hour of trial and bitter sorrow there is nothing that can soothe the mind as effectually as the Christian Faith. 'The Man of Sorrows' taught us not only how to live but also how to die, and those who have been left lonely - ever so lonely - through the war, should be relieved and comforted by the thought that their husbands and sons have helped by their service and sacrifice to sweeten the world and to quicken its ideals.

On Sunday evening the Rev Cannon C. W. G. Wilson held another touching memorial service in Cuckfield Parish Church for those fallen in the war and especially for the following men who have recently given their lives for their King and Country:-

John M. Ansell
Gerald Edward Drake
Albert H. Hole
Henry T. Knapp
Jesse Pelling
William Rhodes
Charles Selby

Jack Bates
Harry Etherton
Oliver S. Huckett
Ernest Lander
Captain Stuart K. Reid, M. C.
Sergeant Albert E. Selby M. M
A. Franklin Young

Muffled bells summoned the people to the church, and prior to the start of the service the sacred edifice was packed. We noticed in the congregation, residents of Ansty, Staplefield, Lindfield, Balcombe and Haywards Heath, and their presence showed how they regard these memorial services. With the Volunteers were Captain L. L. Roberts,

- 56 -

Lieutenant H. E. Stewart and Lieutenant R. Newton and the Boy Scouts were under the command of Acting Scoutmaster A. T. Rapley. A number of wounded soldiers were also present.

The processional hymn was 'Let Saints on earth in concert sing with those whose work is done'. The cross was carried by Mr William Knight, and the flag bearers were Jack Etherton (son of the late Private H. Etherton) and W. Clarks. The lessons were impressively read by Mr B. Y. Bevan J. P. and Lieutenant H. E. Stewart, and, with compassionate tenderness, Canon Wilson read the prayers. How helpful they were. How soothing to the bereaved.

At the end of the second lesson the congregation arose and Canon Wilson read out the names of the fallen heroes recorded above, after which there was sung John Arkwright's beautifully worded hymn, 'Father we bring our dead to Thee'. Prior to the Bidding Prayer, 'On the Resurrection Morning' was sung, and before the close many eyes were dimmed with tears. The address was given by Cannon Wilson and was much appreciated. The Rev gentleman knows how to comfort, how to cheer, and it is because he strikes a human note that the people love to hear him.

He prefaced his remarks by alluding to the Sussex Prisoners' of War Fund, to which the offertory was to be given, and recalled to mind that the German prisoners in England were better treated than our poor men who were prisoners in Germany. The lot of prisoners of war, he proceeded to state, was hard at any time, and it was especially hard if aggravated by want of proper food and clothes. 'We know the needs of our men, we know how they are helped, and how life is made possible for them by the parcels they receive from home. It is a tremendous encouragement and a source of consolation to them to know that we at home do not forget them, and in doing what we can to help them we can show our gratitude for what they have done for us.'

The faces of the congregation, whose eyes were riveted upon the vicar, indicated that they thought the words well spoken.

At the outset he pointed out why these memorial services - the one that night was the eighth in three years - were held. They were not held to arouse afresh the grief and to harrow the feelings of those who have been bereaved. That would be unworthy. They were held for a purpose higher and better than that. They at Cuckfield met together to pay their tribute of honour and regard to those brave men who had laid down their lives for the defence of their country and to give them in their Old Parish Church, where many of them had been christened and so often had met together for worship, 'a service in which we commemorate them before God and man, and to remind ourselves of the greatness of the debt which we owe to them, and the noble nature of the death which they have died'. Their lives had not been wasted; but given in the noblest of causes - in the defence of a glorious heritage - the common property of themselves and us. Passing on, the preacher said we had reason to be proud, and thankful to belong to the English race.

Who would not repeat those words of the Psalmist - 'The lot is fallen unto me in a fair ground: yea, I have a goodly heritage.'. What the heritage was, Canon Wilson ably set forth, and he pictured what would have happened to this fair land had Germany been allowed to invade it, and ended by pointing out that it was to defend and protect their heritage and ours that the brave lads of Cuckfield, together with those from other parts, had fought and died. 'Let us see to it that our men shall not have died in vain.'

At the close of the sermon the congregation sang, 'Abide with me', and here the offertory was taken. The hymn finished, Canon Wilson called upon those before him to join him in thanking God for the success to our arms and the arms of our Allies and at the end he pronounced the Benediction.

A verse of the National Anthem followed, and very heartily it was sung. Then came a hush and presently the silence was broken by the solemn strains of the Dead March in 'Saul'. Sacred memories stored in the treasure house of the heart were touched as Mr Attewell played, but we will not dwell upon them, for where there is sorrow there is holy ground. The final pathetic note was sounded by Sergeant-Bugler F. Hounsell, and it was 'The Last Post'.

In closing we feel it right to add that Canon Wilson is deserving of grateful thanks for holding these memorial services, and we know of many who have been helped by them as well as strengthened to bear their cross.

TWO MINUTES SILENCE

At the suggestion of the King a silence of two minutes was kept at 11.00a.m. on Armistice Day (November 11th) throughout the Empire in memory of those who died in the war. We observed the silence in the Church at Cuckfield and it was followed by a well attended short service.

Cuckfield Parish Magazine - December 1918

THE END OF THE WAR

November 11th, 1918, the Festival of St Martin, the Soldier Saint, will be for ever memorable throughout Great Britain and the Empire as the day which saw the practical conclusion of the Great War, owing to the signing of the Armistice with the last and greatest of our enemies, and the assurance of a victorious Peace.

The news was received with a sense of great relief, as well as joy and thankfulness, which found expression in the outburst of thanksgiving at the service the same evening, when the church was crowded in spite of the very unpleasant weather, and at the services on Thanksgiving Sunday.

The ringing of the bells proclaimed the joyful news to the whole parish and was continued throughout the day and on the Sunday. The names of the Ringers who took part in this joyful celebration were as follows:-

Messrs. F. Hounsell, Sen., F. Hounsell, Jun., W. Gibson, A. Wheale, C. Watson, A. T. Rapley, A. Pix, A. Mitchell, Alfred Robinson, W. Robinson, P. Hillman, T. Jeffery, H. Stoner, Miss Ivy Portway, Miss Lily Roffey and Miss Mary S. Wilson.

To all of them we wish to express the thanks of the parish, and our appreciation of their services.

Mid-Sussex Times - 12th November 1918

CUCKFIELD CONGREGATIONAL CHURCH

In response to the suggestion of the Free Church Council, a thanksgiving service for the signing of the armistice was held in the Congregational Church last Monday evening. Beginning with the Doxology, and closing with 'God Bless our Native Land', the service was one of praise and prayer. The Roll of Honour was read, and the lessons - one from the Psalms and the other from Rev.XX1-XX11 were read by Mr William Stevens, J.P. The Church was filled for the service which was conducted by the Rev S. Maddock (pastor).

Mid-Sussex Times - 12th November 1918

HOLY TRINITY PARISH CHURCH CUCKFIELD

THE JOYOUS ARMISTICE NEWS - filled Cuckfieldians with delight, and when evening came the thanksgiving service at the Parish Church was attended by a crowded congregation, including the Boy Scouts and their band. The service was taken by the Rev. Cannon Wilson and the address he gave struck a fine patriotic note. It was based on a text from the psalms, 'The Lord shall give strength unto His people: the Lord shall give his people the blessing of peace'.

The National Flags were prominently displayed, and the heart was moved as, with the processional cross, the Royal Standard was placed before the altar while the Te Deum and the National Anthem were sung. The hymns selected for the occasion were, 'All People that on earth do dwell', 'Praise my Soul the King of Heaven', and 'The Day thou Gavest Lord is ended'. Altogether it was a memorable service.

Mid-Sussex Times - 19th November 1918

THANKSGIVING SUNDAY

There were crowded congregations at Cuckfield Parish Church last Sunday for the thanksgiving for victory and then cessation of hostilities.

The services began with a celebration of Holy Communion at 8.00 a.m. and there was another celebration after Morning Prayer. The services, which followed the lines laid down in the authorised form were conducted by the Vicar (Canon Wilson) who had the assistance in the morning of the Rev. C. J. B. Webb. The Lessons at both Matins and Evensong were read by Mr B. Y. Bevan J.P.

The services commenced with the procession of the Choir and Clergy, headed by the cross and the flag of St. George and the Union Jack, and opened with the singing of the National Anthem. The sermon, both morning and evening was preached by the Vicar, who on each occasion paid a glowing tribute to those Cuckfield men - they numbered 80 - who had given their lives for their country. All the names were read out, the congregation standing as a mark of respect. The sermon was followed by the special form of thanksgiving which included the, 'Te Deum', for which the Cross and the Flags were brought to the front, and after the blessing, Chopin's Funeral March was impressively played as a tribute to our dead heroes. The offerings at Matins and Evensong amounted to £21.10s. 6d. and were given to the Fund for Disabled Soldiers and Sailors. The evening service was attended by the Girl Guides, under the command of Lieut. Helen Wilson, and also by the Boy Scouts, who paraded with their drum and bugle band. In the absence of Acting Scoutmaster A. T. Rapley, owing to illness, Sergeant M. Anscombe was in command.

The services of this happy day were brought to a fitting conclusion by a peal on the Church bells.

Cuckfield Parish Magazine - March 1919

MEMORIAL PEAL

Many of the members of our Bell Ringers Association have been on service during the war and three of them have fallen -

2nd Lieutenant Ernest Attwater
A.E. Chinnery
George Gibson

We have commemorated them at our Memorial Services, at which muffled peals have been rung, but it was very fitting and appropriate that, as was being done in so many Churches throughout the country, a special memorial peal should be rung on our bells on Saturday February 22nd. It consisted of what is called a 'whole pull and stand' and it was conducted by Mr F. Hounsell, Senior.

CHAPTER 6

CUCKFIELD MEN REMEMBERED

CUCKFIELD MEN REMEMBERED

While, throughout the country, the people in towns like Cuckfield were celebrating the end of the war and welcoming their loved ones home, for many families it was a sad time that their sons and fathers were not part of the celebrations. Yet they could feel very proud that their men folk had given their lives in order for the Great War to be won.

Eighty seven men from Cuckfield died, and in the following pages, in alphabetical order, is told each man's individual story. Seventy three of these histories are accompanied by a photograph. Some of the Army Service Records from World War One were destroyed by fire and water damage during the German bombing of London in 1940. This leaves a big gap in some information, but behind each name is a story - some remain difficult to uncover, but none should be forgotten. I would not wish names carved in stone to be their only legacy.

From historical records diligently compiled by the Commonwealth War Graves Commission, I found the place of enlistment into service, the Regiment joined and the Service number of each man. Although many enlisted with the Royal Sussex Regiment, as war developed and needs changed, many soldiers were transferred to other regiments and some were given another number. Amalgamations of Regiments are noted on Army records and the movements and fortunes of each Regiment can be traced. Some records gave information such as the man's address and name of next of kin.

Most of the men listed on the war memorials were born and brought up in Cuckfield. Information about their families and where they lived was traced through the National censuses. The Parish Magazines and Log Books provided much information on their school life, hobbies, interests and work. All combine to give here a picture of each man and his life before he enlisted.

Probably the most poignant of all are the mens' letters home. They give first hand accounts of what life was really like on the battlefields. Sad are the letters written by the commanding officer or chaplain of the regiment, describing to those at home how their loved one was wounded and killed. Most of these letters were printed in the Mid-Sussex Times newspaper.

The place of death of each man, with the reference position of his grave and/or memorial is also given, which will help anyone who wishes, to visit the grave or memorial site.

Some slight discrepancies in dates will be noted between the date of an event happening and its inclusion in the Parish Magazine or Mid-Sussex Times Newspaper.

A

CORPORAL FREDERICK CHARLES ANSCOMBE

Frederick Charles Anscombe was born in Horsegate Lane, Cuckfield in 1895. He was the son of Alfred. A. Anscombe and Helen Anscombe who was born in Newhaven, Sussex in 1865.

Frederick had an older brother, Michael A. Anscombe, born in 1894, who also enlisted in the Army and sent many interesting letters home. Although wounded by shrapnel Michael survived the war.

They had a younger brother called Claud C. Anscombe who was born in 1897. Father Alfred Anscombe was a house decorator.

Frederick enlisted into the Royal Sussex Regiment in Haywards Heath. His rank was Private, Service number 1385.

He was transferred to the 2nd Battalion Royal Warwickshire Regiment, 7th Regular Division, Service number 241769.

Mid-Sussex Times - 7th March 1916
THE COOLNESS OF THE FRENCH
Mrs Anscombe, of 1 Albany Villas, Cuckfield received last week the following letter, dated 27th February from her soldier son in France:

'The weather this last week has been very bad. It snowed hard for three days and since then we have had a mixture of snow and rain. The ground has been several inches deep with it. For the past three weeks we have been experiencing the joys of barbed wiring under difficulties. Just try and imagine what it is like to be out on a bitterly cold night, pitch dark, with rain pouring down, trying to fix up barbed wire entanglements. The stuff flies all over the shop and hooks up in everything. The man who invented the blooming stuff ought to be hung, drawn and quartered. But there, the Germans will have more cause to grumble over it than we shall, if ever they get their hearts up high enough to try and advance through it. We are now billeted in houses instead of the old barns which were swarming with rats. Although the place is only about a mile from the firing line and the Germans are often shelling it, a lot of the French people still live here. It does not seem to worry them much that a shell may land through the roof of their house any minute.

There was a fine cathedral here but it has been blown to pieces. The Germans must have sent thousands of shells at it. It is a great shame, as it was magnificent'.

Mid-Sussex Times - 25th July 1916
CORPORAL F. ANSCOMBE
of the Royal Warwick Regiment, second son of Mr and Mrs Anscombe, of 1 Albany Villas, has been promoted to the rank of Corporal. Sadly he was wounded by a shot in the right elbow. He arrived at Dover on Saturday and is now in the East Sussex Hospital at Hastings.

Mid-Sussex Times - 23rd October 1917
The sad news is to hand that Private F. C. Anscombe, son of Mr and Mrs A. A. Anscombe of 1, Albany Villas, Broad Street, Cuckfield, was killed in action in France on 7th October. He was called up at the start of the war in the Royal Sussex Regiment and afterwards transferred to the Royal

Warwickshire Regiment with whom he went to France. He was wounded in July 1916 and was in hospital in England for a long time. He returned to France three months ago. His age was 22 years.

A letter of sympathy has been received by his parents from the King and Queen. The deceased was for many years a member of the Parish Church choir and took part in the Empire Day Celebration at the school last May.

Mr and Mrs Anscombe have received the following letter from 2nd Lt F. C. Barton:

'Please accept my deepest sympathy in your sad bereavement. Your son was with me when he was killed. The Huns had put up a strong counter attack one morning and the front line Battalion had used up practically all their ammunition, so I was called on to make up a party of one hundred men with a further supply. The journey was a terrible one but the men were heroes, every one. Your son's death was, from a soldier's point of view, a glorious one. He gave his all to try and help comrades in distress. God will reward him ! God give you his comfort in your sorrow ! Be proud of your son and trust the Creator that all things work together for good'.

Frederick is Remembered with Honour on the Tyne Cot Memorial in Belgium, Panel 23 to 28 and 163A.

His name appears on the war memorial in the Churchyard of Holy Trinity Church, Cuckfield, on the marble memorial inside the Church and on the memorial board in the Queen's Hall, Cuckfield.

LANCE-CORPORAL
JOHN MEREDITH ANSELL

John Meredith Ansell was born into a large extended family all living at Old Beech Farm, Cuckfield at the turn of the century. Head of the family was his widowed grandmother Betsy Haylor who was born in Cuckfield in 1840.

Her son William Haylor born in 1871 and daughter Alice Haylor born in 1868, both single, lived with her. Also at Old Beech Farm were her daughter Harriett Ansell with son in law Albert. E. Ansell.

John Meredith, born in 1897, was one of the children of Harriett and Albert, along with Albert born in 1888, Kate born in 1890, Mildred born 1896 and Annie born in 1900. John's father Albert was a domestic groom on the farm.

John enlisted in Brighton into the Kings Liverpool Regiment, Service number 65011.

He was transferred to the 32nd Battalion, Royal Fusiliers (City of London Regiment) Service number 60666

Mid Sussex Times - 30th October 1917
Missing
Mr and Mrs Albert Ansell, Old Beech Farm, Henmead, Cuckfield, have received official information that their son Lance Corporal J. M. Ansell, Royal Fusiliers, was posted as missing between the 19th and 22nd September 1917. He had only recently rejoined his regiment as he was wounded in the face by a shrapnel splinter earlier in the year.

Mid Sussex Times - 23rd July 1918
JOHN ANSELL
Mr and Mrs Albert Ansell, of Old Beech Farm, have received the sad news that their youngest son, John, aged 20 years, has died. He was reported missing on 19th September 1917 and had not been heard of since.

He was wounded in France in April 1917, was sent to England in May, and returned again to France in July of the same year.

John is Remembered with Honour on the Tyne Cot Memorial, Belgium, panel 28 to 30 and 162A and 163A.

His name appears on the war memorial in the churchyard of Holy Trinity Church, Cuckfield, on the marble memorial inside the Church and on the memorial board in the Queen's Hall, Cuckfield.

GUNNER JAMES ATTREE

James Attree was born in 1880 in Portslade, Sussex, the son of Henry and Charlotte Attree. His elder sisters were Caroline born in 1876 and Alice born in 1878.

His father was a journeyman miller at flour mills and in the 1901 census is shown aged 54, living with his wife at the 'Old Mill', High Bridge, Cuckfield, where there was a flour mill.

James enlisted in Brighton with the Army Veterinary Corps, Service number 2952. He then transferred to the 'V' 1st Trench Mortar Battery, Royal Horse Artillery and Royal Field Artillery No 156088.

He saw action in France and Flanders and was killed in action at Ramscappelle on 27th June 1917 aged 36 years.

James is buried in the Ramscappelle Road Military Cemetery, Belgium - grave reference Nieuport-Bains Cemetery Memorial 3.

His name appears on the war memorial in the churchyard of Holy Trinity Church, Cuckfield, on the marble memorial inside the Church and on the memorial board in the Queen's Hall, Cuckfield.

SECOND LIEUTENANT ERNEST ATTWATER

Ernest Attwater was born in Church Street, Cuckfield in 1888, the son of Alfred and Frances Attwater. He had an elder brother Frank, born in 1885. Alfred was a whitesmith.

Ernest was the husband of Mrs. A. E. Light, formerly Attwater, of 4, Fitzalan Terrace, Arundel, Sussex.

He enlisted into the 58th Company, Machine Gun Corps (Infantry).

Mid-Sussex Times - 25th January 1916
GRANTED A COMMISSION

On Friday, Mrs Attwater of Albany Villas, received the news that her son Ernest, a sergeant in the machine gun section of the 9th Battalion Royal Sussex Regiment, had received a commission.

When at Cuckfield he rendered excellent service as a bell ringer, and was a member of the Church choir. He was also well known as a member of the football and cricket clubs. Soon after war broke out he left his position of ground bowler to the Surrey County Cricket Club and entered upon the large field of action in which he is now engaged, and he will have the good wishes of the whole of Cuckfield in his new appointment.

Mid Sussex Times - 2nd April 1918
LIEUTENANT. E. ATTWATER

Sad News - We hear that Second Lieutenant E. Attwater, Machine Gun Corps, who was well known in the town as a cricketer and footballer, has met his death in the recent great offensive in France. He was a young man of sterling character and very popular in Haywards Heath as well as Cuckfield. He was a member of the Cuckfield Church Choir and also a bellringer.

Cuckfield Parish Magazine

On Good Friday the sad news was received that Lieutenant Ernest Attwater was killed in action on 22nd March. He joined up on the outbreak of war and saw much fighting at Ypres, Loos and the Somme, where his good work as a machine gunner earned for him the recommendation for a commission. He was very well known in Cuckfield, being a member of the Church choir and also a bellringer. He was a good cricketer and footballer and ever ready to help in any good cause. He was, as one who knew him said, 'one of the best', and his death is deplored by his many friends. His mother died last December, and so she has been spared this sorrow, but we should like to express our sincere sympathy with his brothers and sisters and especially with his young widow with her infant son.

Ernest was killed in action on 22nd March 1918 age 29 years and is buried in the south west corner of Foucaucourt Communal Cemetery.

His name appears on the war memorial in the churchyard of Holy Trinity Church, Cuckfield, on the marble memorial inside the Church and on the memorial board in the Queen's Hall, Cuckfield.

B

PRIVATE ARTHUR JOHN BALLARD

Arthur John Ballard was born in 1887 in Basingstoke, Hampshire.

He was the son of Mrs Jane Ballard of Basingstoke and had a brother George born in 1888. He was the husband of Rose Florence Ballard, who later married again to become Rose Florence Hillman, of 6, Chatfield Road, Cuckfield.

Arthur had moved to Cuckfield before he enlisted into the Royal Sussex Regiment in Brighton, Service number 140 .

He was later transferred to the 2nd Battalion Lincolnshire Regiment, 21st Division, Service Number 44934, with whom he saw action in France and Flanders.

Mid-Sussex Times - 15th August 1916
SERIOUSLY WOUNDED
Last Tuesday evening Mrs Ballard, of Ockenden Lane, received the sad intelligence that her husband Private A. J. Ballard, Royal Sussex Regiment, was in hospital at Rouen, having been shot through the head.

His condition was regarded as serious. On enquiry yesterday we were informed by Mrs Ballard that she had received no further news. Her husband joined the Army in August 1914, and had been in France some fourteen months. For several years he was in the employ of Mr Symons as a carter.

Mid-Sussex Times - 22nd August 1916
BETTER NEWS
Mrs Ballard, of Ockenden Lane, heard from her husband, Private Ballard, a day or two ago, stating that he was in hospital in Leeds and making a good recovery from the wound in his head. He had a most marvellous escape from death. A shell blew him from one trench to another, and but

for the gallantry of a Sergeant he would have been taken prisoner by the Germans.

Cuckfield Parish Magazine - July 1919
Official notification has been received of the death of Private A. J. Ballard, 2nd Lincolnshire Regiment, formerly Royal Sussex Regiment, but no actual date has been given or details of his death. A different report states that Arthur was killed in action on 27th May 1918 aged 31 years.

In January 1920 Mrs Ballard received notification that her husband's grave had been located and he is buried at Queen's Bacquoy Cemetery, near Bapaume.

He is Remembered with Honour on the Soissons Memorial.

His name appears on the war memorial in the churchyard of Holy Trinity Church, Cuckfield, on the marble memorial inside the Church and on the memorial board in the Queen's Hall, Cuckfield.

PRIVATE FRANK BATES

Frank Bates was born in Cuckfield in 1894, the son of William James and Sarah E. Bates of Ockenden Lane, Cuckfield. William was born in Balcombe and worked from his home as a tailor.

Frank was their fourth child. Norman the eldest was born in 1888, Jack in 1889, Maggie in 1891 and the youngest sister Bessie was born in 1897.

Frank enlisted in Horsham into the 4th Battalion Royal Sussex Regiment, Service number TF/2020.

He died at his home on 31st January 1915 aged 21. According to the Parish Records Roll of Honour he died as a result of a chill caught on duty.

Mid-Sussex Times - 31st January 1915
PRIVATE FRANK BATES - Died of Sickness

A young Cuckfield soldier, Private Frank Bates, of 'A' Company, 4th Battalion Royal Sussex Regiment, died at his home on Sunday as the result of a chill contracted while doing duty with the Battalion at Newhaven.

He was the youngest son of Mr and Mrs W. J. Bates of Clock House, and was only twenty-one years of age.

It can be truly said that he gave his life for his country, for he responded to its call in August, temporarily leaving the service of Mr and Mrs L. Messel, of 'Nymans', Staplefield, for that purpose. He was much liked in that district and his death will be deeply deplored. It was about a month ago that he returned to his home, and for a few days prior to Sunday the doctors realised that his life could not be spared and the end came peacefully shortly after noon.

Mid-Sussex Times Account
DIED OF SICKNESS
A TERRITORIAL'S FUNERAL AT CUCKFIELD
Impressive scenes

These lines occurred to the writer as, along with a large crowd of sad faced Cuckfieldians, he stood watching the last scenes at the funeral of one of the old town's soldier sons in the local churchyard on Thursday afternoon. The dead soldier was Private F. Bates, of 'A' Company 4th Battalion, Royal Sussex Regiment, who died as the result of a chill caught at Newhaven some weeks ago. He was buried with the usual honours accorded to a soldier.

The whole ceremony made a deep impression on the large crowd that lined the High Street or assembled in the churchyard, and not the least sad feature was the presence in the church, of relatives of another Cuckfieldian who perished while serving his King and Country on far-off seas.

About a hundred and fifty Territorials took part in their dead comrade's funeral, a procession forming up in the High Street for the short journey to the Church. First came the firing party - men of his own company - with arms reversed, and following them was the Battalion band, under Bandmaster H. M. Carr, then came the buglers of the Post Office Rifles and of 'A' Company of the 4th Royal Sussex. Immediately following was the coffin, covered with the Union Jack, borne on the shoulders of six of his comrades, and the principal mourners followed it. They were Mr and Mrs Bates (father and mother), Mr J. Bates (brother) Miss B. Bates (sister) Mrs Bates and Miss Bates (aunts), Mr Botting (uncle) Mr and Mrs Botting and the Misses Bates (cousins) Mr L. Tester

(Newhaven) Miss Scott, Mr F. Bleach, Mrs Anderson, Mrs Grey, and Mrs Nailor.

After them came 'A' Company of the 4th Royal Sussex, under Captain Warren and Captain Wrightson, Sergeant - Major Jackson and twenty four men of the Post Office Rifles preceded Assistant Scoutmaster Rapley and Patrols of the Cuckfield Boy Scouts. The procession moved off at a slow march, the band playing Chopin's March Funebre, and numerous men of the Post Office Rifles among the crowd came rigidly to the salute as the coffin passed their standpoint. The band and the buglers divided their ranks in Church Street for the cortege to pass down by the School wherein the deceased soldier had learnt that love of a country which his action of six months ago proved he never forgot. Inside those walls too, he probably sang many times the lines quoted above, and we noticed the school flag drooping at half mast in honour of a worthy 'old boy'.

The band ceased, and then the Vicar's voice was heard speaking those hopeful opening sentences of the Church's beautiful burial service.

Frank is buried in Cuckfield Cemetery Ref 11(W) 323

His name appears on the war memorial in the churchyard of Holy Trinity Church, Cuckfield, on the marble memorial inside the Church and on the memorial board in the Queen's Hall, Cuckfield.

PRIVATE JACK BATES

Jack was born in Cuckfield in 1889, a brother of Frank Bates who also died during service. His father was William James Bates, a tailor, originally from Balcombe and mother Sarah of Cuckfield.

Jack was married to Marguerite Ethel Bates of 'Hope Cottage', Balcombe.

MARRIAGE OF BATES AND BATES

31st May 1916, at Balcombe Parish Church by the Rev D. L. Secretan, Rector, Jack, son of Mr and Mrs W. Bates of 'Clock House', Cuckfield to Marguerite Ethel, eldest daughter of the late Mr Edward Bates and Mrs E. Bates of 'Kemp Cottage', Balcombe.

Jack enlisted in Haywards Heath into the Royal Fusiliers, 58th London Division, City of London Regiment, Service number 68386.

He was later posted into the 2nd/4th Battalion, The London Regiment.

He saw action in France and Flanders and died of his wounds at Danizy on 16th April 1918 age 29 years.

Jack died of wounds at a German dressing station on some day at the end of March or the beginning of April. The long and weary time of anxious suspense during the time he was missing is now brought to an end, and great sympathy is felt for the young widow and also for Mr and Mrs Bates, who have now lost both of their sons in the war.

Jack is buried in Chauny Communal Cemetery British Extension, Ref 4. A. 5

His name appears on the war memorial in the churchyard of Holy Trinity Church, Cuckfield, on the marble memorial inside the Church and on the memorial board in the Queen's Hall, Cuckfield.

PRIVATE GEORGE ERNEST BENNETT

George Ernest (Henry) Bennett was born in Cuckfield, the son of Alfred and Anne Bennett. On the 1901 census he was living with his grandmother Ellen Bennett at Churchyard Cottages, Cuckfield.

George enlisted in Bolney into the 4th Battalion Royal Sussex Regiment, Service number TF/1690

He died of wounds in Newhaven, Sussex on 23rd March 1915 aged 20 years.

Mid-Sussex Times - 23rd March 1915
DEATH OF PRIVATE G. E. BENNETT

Last Tuesday there passed away in the hospital at Newhaven, Private George E. Bennett, eldest son of the late Mr and Mrs Alfred Bennett of Cuckfield.

The deceased, prior to joining 'A' Company, 4th Battalion, Royal Sussex Regiment some two years ago, acted as a telegraph boy at the Cuckfield Post Office and later entered the employ of Mr. B. Y. Bevan at 'Woodcroft'. He was also a Boy Scout when the Rev. R. H. C. Mertens was interested in the movement. He was but 20 years of age at the time of his death, and his loss - so unexpected - was deeply regretted by his comrades.

The funeral took place on Friday afternoon at Cuckfield Church in the presence of a large number of people.

Captain Warren and 32 men belonging to 'A' Company, 4th Battalion Royal Sussex Regiment attended, and six of the men bore the coffin, which was covered with the Union Jack, to its final resting place. Twenty three of the Cuckfield Scouts, under Acting Scoutmaster Rapley, joined in the procession, as also did a number of Buglers attached to the Post Office Rifles.

The chief mourners were Mrs Constable (aunt), Mr and Mrs John Bennett (uncle and aunt), Mr Isaac Croucher (grandfather). Miss Pattenden (great aunt), Miss Elliott, the Misses N and L Constable, Miss M. Bennett and Mr John Bennett (cousins), Mr Croucher and Nurse Stoner.

The School flag floated at half mast, and the school boys witnessed the coffin being taken into the Church, where the service was conducted by the Rev Robert Fisher (Vicar) and the Rev E. V. Fenn.

At the close of the service at the graveside three volleys were fired and the 'Last Post' was sounded, and thus ended another soldier's funeral.

Amongst others, floral tributes were received from the Officers and Comrades of the 4th Battalion Royal Sussex Regiment.

Through this medium, Mrs Constable, Mr Bennett and family wish to return thanks for all the kind sympathy shown by friends.

George is buried in Cuckfield Cemetery Ref 10 (W) 299

His name appears on the war memorial in the churchyard of Holy Trinity Church, Cuckfield, on the marble memorial inside the Church and on the memorial board in the Queen's Hall, Cuckfield.

LANCE CORPORAL GEORGE ERNEST BOTTING

George was born in 1899, the youngest son of James W. Botting of Cuckfield and his wife Louisa born in West End, London. James was a gardener/domestic servant and the family lived in Holmstead Cottages, Cuckfield.

George was the youngest of six children, Amy Louisa born 1889, Alfred W. born 1891, Charles V. born 1892, Percy H. born1894, and Robert S. born 1895. All the children were born in Cuckfield.

Prior to enlisting he worked for Messrs Charlesworth & Co.

A year before he enlisted in the army, George married Dora May Wells of 4, Jubilee Cottages, Broad Street, Cuckfield.

Mid-Sussex Times - 15th February 1916
MARRIAGE OF BOTTING AND WELLS

9th February at Holy Trinity Church, Cuckfield, by the Rev. C. W. G. Wilson (Vicar), George Ernest, son of James W. Botting, to Dora May, daughter of William Wells of Broad Street, Cuckfield.

George enlisted into the Royal Marine Light Infantry, 2nd. R.M. Battalion, 63rd Royal Naval Division, Service number PO/1451(S)

He was killed in action on 23rd August 1917 aged 29 years.

Mid-Sussex Times - 4th September 1917
LANCE-CORPORAL GEORGE ERNEST BOTTING

It is with deep regret that we have to chronicle the death of Lance Corporal G. E. Botting R.M.L.I. as his widow who lives in Broad Street has received the following letter from Lt Colonel R. C. Hawkins.

'I very much regret having to send you the sad news of the death of your husband Lance Corporal G. E. Botting R.M.L.I who was killed on the 23rd August in a bombing accident. He was struck through the heart and died instantly. Fortunately he did not suffer any pain and I honestly believe he knew nothing of the accident.

Your husband was a magnificent instructor and was much admired and loved by his men. He was carrying out his duties on the morning of the accident and was instructing men in how to throw live grenades. All possible precautions were taken, but the accident occurred through a premature exploding in the recruit's hand causing the death of your husband and serious injuries to two other men.

He was buried in the British cemetery at.... where his grave could be seen if you should visit the area after the war. I am deeply distressed at the accident, and the loss of Lance-Corporal Botting is severely felt. Please accept my deepest sympathy'.

Other officers have written the widow sympathetic letters. Writing to his mother in Pentlands Road, Haywards Heath, Captain Edwards said -

'I can scarcely express my deep sympathy for you in your sorrow and my own grief at loosing such a fine man and splendid soldier. Lance Corporal Botting was next to me at the time of the accident and was teaching a recruit how to throw bombs. The recruit took the bomb in his hand to throw it and it exploded prematurely. A small piece entered your son's body just over the heart and he died practically instantaneously and without pain. The man who threw the bomb and a sergeant instructor were also wounded, I fear fatally. I cannot say how deeply we regret this terrible tragedy but you may rest assured it was an accident which no amount of care on our part could have avoided. Every possible precaution was taken but the accident was due entirely to a faulty bomb. As belonging to the same battalion as your son and sharing many dangers with him I should like to express my admiration for him as a thoroughly efficient and courageous man, and I should like you to know how popular he was with all his comrades. The Battalion never had a finer man and many of us have lost a dear friend'.

Writing a letter of sympathy to his parents, Messrs Charlesworth and Company said:

'Your son was held in high esteem by us all and we sincerely mourn the loss of a loyal and respected employee who had endeared himself to all his fellow workers and who we feel sure would have done well in our profession had he been spared to return'.

George was a member of the Cuckfield Football team 1907 - 8 which won the Mid-Sussex Junior League cup. He was also an athlete and as a member of the Haywards Heath Athletic Club won many prizes.

Mrs G. E. Botting desires through this medium to express her heartfelt thanks for the many kind message of sympathy she has received which have touched her deeply.

George was buried at Lapugnoy Military Cemetry reference V.D.14

His name appears on the war memorial in the churchyard of Holy Trinity Church, Cuckfield, on the marble memorial inside the Church and on the memorial board in the Queen's Hall, Cuckfield.

PRIVATE THOMAS CHARLES BOURNE

Thomas Bourne was the second son of Charles. T. Bourne who was born in Balcombe in 1863, and his mother Annie who was born in Slaugham, Sussex in 1868. Thomas was born in Slaugham in 1890, his elder brother William was born there in 1888. His younger brothers were all born in Bolney; Ernest born in 1892, Frederick born in 1895, Sidney born in 1897, Albert born in 1899 and Percy born in 1900. Charles was a cooper - smart hoop maker in 1891 but by 1901 was an agricultural labourer. The family lived at 'Chatfields', Bolney and later moved to 'New England Cottage', Beech Farm, Cuckfield.

Thomas enlisted in Horsham into the 2nd Battalion Royal Sussex Regiment - 1st Regular Division. Special Reservist. Service number S/414.

Mid-Sussex Times - 7th December 1915
PRIVATE T. C. BOURNE

Having been reported as missing since October 1914, Private T. C. Bourne, 3rd Royal Sussex Regiment, has now been reported killed in action at that time. He was 25 years of age and had been in the Army for seven years, going out to the front on the outbreak of hostilities. He was killed in action while with the British Expeditionary Force near Ypres on 31st October 1914 and is Remembered with Honour on the Ypres (Menin Gate) Memorial Panel 20.

His name appears on the war memorial in the churchyard of Holy Trinity Church, Cuckfield and on the marble memorial inside the Church.

This is the second son Mr and Mrs Bourne have lost, as on the 27th January of this year, Private William. E. Bourne, 2nd Battalion Royal Sussex Regiment was killed at La Bassee, at the age of 28. He was married and lived in Lindfield and left a widow and one child.

LANCE-CORPORAL CECIL ALFRED BOWELL

Cecil was the son of Henry and Anne Bowell of 'Woodcroft Villas', Whitemans Green, Cuckfield. Henry was a carpenter, born in Warwickshire and his wife Anne was born in Hampshire. Cecil was their eldest son, born in 1895; his brother Norman was born in 1898.

He enlisted at Chichester, Sussex in 1913 into the 3rd Battalion, Royal Sussex Regiment, Service number G2031.

He later transferred to the 71st Field Company, the Royal Engineers Mesopotamian Expeditionary Force, Service number 26402.

Mid-Sussex Times - 31st July 1917
LANCE-CORPORAL CECIL BOWELL - Died of Heatstroke

Official news was received yesterday evening that Lance Corporal Cecil Bowell R. E. died in hospital in Basra in the Persian Gulf on 22nd July, cause of death being heat stroke. The eldest son of Mr and Mrs H. Bowell, of 'Woodcroft Villas', Whitemans Green he was for a time a clerk on the railway, but he joined the army in 1913.

He was in the fierce fighting in Flanders in the early part of 1915 and was wounded in the leg at Hill 60.

He was invalided home and when he was again fit for duty he volunteered for service in Mesopotamia. He was with the force which captured Baghdad where he was again slightly wounded. He has written many interesting letters home lately descriptive of Baghdad and the people. Much sympathy is felt for Mr and Mrs Bowell whose second son Norman is now fighting in France.

Cecil died in a Basra hospital in Mesopotamia and is buried in Baghdad (North Gate) War Cemetery, Iraq.

His name appears on the war memorial in the churchyard of Holy Trinity Church, Cuckfield, on the marble memorial inside the Church and on the memorial board in the Queen's Hall, Cuckfield.

LANCE-CORPORAL
WILLIAM CHARLES BOWLEY

William was born in 1895 in West Grinstead, Sussex, the son of Charlie and Elizabeth Bowley of Church Street, Cuckfield. His father was a gardener, born in Arundel, and his mother Elizabeth was born in Crawley. William had a stepbrother named John. H. Steer born in 1891, and a sister Kate born in 1893.

William enlisted in Haywards Heath into the 9th Battalion Royal Sussex Regiment, 24th New Army Division, Service number G/3391.

Previous to the war, William was in the service of Mrs Bigg, 'The Hyde', Handcross, as footman, and he enlisted in September 1914.

Before going to France, just a year after his enlistment, he was made a Lance-Corporal.

He was killed in action with the British Expeditionary Force on 28th September 1915 aged 20 years.

Mid-Sussex Times - 12th October 1915
LANCE - CORPORAL W. BOWLEY

Letters written home by Cuckfield men last week were the means of conveying to Mr and Mrs C. Bowley, of Church Street, Cuckfield, the sad news that their younger son, Lance-Corporal William Bowley No 3391, 'B' Co, 9th Battalion Royal Sussex Regiment, had been killed during the advance of a fortnight ago. As his parents have received no tidings from him since the encounter it is feared the information must be accepted as true, but his relatives are anxiously awaiting an official announcement.

Lance-Corporal Bowley, who was in his twenty-first year, was born at West Grinstead, but came to Cuckfield with his parents when he was three years old. He attended the Church School, and for some years was a choir boy at the Parish Church.

With his clever impersonation of a farmer when attired in a smock frock, he gave recitations in the Devonshire dialect at concerts several years ago, which will be remembered by Cuckfieldians, and he will also be remembered by the 'old folks', who still cherish happy memories of his humorous portrayal of 'The Hunt Dinner'.

He is Remembered with Honour on the Loos Memorial, Panel 69 to 73

His name appears on the war memorial in the churchyard of Holy Trinity Church, Cuckfield, on the marble memorial inside the Church and on the memorial board in the Queen's Hall, Cuckfield.

LIEUTENANT ALFRED RICHARD BURNESS

Alfred, who was born in 1888, was the son of Isabella J. Farquharson (formerly Burness) of 'Northlands', Haywards Heath, Sussex and the late Mr A. J. Burness of London.

He was a Lieutenant in the 2nd Battalion Seaforth Highlanders (Ross-shire Buffs, the Duke of Albany's) 4th Regular Division.

Alfred was killed in action near Langemark on 25th April 1915 aged 27 years.

Mid-Sussex Times - 18th May 1915
LIEUTENANT A. R. BURNESS

Notification has been received of the death, in action, of Lieutenant Alfred Richard Burness, of the 2nd Battalion Seaforth Highlanders.

He was the only son of the late Mr A. J. Burness, of 138 Leadenhall Street London E.C. and of Mrs Farquharson, (formerly Burness) wife of Major C. H. Farquharson, J.P. of 'Ruthven Lodge', Cuckfield. In an account received from the Adjutant of the regiment, who was with him at the time, Lieutenant Burness was wounded in the spine near Ypres on April 25th and died soon after.

The young officer was born on May 29th 1888, and was thus nearing his twenty-seventh birthday.

After being educated at Eton, he went into the Special Reserve, and from there he received his commission as Second Lieutenant in July 1910, being promoted to Lieutenant three years later. He had been in France since last August.

Alfred is buried in Seaforth Cemetery, Cheddar Villa, Belgium, memorial reference A3.

His name appears on the war memorial in the churchyard of Holy Trinity Church, Cuckfield and on the marble memorial inside the Church

C

ABLE SEAMAN JOSEPH CARD

Joseph was born in Chelsea, London in 1885. He was the son of William Card who in the 1901 census is shown as a retired Police Officer married to Susan. William was born in Wivelsfield and Susan was born in Brighton. Both Joseph and his elder brother, Thomas born in 1880, were barmen living with the entire family at 'Albert House', Cuckfield. They had two younger sisters, Ellen born in 1890 and Rose born in 1892.

Joseph joined the Royal Naval Volunteer Reserve, Nelson Battalion R. N. Division. Service number Sussex 2/293.

For many months Joseph was reported missing. His wife, Lilian Mary, refused to give up hope of him being found and coming home. But on 9th July 1916, after a very short illness, she passed away at her home at Whiteman's Green aged 28 years. Just a few days afterwards an official intimation was received that it had now been assumed by the Admiralty that Joseph was killed in action on the Gallipoli Peninsula on July 13th 1915.

Mid-Sussex Times - 24th August 1915

Joseph Card, A.B., 2/293, Nelson Battalion, 7th Royal Naval Division, who has been reported wounded and in hospital at Alexandria, is the younger son of Mr and Mrs Card, formerly of Cuckfield and Haywards Heath.

He was reported wounded on July 13th, since when no news has been received of him. His wife is residing at Cuckfield, and his elder brother, Mr T. Card is the landlord of 'The Ship'.

He is Remembered with Honour on the Helles Memorial panel 8 to 15.

His name appears on the war memorial in the churchyard of Holy Trinity Church, Cuckfield, on the marble memorial inside the Church and on the memorial board in the Queen's Hall, Cuckfield.

PRIVATE HUBERT WILLIAM CARTNER

Hubert William was born in 1896 in Keswick, Cumberland, the son of James Cartner who came from Carlisle and Dinah Cartner who came from Keswick. On the 1901 census when Hubert was 5 years old, the family lived at 'Northwood Cottage', Fairfield, Buxton, Derbyshire where James worked as a groom domestic.

Hubert had an elder sister Imogen born in 1894, also in Keswick.

By the time of the outbreak of war it is presumed the family had already moved to 'Mytton Lodge', Cuckfield, as Hubert was working on the staff of the Mid-Sussex Times newspaper in Haywards Heath (see below)

He enlisted in Haywards Heath into the 2nd Battalion, The Royal Sussex Regiment, 1st Regular Division, Service number G/1477.

Mid-Sussex Times - 16th November 1915
PRIVATE HUBERT CARTNER

Private Hubert W. Cartner, 3rd Battalion Royal Sussex Regiment, son of Mr James Cartner of 'Mytten Lodge', Cuckfield, who had returned to the Western front after a spell in hospital suffering from frozen feet, is now in hospital at Leicester with bad feet. He is one of the numerous members of the Mid-Sussex Times staff who answered the call of King and country.

Mid-Sussex Times - 10th October 1916
HUBERT WILLIAM CARTNER - DIED IN HONOUR

We deeply regret to have to record the death of Private Hubert W. Cartner, Royal Sussex regiment, only son of Mr and Mrs James Cartner of 'Mytten', who was killed in action on September 9th. He was in his 21st year. A War Office communication to the parents said he was posted as 'missing' but the worst fears were realised when the following letter, dated September 28th was received:

'Dear Mrs Cartner,

It is hard to be the bearer of sad news, but I think you would rather hear from me of the death of your gallant son - 1477 Private H. Cartner, Royal Sussex - and any particulars I can give, than get the first bare intimation which you will receive in a few days (if you have not done so already) from the War Office.

I found his body yesterday, about 300 yards south-----------(you will know where that is) and there he is buried. All I found upon him was the pocket book which I enclose. I said some of our Church prayers, so full of faith and hope, and placed a rough cross on the spot. More it was impossible to do, as heavy shell fire was going on all around.

I'm sure your son must have been a very gallant fellow. He has in the highest sense got his promotion very early. His pay book I also found, and this I have forwarded to the proper authority.

With kind sympathy, believe me,
Yours truly

Cecil L. Money-Kyrle (Rev) S.C.F. Headquarters 1st Division

The unfortunate soldier lad was almost 21 years of age, and was well liked by all who knew him. He was a member of the Mid-Sussex Times staff when war broke out, and feeling it to be his duty he joined up very soon after hostilities commenced. During the first winter he suffered from 'trench feet', and was invalided home, and on returning to the Front became a bomb thrower. He was constantly in the firing line. Later he returned to the base for instruction in machine gun work, and it was probably while on this work that he met his death.

Hubert is Remembered with Honour on the Thiepval Memorial, Pier and Face 7C.

His name appears on the war memorial in the churchyard of Holy Trinity Church, Cuckfield, on the marble memorial inside the Church and on the memorial board in the Queen's Hall, Cuckfield.

Mr and Mrs Cartner desire to express their heartfelt thanks for the many expressions of sympathy they have received.

LANCE-CORPORAL FRANK CHATFIELD

Frank was born in 1887 at 'Stroods', Brook Street, Cuckfield, the son of George Richard Chatfield, a farmer, and Clara Ellen Chatfield who was born in Henfield, Sussex. By the time the war started the family were living in Pickwell Lane, Cuckfield.

Frank was the fourth child listed in the family on the 1891 census. Eldest was Albert born in 1879, then Emily born in 1882 and Mabel born in 1886.

He was an agriculture labourer and then an attendant at the Brighton County Asylum in Haywards Heath.

Lance-Corporal Chatfield, who joined the army soon after the outbreak of war, enlisted in Haywards Heath with the 2nd Battalion Royal Sussex Regiment, 1st Regular Division. Service number G/1475

Mid-Sussex Times - 25th May 1915
LANCE-CORPORAL F. CHATFIELD
News has been received by Mr and Mrs Chatfield, of Pickwell Lane, Cuckfield, that their son, Lance-Corporal Frank Chatfield is wounded and missing.

Mid-Sussex Times - 1st June 1915

LANCE-CORPORAL F. CHATFIELD

It was reported in this column last week that Lance-Corporal Frank Chatfield was wounded and missing. The news was received unofficially by his parents from a comrade, but notification has now been received from the War Office that he was killed in action at Richebourg l'Avoué on May 9th.

Lance-Corporal Chatfield was the second son of Mr and Mrs G. R. Chatfield of Pickwell Lane, Cuckfield, and was born at Brook Street in the same Parish on December 9th 1887, he thus being in his 28th year.

As a boy he attended the local Church Schools and was also in the Brook Street Mission Church Choir.

For some years he was in the employ of Colonel Stephenson R. Clarke as footman, and for the last five years had been an attendant at the Brighton County Borough Asylum at Haywards Heath. It was from here that he joined the 3rd Battalion Royal Sussex Regiment on September 3rd last, and went to France on January 11th being attached to the 2nd Battalion. He went safely through the battles of La Bassée and Neuve Chappelle, and received his stripe while abroad.

He was killed in action at Richebourg L'Avoue with the British Expeditionary Force on 9th May 1915, aged 28 years.

He is Remembered with Honour on Le Touret Memorial, Richebourg, Panel 20 and 21.

His name appears on the war memorial in the churchyard of Holy Trinity Church, Cuckfield, on the marble memorial inside the Church and on the memorial board in the Queen's Hall, Cuckfield.

SAPPER ALBERT EDWARD CHINNERY

Albert was born in Staplefield, Sussex in 1885 the son of Thomas and Louisa Chinnery. Thomas was born in Norfolk and was an agricultural labourer. Louisa was born in Cuckfield.

Albert was the second son. The eldest son was Walter, born in 1884, and after Albert came George born in 1887, Ethel was born in 1889 and Florence was born in 1890. Matilda was born in 1892, then Mabel in 1895 and Arthur in 1900.

Before enlisting, Albert had a job as a wheelwright.

In 1891 they all lived at 'Dorcas Cottages', Staplefield where Walter the eldest son was a gardener. By 1901 the family had moved to 'Rooke Cottages', Cuckfield.

Albert enlisted in Haywards Heath into the 106th Field Company, The Royal Engineers, Service number 57278.

He was married in 1915 to Miss Charlotte Blowers who was from Kippilaw, St Boswells, Roxboroughshire.

Shirley Bond

Mid-Sussex Times - 14th August 1917
ALBERT CHINNERY R. E.

On Friday the sad news was received by Mr and Mrs T. Chinnery, of High Street, Cuckfield, that their second son Albert Chinnery R. E. was killed on the previous Sunday. He was home on leave very recently and returned to his duties on August 4th and on the next day he met his death.

He was a waiter in the officers' mess and was on duty in the mess room when a shell landed in the house and wounded him so severely that he died without regaining consciousness and before his wound could be dressed. Several other men in the cook house at the time were buried by the debris for a while, but Albert was killed instantly being wounded in the chest.

Before the war he worked for Mr. S. Knight as a wheelwright and he was a bell-ringer at the Parish Church. He joined up as soon as war broke out and went to the front in September 1915.

Writing to his widow, the Major commanding, speaks of the sadness of it all, and adds, 'He looked after us all with such care, and we often wondered when he slept. His death has been a great blow to his whole company. Your husband was so popular - always cheery and so hard working. I know that your husband's death must be a very great blow to you and I beg that you may accept the deepest sympathy from the officers and men in your great sorrow.'

Albert served in France and Flanders but was killed, as described above, on 5th August 1917 aged 32.

He is buried in the Belgian Battery Corner Cemetery, Ypres, Grave Reference I.M.12

He is remembered on the war memorial in the churchyard of Holy Trinity Church, Cuckfield, on the marble memorial inside the Church and on the memorial board in the Queen's Hall, Cuckfield.

PRIVATE ALBERT CROUCHER

Albert was born in Cuckfield in 1898, the son of Issac Croucher, a general labourer and his wife Esther. He had an elder brother Alfred born in 1895. The family lived at 5, Burrells Cottages, Whitemans Green.

Albert enlisted in Cuckfield into the 8th Battalion, (Pioneer Battalion) Royal Sussex Regiment, 18th Eastern Division, Service number G/2664.

He was killed in action with the British Expeditionary Force at Bernafay Wood on 14th July 1916 aged 18 years.

Mid-Sussex Times - 1st August 1916
THE LATE PRIVATE CROUCHER

Mrs Farrow, of Whiteman's Green, has received the following letter from an officer of the Company of the Royal Sussex Regiment of which her brother, the late Private Croucher - whose death we have already announced - was a member -

'It is my painful duty to inform you of the death of your brother, Private Croucher, who was killed in action on the night of July 13th. He met his end bravely, whilst holding an exposed trench under heavy shrapnel fire. May I assure you of my deepest sympathy in your great loss'.

Albert is Remembered with Honour on The Thiepval Memorial. Pier and Face 7C.

He is remembered on the war memorial in the churchyard of Holy Trinity Church, Cuckfield, on the marble memorial inside the Church and on the memorial board in the Queen's Hall, Cuckfield.

D

CORPORAL THOMAS HENRY DANCE

Thomas was born in Lancing, Sussex in 1896, the son of Emily J. Dance and the late James Dance. In 1901 the family lived at 'Great Bentley Cottage', Cuckfield where James was a carter on a farm. They later moved to 'Barracks Cottage', Brook Street, Cuckfield.

Thomas was their third son; William was born in 1889 and James was born in 1891. Sisters Annie and Lucy were born in 1893 and 1898.

Thomas enlisted in Haywards Heath into The Royal Sussex Regiment, Service number 4523.

He later moved to the 58th Battalion, The Machine Gun Corps (Infantry) Service number 5842.

Mid- Sussex Times - 26th September 1916
PRIVATE T. H. DANCE - 'GASSED'
Mrs Dance, of 'Barracks Cottages', Brook Street, received news on Friday that her third son, Private T. H. Dance, Machine Gun Corps, has been gassed and is in the First Australian General Hospital. Nothing has been heard as to his condition. Little was heard of him until he was reported missing killed in action during the German Spring offensive 22nd March 1918 when he was aged 22 years.

Mid-Sussex Times - 30th April 1918
Missing
Mrs Dance, 'Barracks Cottages', Brook Street, has received official news that her son Corporal T. H. Dance, Machine Gun Corps, has been missing since 22nd March 1918. He joined up in November 1914 and was wounded on April 24th of last year.

Cuckfield Parish Magazine - July 1919
After many months of weary and anxious waiting, Mrs Emily Dance of 'Barracks Cottages', has received from the War Office a notice that her son, Corporal Thomas Henry Dance, Machine Gun Corps, is presumed to have been killed at Quessy on March 22nd 1918.

He is Remembered with Honour on Pozieres Memorial, Panel 90 to 93.

He is remembered on the war memorial in the churchyard of Holy Trinity Church, Cuckfield, on the marble memorial inside the Church and on the memorial board in the Queen's Hall, Cuckfield.

PRIVATE ELLIS ALBERT DANCY

Ellis was born in Cuckfield in 1884. He was the second son of William and Eunice Dancy who lived at Whitemans Green, Cuckfield. William was a house painter. Ellis's elder brother Alfred W. Dancy was born in 1882, his younger brother Edward was born in 1887, his sister Alice born in 1889, Frederick in 1891, Eunice in 1894 and William H. born in 1897. They were all born in Cuckfield and the elder boys were all gardeners.

Ellis was the husband of Nellie Dancy of Brainsmead, Cuckfield and at the time of his death they had small children.

He enlisted in Haywards Heath into the Royal Sussex Regiment, Service number 660, and later transferred to the 6th Battalion, Queen's Own Royal West Kent Regiment, 12th Eastern Division, Service number G.7341

He had been promoted to Lance-Corporal in the Royal West Kent Regiment.

Ellis died of gunshot wounds suffered during the Arras offensive on 9th May 1917. He was aged 33 years.

Cuckfield Parish Magazine - June 1917
Ellis was the second son of Mr and Mrs Dancy who have twice suffered bereavement as their youngest son William Henry was killed in September 1915 at the Dardanelles. Their third son, Private Edward E. Dancy has been wounded while serving with the Egyptian Expeditionary Force.

Ellis is buried in the Duisans British Cemetery, Etrun, Ref 111. K. 45

He is remembered on the war memorial in the churchyard of Holy Trinity Church, Cuckfield, on the marble memorial inside the Church and on the memorial board in the Queen's Hall, Cuckfield.

PRIVATE WILLIAM HENRY DANCY

William Henry was born in 1897, the son of William Dancy of Brainsmead, Whiteman's Green, Cuckfield and the late Eunice Dancy of Brainsmead, Whitemans Green, Cuckfield. He was the brother of Ellis Albert Dancy born in 1884 who died in the war in 1917.

They were a large family. Alfred was born in 1882, Ellis in 1884, Edward in 1887, Alice in 1889, Frederick in 1891 and Eunice born in 1894.

Before enlisting, William was employed by Mr. W. G. Trethewey at 'Holmstead Place' as a gardner.

He was only 19 years of age when he joined the Territorials. He was the youngest of four brothers who were also in the Army, one being in France with the West Surrey Regiment and two others at Tring with No 6 Supernumerary Company of the 4th Battalion Royal Sussex Regiment.

He enlisted in Horsham into the 4th Battalion Royal Sussex Regiment, 53rd Welsh Division Service number TF/3219.

William was killed in action in Sulva Bay, Gallipoli on 26th August 1915 aged 19 years. He is buried in Azmak Cemetery, Sulva Bay, Gallipoli Ref 11.D.1

Mid-Sussex Times - 14th September 1915
PRIVATE WILLIAM HENRY DANCY

The sad news has been received by Mr and Mrs W. Dancy, of Whitemans Green, Cuckfield, that their youngest son, Private William Henry Dancy, 4th Battalion, Royal Sussex Regiment, has been killed in action in the Dardenelles.

The information was conveyed to them in a tragic manner for it was a scribbled note by his commanding officer on the back of a letter written by the young soldier two days before his death, which took place on 26th August 1915. The letter, which had not been posted when he was killed, reached Cuckfield on Saturday evening. It ran -

'Just a few lines, hoping you are all quite well, as this leaves me in the best of health. We are in the trenches now; we came into them on Sunday last. There are plenty of shells going about. I am sitting in a trench writing this letter in my spare time. It does seem funny living in the trenches night and day. The sooner it is over the better, so we can get back again. I don't think it will last very much longer out here; I hope not. I think I have not much more to say this time, will write again before long. Hope to see you again soon.'

The officer's message on the back was,

'I regret to inform you that Private Dancy was killed on duty this morning. It may be of some comfort to you to know that he will be given a decent burial tonight by his comrades and have the service read by the Chaplain. Assuring you of my deepest sympathy and that of the officers and men of his Company, believe me.'

Yours sincerely,

Arthur N. H. Weekes, Captain, Commanding 'A' Company.

William is remembered on the war memorial in the churchyard of Holy Trinity Church, Cuckfield, on the marble memorial inside the Church and on the memorial board in the Queen's Hall, Cuckfield.

PRIVATE FREDERICK DIVALL

Frederick was born in 1887, in Norlington Lane, Ringmer, Sussex, the third child of Thomas a farmer, and Fanny Divall, later of 'North House', London Road, Burgess Hill, Sussex.

His elder brother William was born in 1883, sister Fanny was born in1885, younger brother Ernest in 1889, Edith in 1890, Lilian in 1893, Berin born in 1895, Beatrice in 1897 and Gertrude born in 1898. They were all born in Ringmer, Sussex.

At a later date the family moved to Westup Farm, Cuckfield and Frederick was working at home, probably helping his father on the farm. Before enlisting, he worked as a gardener in the employ of Mr Richard Worsley of 'Broxmead'.

Frederick enlisted in Lewes, Sussex into the 6th Battalion, Queen's Own (Royal West Kent Regiment) Service number G/13396.

On 5th October 1915 he was officially reported as having been wounded in the Dardanelles. On 5th December 1916 he was killed in action aged 29 years.

He is remembered with Honour in Wailly Orchard Cemetery in the Department of the Pas-de-Calais. Memorial ref I.H.6.

He is remembered on the war memorial at Ringmer as well as the memorial panels in the Queens Hall, Cuckfield.

ABLE SEAMAN CHARLES FRANK DOICK

Charles was born in 1895 at 'Mizbrooks', Cuckfield, the son of William who was born in Pulborough and his wife Ellen who was born in Lindfield. William was a stockman on a farm. Their eldest son was John, born in 1881, then Maud who was born in 1888, Alice born in 1890, Harry born in 1892, then Charles and lastly Ada born in 1898.

Charles joined 'H.M.S. Black Prince' of the Royal Navy, Service number J/9484.

He was killed on 31st May 1916 aged 22 years, when his ship was lost with all hands at the Battle of Jutland.

He is commemorated on the Portsmouth Naval Memorial, Southsea, Hants - ref 12

His name also appears on the war memorial in the churchyard of Holy Trinity Church, Cuckfield, on the marble memorial inside the Church and on the memorial board in the Queen's Hall, Cuckfield.

E

CAPTAIN CHRISTOPHER ERLE

Christopher was born in Cuckfield in 1873, the first son of Twynihoe William Erle and Mary Erle who in 1917 were living at 17, Parkside, Albert Gate, Knightsbridge, London.

His father was a Master of the Supreme Court of Justice which may have been the reason for the family moving around the country. In 1891 they were living at 1 Cambridge Gate, St Pancras, London.

Christopher's father was born in Middlesex and his mother was born in Glasgow. Christopher was born in Cuckfield as was his sister Violet born in 1877. He had two elder sisters, Lillian born in 1878 and Sybil born in 1881, both born in St Pancras, Middlesex.

Christopher enlisted in the 1st Garrison Battalion Northamptonshire Regiment.

He served in the South African Campaign and was killed on 10th February 1917 aged 44 years.

He is Remembered with Honour in the Alexandria (HADRA) War Memorial Cemetery Ref. B8.

His name is not listed on any of the War Memorials in Cuckfield but his photograph is amongst those men from Cuckfield who died in the war.

PRIVATE HARRY ETHERTON

Harry was the son of Edwin and Louisa A. Etherton of 2, Anstye Lane, Cuckfield. Born in 1872 he was their eldest son. He had a younger brother Thomas born in 1879 followed by two sisters, Annie born in 1881 and Louisa born in 1884. Father Edwin was an agricultural labourer.

By the time he enlisted in Haywards Heath, Harry was married to Annie and they were living in South Street, Cuckfield. Harry was a roadman for the Urban District Council.

He enlisted in Haywards Heath into the 15th Battalion, Royal Sussex Regiment, Service number 6940 and later transferred to the 409th Company, The Labour Corps, Service number 499177.

Harry died of meningitis at the Northern Hospital, Lincolnshire after a long illness and was brought home to 1, Jubilee Cottages, Broad Street, Cuckfield, on 30th June 1918 aged 46 years.

Mid-Sussex Times - July 9th 1918

FUNERAL OF PRIVATE HARRY ETHERTON

On Wednesday the mortal remains of Private Harry Etherton, Royal Sussex Regiment, were laid to rest in Cuckfield churchyard. The deceased who passed away at the Northern Hospital, Lincolnshire, from meningitis, was formerly in the National Reserve and also in the employ of the Cuckfield Urban District Council. He joined up just over three years ago.

Under the command of Major Lister the Volunteers attended. Sergeant Ferguson was in charge of the firing party and there acted as bearers Corporal Carter, Corporal Brigden, Private Willsden and Private Turville.

Several of the Cuckfield Boy Scouts, under acting Scoutmaster A.T. Rapley, also attended the funeral, and the flag on the church tower was at half mast.

Among the many present in the church were Miss Berly, Miss Best, Mrs Cooper, Mr Wells, Mrs Conway, Mrs Reid, the Rev. Dr. Richards, Mrs Botting, Mrs H. Rowland, Mrs Jupp, Mrs A. Browne, Mrs Morfee, Mrs A. Burtenshaw, Mrs Fuller, Mrs Pennifold and Miss Osbourne.

The Rev. J. H. Layton conducted the service. The chief mourners were Mrs Etherton (widow), Masters Jack and Leslie Etherton (sons), Misses Winnie, Sybil and Ivy Etheron (daughters), Mr Etherton (father), Mrs Edwards, Mrs Peacock, Mrs Harmer (sisters) Mr Pennifold (father-in-law), Miss Pennifold, Mrs Johnson, Miss L. Pennifold, Mrs A. Henley (sisters-in-law), Miss Stone (niece) and Mrs A. Upton (cousin).

The coffin, which was covered with the Union Jack, bore the following inscription -

Private Harry Etherton
Died June 30th 1918
Aged 46 years

At the close of the committal service the 'Last Post' was sounded by Sergeant-Bugler F. Hounsell. The floral tributes were sent by his sorrowing wife and his children, his loving father and brothers and sisters Mrs Harry Preston with Emily and Arthur, Mr and Mrs A. Browne, Mr and Mrs H. Rowland, Mr and Mrs Mays, Mrs Wells and family, Mr and

Mrs Day and daughters, Mr and Mrs Murrell, Mr and Mrs Brigden, Mr and Mrs Thomsett, M. Stone, and Mr and Mrs Bone of Felvedon Essex.

Harry is buried in Cuckfield Cemetery Ref 10 (W) 296

His name also appears on the war memorial in the churchyard of Holy Trinity Church, Cuckfield, on the marble memorial inside the Church and on the memorial board in the Queen's Hall, Cuckfield.

F

SECOND LIEUTENANT
WILFRED FREDERICK FISHER

Wilfred Frederick was born in 1898, the son of Canon Robert and Mrs Mary Frances Fisher (formerly of Cuckfield).

In 1901 the family were living in the Vicarage at Withyham in the Rural District of West Grinstead where Wilfred's father was the clergyman. Frances was the eldest son born in 1889, Etheldreda was born 1890, Dorothea was born in 1894 and then Wilfred born in 1898.

Wilfred enlisted with the 3rd Battalion, Royal Sussex Regiment, 39th New Army Division.

Mid-Sussex Times - 2nd October 1916
SECOND LIEUTENANT WILFRED F. FISHER - WOUNDED

Second Lieutenant Wilfred. F. Fisher (Royal Sussex Regiment), younger son of the Rev. Cannon Fisher, is now at home on sick leave. He was shot in the left arm at close quarters. He spent ten hours in a shell hole waiting for darkness before he could return to his lines. He was in hospital for five days and was then sent home. The wound is not severe, and he is making good progress.

(Canon and Mrs Fisher are shortly going to take up their residence at Chichester)

Mid-Sussex Times - 9th October 1917
DEATH OF SECOND LIEUTENANT W. F. FISHER

Died in France on July 24th 1917, Second Lieutenant W. F. Fisher Royal Sussex Regiment, younger son of the Rev Cannon and Mrs Robert Fisher of 'The Elms' Chichester, and formerly of Cuckfield.

Much sympathy is felt for Cannon and Mrs Fisher, they having on Friday received a telegram to say that their younger son Wilfred Frederick Fisher, Royal Sussex Regiment had died in France on July 24th. He was reported missing during a trench raid on July 20th prior to the Third Battle of Ypres near St Julian and was killed in action on 24th July 1917.

No further particulars have been received so far.

He is Remembered with Honour on the Ypres (Menin Gate) Memorial, Panel 20.

His name appears on the war memorial in the churchyard of Holy Trinity Church, Cuckfield, on the marble memorial inside the Church and on the memorial board in the Queen's Hall, Cuckfield.

Wilfred is remembered in Cuckfield because his mother Mary was born and brought up in Cuckfield, and Canon Fisher was the Church of England vicar in the Parish for some time.

Cuckfield Parish Magazine - January 1919
The Vicar and churchwardens wish to acknowledge, with very many

thanks, a gift which has been made to the Church and which was used for the first time on Christmas Day.

A handsome brass processional cross with facets of rock crystal, the gift from Miss Maberly, bears the following inscription -

'For the Glory of God and in dear memory of Wilfred F. Fisher, 2nd Lieutenant, Royal Sussex Regiment, son of R. Fisher, some time Vicar of Cuckfield, who gave his life in Flanders 24th July 1917. This cross is presented to the Church of Holy Trinity, Cuckfield by L. E. Maberly'.

We are fortunate in now possessing two processional crosses, both of them beautiful and both of which we shall be glad to use on appropriate occasions.

PRIVATE GEORGE SAMUEL FRANKS

George Samuel was born in 1891 in Worth, Sussex, the son of George and Mary Ann Franks. He had an elder sister Annie born in 1888 and three younger sisters, Cicely born in 1892, Florence born in 1894 and Caroline born in 1897. Their father was a gardener.

George enlisted in Brighton into the 2nd/6th Battalion Royal Sussex Regiment Service number TF/265403.

He later joined the Indian Army and was based in India where he died of disease on 17th August 1917.

He is buried in the Tank Cemetery 23 in India and is Remembered with Honour on the Delhi Memorial (India Gate) Face 1-23.

Mid-Sussex Times - 16th October 1917
Private G. Franks who before joining up was a gardener at Moon Hill, has died in India. It may be because of his connection with Moon Hill that he is remembered on the war memorial in the churchyard of Holy Trinity Church, Cuckfield, on the marble memorial inside the Church and on the memorial board in the Queen's Hall, Cuckfield.

As his family came from Worth in Sussex, George is also remembered on Crawley War Memorial and Ifield Parish Church War Memorial.

PRIVATE LEONARD THOMAS FUNNELL

Private Leonard Funnell was born in 1889, the younger son of Mr William Funnell of 'Lauriston House', Cuckfield. William Funnell was shown as an ironmonger and blacksmith in Seaford, Sussex in the 1891 and 1901 census. He lived there with his wife Harriett. The eldest son William was born in Seaford in 1881, Leonard was born in 1889 and sister Olive was born in 1892. On moving to Cuckfield, William became the caretaker of the Cuckfield Club.

Leonard moved to Canada some few years before, but on the outbreak of war he and his elder brother William both joined the Army. He enlisted into the 78th Battalion, 4th Canadian Infantry Division, (Manitoba Regiment), Service number 1000261.

He was killed in action at Passchendale on 30th October 1917 aged 28 years.

Leonard gave his life in defence of his Motherland and is remembered on the Ypres (Menin Gate) Memorial Panel 24-26-28-30.

His name appears on the war memorial in the churchyard of Holy Trinity Church, Cuckfield, on the marble memorial inside the Church and on the memorial board in the Queen's Hall, Cuckfield

G

BOMBADIER JESSE GANDER

Jesse was born in 1887 in Cuckfield, the son of Albert and Annie Gander of 37, Jesamine Cottages, Brook Street, Cuckfield. He had a younger brother Henry born in 1890 and a sister Esther also born in 1890.

Like his father, Jesse was an agricultural labourer before enlisting in Haywards Heath into the Royal Garrison Artillery, 60th Heavy Battery, Service number 23501.

Mid-Sussex Times - 4th January 1916
Sad News
We regret to have to announce that news was officially received on Saturday by Mr and Mrs Albert Gander, of Brook Street, Cuckfield, that their son Jesse Gander, 60th Battery, R.G.A, had been accidentally shot

through the heart at Barca Camp, Roorkee, United Provinces, India. He died on 28th December, 1915 aged 28 years and is buried in Roorkee Cemetery, India.

Mid-Sussex Times - 26th January 1916
SOLDIERS DEATH IN INDIA

In our issue of the 4th inst. we announced the death, in India, of Jesse Gander, 60th Battery, R.G.A. His parents who reside in Brook Street, Cuckfield, have since received a letter (dated December 31st 1915) from Lieutenant H. C. R. Caudle, who, writing from the R. A. Mess, Roorkee, United Provinces, states that the soldier met with a fatal accident two days previously.

'He was cleaning his revolver and had forgotten there was a round in it. It went off and shot him through the heart. He died at once, and suffered no pain. His death has been a very great loss to the Battery, as he was greatly loved by all the men, and during his two years serving under me I have seldom met a man who I liked better. The officers and men of the Battery desire to express their greatest sympathy with you in your loss. Your son, who was buried in Roorkee Cemetery, will not be forgotten by the gunners in Rookee'.

He is remembered on the Madras 1914 - 1918 war memorial in Chennai, Face No 5.

Jesse is remembered on the war memorial in the churchyard of Holy Trinity Church, Cuckfield, on the marble memorial inside the Church and on the memorial board in the Queen's Hall, Cuckfield

PRIVATE GEORGE GIBSON

George was born in 1892, the son of William and Kate Gibson of 'Harradines', Cuckfield. He had two older sisters, Kate born in 1887 and Margaret born in 1888. A brother Robert A. followed in 1894 and sister Agnes M. in 1895.

William, George's father, was a joiner/carpenter born in Scotland and mother Kate was born in Pulborough, Sussex.

George enlisted in Haywards Heath into the 8th Battalion, (Pioneer Battalion) Royal Sussex Regiment, 18th Eastern Division, Service number 2779. He served in the British Expeditionary Force.

The Mid-Sussex Times - 25th July 1916
PRIVATE GEORGE GIBSON KILLED

Cuckfieldians will hear with regret that Mr and Mrs W. Gibson received news on Saturday that their eldest son, Private George Gibson, of the Royal Sussex Regiment, had died as a result of wounds received on July 13th.

From a letter written by one of his companions it appears that while digging a new trench the men were heavily shelled, and that among those who were hit were several Cuckfield men.

The deceased, who was 24 years of age, joined up on the outbreak of war. He was well known in Cuckfield having for several years been a regular member of Cuckfield Football team, and he was deservedly popular both with players and spectators. He also occasionally played for the local Cricket Club and he was a member of the Town Band and the Bell Ringers Society. It will be remembered how he and the other members of the Town Band played themselves away when they left Cuckfield to join up at the beginning of the war.

George is buried in Peronne Road Cemetery, Maricourt. Ref I.C.12

He is remembered on the war memorial in the churchyard of Holy Trinity Church, Cuckfield, on the marble memorial inside the Church and on the memorial board in the Queen's Hall, Cuckfield

Mr and Mrs Gibson and family wish to take this opportunity of expressing their gratitude to all who have sent them letters or messages of sympathy in their great bereavement.

H

PRIVATE WILLIAM HAYLOR

William was born in Cuckfield, Sussex in 1891 the son of John Haylor and Harriett Kate Haylor. His older brother John was born in 1879, George in 1883 and elder sister Rose Emma was born in 1889. His father worked as a general labourer and at the time of the 1901 census the family lived in Horsham Road, Slaugham near Cuckfield.

William married Florence and they lived at 8, Highlands, Cuckfield.

He enlisted for service in Brighton into the 2nd Battalion, Royal Sussex Regiment, Service number, 20628. For seven years he served in the Royal Artillery and five years in the Reserve.

While serving with the British Expeditionary Force, he was killed in action on 25th December 1915 aged 23 years.

Mid-Sussex Times - 4th January 1916

A MILITARY FUNERAL

A military funeral was accorded last Tuesday to the remains of Mr William Haylor of 'Highlands', he having been a member of what was known as the National Reserve, No 6 Supernumerary Company, 2/4th Royal Sussex Regiment, under the command of Colonel C. H. Coles who attended and Sergeant Brookshaw was in charge of the firing party. Ex-Sergeant-Bugler Hounsell sounded the 'Last Post'. The Rev. C.W.G. Wilson (vicar) and the Rev. J. H. Layton conducted the service which made a deep impression on all those present.

William is buried in Cuckfield Cemetery Ref. 11(S) 16

His name appears on the Memorial panels in the Queens Hall Cuckfield.

PRIVATE JOHN EDWARD THOMAS HAYWARD

John was born in Cuckfield in 1888, the son of John Edward and Eliza Hayward of Cuckfield. He had a younger sister Edith born in 1890. Father John was a bricklayer born in Lewes and the family lived in 'Stocklands'.

John enlisted in Cuckfield into the 8th Battalion, Royal Sussex Regiment, Service number G/2448.

Mid-Sussex Times - 5th November 1918
JOHN EDWARD HAYWARD - KILLED BY A SHELL
News has reached Cuckfield that John Edward, only son of John and Elizabeth J. E. Edward, late of 'Stocklands', was instantaneously killed by a shell during the fighting near Le Cateaux on 23rd October 1918. He was serving with the British Expeditionary Force during the Battle of Selle and was 32 years of age. His commanding officer, when communicating the sad news, added these words, which are a splendid tribute to Edward Hayward's good qualities.

'Private Hayward was a very fine soldier and the very best of men and will be much missed by all who knew him out here. I can only say he has fought for his country and lived a splendid life out here.'

This is a record which anyone might well be proud to have, and it will be a consolation to Miss Hayward and her sisters who have the sympathy of us all.

He is buried in Pommereuil British Cemetery - Memorial ref B 24.

He is remembered on the war memorial in the churchyard of Holy Trinity Church, Cuckfield and on the marble memorial inside the Church.

PIONEER ALBERT J. HENLEY

Albert was born in 1875 to Caleb and Ann Henley of Anstye Lane, Cuckfield. Caleb was an agricultural labourer. Ann was born in Slaugham.

Albert was the youngest of a large family. The oldest brother George was born in 1855, Charles ws born in 1857, Fanny in 1859, Ann in 1862, Rose in 1868 and Emma in 1872.

Albert was the husband of Mrs S. Frost (formerly Henley) of 8 Chatfield Road, Cuckfield.

Albert enlisted with the Royal Engineers, 307th Road Construction Company, Service number WR/21333.

He died on November 20th 1918 of acute bronchitis in a military hospital at Dover, to which he was brought only the day before from Boulogne. He was 43 years old.

He was buried with military honours in Cuckfield Churchyard on November 25th. Cemetery ref. 11 (W) 337

He is remembered on the war memorial in the churchyard of Holy Trinity Church, Cuckfield, on the marble memorial inside the Church and on the memorial board in the Queen's Hall, Cuckfield

PRIVATE AMBROSE WILFRED HENLEY

Ambrose Wilfred was born in Cuckfield in 1899, the son of Henry Henley born in Burgess Hill and his wife Susan who was born in Horsham. Ambrose had a sister Bessie born in 1898.

Henry was a farmer and the family lived in 'Merrifields', Cuckfield.

Ambrose enlisted in Brighton into the 7th Battalion, Queen's (Royal West Surrey Regiment) 18th Division, 'C' Company, Service number G/25409.

Mid-Sussex Times - 26th April 1918
KILLED IN ACTION
Mr and Mrs Henley of 'Merrifields Farm', Cuckfield, have received sad news of their son, Private Ambrose Henley, Queen's Regiment. His officer states -

'It is with profound regret that I have to write and inform you of the death of your son, Private A. Henley of my platoon. At the time we were holding an advanced post at St Quentin. On the 23rd March, during the morning, we came under a severe barrage of the enemy artillery.

Unfortunately one shell dropped right in the part of the trench occupied by your son, and the three or four standing there were all either killed or wounded, including your son. This was very distressing to me, especially as your son was such a young brave lad and all his friends in the company join me in their deepest sympathies in your irreplaceable loss'.

Since hearing from his officer, the news has been confirmed from the War Office. Private Henley, who was 19 years of age, was Mr and Mrs Henley's eldest son.

He is Remembered with Honour on Pozieres Memorial, panels 14 and 15.

His name also appears on the war memorial in the churchyard of Holy Trinity Church, Cuckfield, on the marble memorial inside the Church and on the memorial board in the Queen's Hall, Cuckfield

PRIVATE ERNEST HENLEY

Ernest was born in 1893 in Cuckfield, the son of Charles and Edith Caroline Henley of 4, Lavender Cottage, Anstye Lane, Cuckfield. His elder brother Albert also enlisted for service in the war.

The 1901 census shows that Thomas was born in 1879, William in 1880, Albert in 1885, Frank in 1887, Alice in 1889, Ernest in 1893 and Beatrice born in 1898.

Ernest enlisted in Haywards Heath into the 9th Battalion Royal Sussex Regiment, 24th New Army Division. Service number G/3583.

Mid-Sussex Times - 12th October 1915
PRIVATE E. HENLEY

Private Ernest Henley, 9th Battalion, Royal Sussex Regiment, son of Mr and Mrs Charles Henly of Ansty Lane, Cuckfield, is unofficially reported missing. The news was contained in a letter written home last week by a friend, who stated, 'I am very sorry that poor Ern. Henley is missing; we cannot hear anything of him at all.'

A year later in Cuckfield Parish Magazine, August 1916, Ernest was still reported missing, yet it transpired that he was killed in action while with the British Expeditionary Force at Loos on 25th September 1915. He was aged 22 years.

He is remembered with Honour on the Loos Memorial panel 69 to 73.

His name also appears on the war memorial in the churchyard of Holy Trinity Church, Cuckfield, on the marble memorial inside the Church and on the memorial board in the Queen's Hall, Cuckfield

Cuckfield Parish Magazine - May 1920
MEMORIAL BRASS

A brass tablet has recently been fixed on the Chancel wall in Ansty Mission Church in memory of the late Private Ernest Henley, who fell at Loos, and who was for 10 years a Choir boy at Ansty. The brass is the gift of Miss Best, and Mr Arthur Randall provided the wooden block for it and fixed it. On Sunday, June 13th there will be a Service of Dedication at Evensong, when the tablet will be unveiled. The ceremony will be performed by Miss Best and an address will be given by the Vicar. It is hoped that the Ansty ex-servicemen will make a point of being present and that the little ceremony will be impressive and worthy of the occasion.

PRIVATE FRANK HENLEY

Frank was born in 1887 in Anstye Lane, Cuckfield, Sussex, the fourth son of Charles and Edith Henley. He was one of a large family as documented under the entries for Albert and Frank Henley his brothers.

He was the husband of Rosina Bigg (formerly Henley) of 50, Old Ruttington Lane, Canterbury.

Frank enlisted in Hurstpierpoint into the 9th Lancers (Queen's Royal) Household Cavalry and Cavalry of the Line (including Yeomanry and Imperial Camel Corps) Service number 1119.

Mid-Sussex Times - 3rd November 1914
A CAVALRYMAN'S LETTER

Mr and Mrs Charles Henley, of Ansty, have received a letter from their son, Private F. Henley, 9th (Queen's Royal) Lancers. In it he says -

'I am still quite well. I am sorry I have not written before, but we have been very busy out here, and after we have been out all day fighting I do not feel like writing letters. We have to start out at day-break every morning and do not get to the place we are bound for until dark. I must tell you the weather out here is none too good for our work. We have a lot of the Indian troops out here, and they look very funny with our troops. There has been some very severe fighting, but I am thankful to say we have come out best so far. The French are going on fine and the Russians have also had a great victory over the Germans, so I don't really think the war can last much longer as they are losing a lot every day by one or the other.'

Mid-Sussex Times - 1st December 1914
PRIVATE F. HENLEY
Mr and Mrs Henley of Ansty, Cuckfield, received official intimation during the weekend that their son, Private F Henley, No 1119, 9th Lancers had been slightly wounded in action.

Mid-Sussex Times - 20th April 1915
WOUNDED AND MISSING - PRIVATE F. HENLEY
Private Frank Henley, 9th Lancers, son of Mr and Mrs Henley of Ansty Lane, Cuckfield, has been missing since the end of November. From the time of receiving an official communication from the War Office saying he was slightly wounded on November 27th, his relations have had no tidings from him. His wife's brother, who is attached to the Motor Ambulance Corps, wrote home a week or two ago and said he had seen the 9th Lancers, and on questioning some of them had gained the information that the Germans advanced so rapidly when Henley was wounded that he could not be rescued, so it must be presumed he fell into their hands and was made prisoner.

Mid-Sussex Times - 15th June 1915
PRIVATE F. HENLEY
The silence concerning the fate of Private Frank Henley, 9th Lancers, since he was wounded last October, has now been broken by the receipt of information that he died on November 9th 1914 while a prisoner of war in Germany. He was the fifth son of Mr and Mrs Henley of 'Lavender Cottage', Ansty Lane, Cuckfield and his parents had caused enquiries to be made about him by the British Red Cross Society.

Under date of June 9th the Society wrote to his mother:

'We deeply regret to have to inform you that according to the following official communication from Germany dated 17th April, and sent to us through the Red Cross at Geneva, that Frank Henley, 9th Lancers, is reported to have died on the 9th November 1914 in a reserve lazaretto at Munster. The wound was a shot wound in the left upper thigh. He was buried at Munster'.

An earlier communication from the Society states that from enquires made of a comrade in the same regiment, Private Henley was wounded at Messines and taken to a dressing station, but the Germans advanced quickly, and it was feared he fell into their hands.

Mr and Mrs Henley have also received official notice of their son's death from the War Office, and the usual expressions of sympathy from the King and Queen and Lord Kitchener.

Trooper Henley was twenty seven years of age and leaves a widow and one child who reside at Canterbury.

He is buried in Cologne Southern Cemetery, Germany Ref XV111. A. 18

His name also appears on the war memorial in the churchyard of Holy Trinity Church, Cuckfield, on the marble memorial inside the Church and on the memorial board in the Queen's Hall, Cuckfield

PRIVATE THOMAS HENLEY

Thomas was born in Ansty in 1879, the son of Charles William and Edith Caroline Henley of Ansty, and husband of Alice Jane Henley of 'Hazeldene', Ansty Lane, Cuckfield.

On the 1901 census Thomas is shown as the eldest son, aged 22, and working as an agricultural labourer. The next son was William born in 1880, Albert born in 1884, Frank born in 1887, sister Alice born in 1889, Ernest born in 1893, Edith born in 1895 and Beatrice born in 1898.

Thomas enlisted in Brighton into the 13th Battalion, Royal Sussex Regiment, 39th New Army Division. Service number SD/3142

Mid-Sussex Times - 15th August 1916
PRIVATE T HENLEY

Private T Henley of the Royal Sussex Regiment, and of Ansty, is officially reported as missing, his name appearing in a list published last week. It transpired that Thomas was killed in action and therefore appeared on the missing lists for two months before being found. It is presumed he was killed in action with the British Expeditionary Force at Rue de Bois on 30th June 1916 aged 40 years.

He is buried in Cabaret-Rouge British Cemetery, Souchez Mem Ref XV.N.28

His name also appears on the war memorial in the churchyard of Holy Trinity Church, Cuckfield, on the marble memorial inside the Church and on the memorial board in the Queen's Hall, Cuckfield

PRIVATE ARTHUR EDWARD HOLDEN

Arthur Edward was born in 1884 to William and Augusta Martha Holden of 11, Glebe Road, Cuckfield. William was a road maker. Arthur had a younger sister Kate born in 1893. He enlisted in Haywards Heath into the 11th Battalion, Royal Sussex Regiment, 39th New Army Division, Service number G/9592. He served in the British Expeditionary Force and died on 16th June 1917 aged 33 years.

Mid-Sussex Times - 26th June 1917
WILLIAM HOLDEN - Died in hospital -
Mr William Holden of 'Little Mizbrooks', Cuckfield has had the sad news conveyed to him of the death of his only son, Arthur Edward Holden at the Seventh General Hospital France.

He is buried in Longuenesse (St Omer) Souvenir Cemetery - Grave ref. 1V.C.31
   Arthur is also remembered on the war memorial in the churchyard of Holy Trinity Church, Cuckfield, on the marble memorial inside the Church and on the memorial board in the Queen's Hall, Cuckfield

LIEUTENANT ARNOLD WALTER HUCKETT

Arnold was born in 1892 in Antananarivo, Madagasca. He was a son of the Rev. Walter Huckett and Margaret Huckett of 'Meadfoot', Cuckfield. The 1901 census shows Arnold at a Mission School in Blackheath Village, London, with many other young boys who had been born in many different parts of the world due to their fathers serving as missionaries in different countries. At boarding school with Arnold was a Hugh C. Huckett born in 1891 in Antananarivo, Madagasca. He is thought to be another son of the Rev and Mrs Huckett.

Arnold enlisted into the 5th Battalion Wiltshire Regiment after receiving his commission.

Mid-Sussex Times - 1st September 1914
Mr. A. W. Huckett of Wadham College, Oxford, son of the Rev. Walter Huckett of 'Meadfoot', Cuckfield, has received his commission as Second Lieutenant in the 5th Battalion Wiltshire regiment and has left for the training camp at Churne, Berkshire.

Mid-Sussex Times - 15th August 1915
LIEUTENANT HUCKETT PRESUMED KILLED

Lieutenant Arnold W. Huckett, Wiltshire Regiment, who was reported missing during the Gallipoli operations, is now presumed to have been killed in action on 10th August 1915 on the Gallipoli Peninsula.

He was the second son of the Rev. Walter Huckett (L.M.S. missionary) and Mrs Huckett of 'Meadowfoot', Cuckfield and was 23 years of age.

Mid-Sussex Times - 31st August 1915
LIEUTENANT A. W. HUCKETT

Lieutenant Arnold W. Huckett whose name has appeared in the official lists as missing, is the second son of the Rev W. Huckett, of Meadcroft, Cuckfield. The reverend gentleman is at present in Madagascar on behalf of the London Missionary Society. Lieutenant Huckett received his commission in the 5th Battalion, Wiltshire Regiment, in the early stages of the war and went to the Dardanelles about two months ago. He has been missing since August 10th along with four other officers of the same battalion, including the Lieutenant- Colonel.

Arnold is remembered with honour on the Helles memorial - ref panel 156 to 158.

His name also appears on the war memorial in the churchyard of Holy Trinity Church, Cuckfield, on the marble memorial inside the Church and on the memorial board in the Queen's Hall, Cuckfield.

RIFLEMAN OLIVER SHARMAN HUCKETT

Oliver was born in Samoa in the Pacific, the younger son of the Rev. Walter Huckett a missionary, and Margaret Huckett of 'Meadfoot' Cuckfield.

He enlisted in Bishop's Stortford, Hertfordshire, in the 1/8th London Regiment, Rifle Brigade (The Prince Consort's Own) 14th Light Division. Service number 48084

Oliver saw action in France and Flanders. He was killed by a shell on 27th April 1918 when he was in the trenches while fighting in France. He was aged 19 years.

He is commemorated on The Pozieres Memorial, Panel 81 to 84.

He is remembered on the war memorial in the churchyard of Holy Trinity Church, Cuckfield, on the marble memorial inside the Church and on the memorial board in the Queen's Hall, Cuckfield.

His brother Arnold was killed on 10th August 1915 while serving his country and another brother who is now in Canada has been invalided out of the Army having been severely wounded.

I

PRIVATE GEORGE IZZARD

George was born in 1878, the son of Mr Henry Izzard and Mrs Susan Izzard of East Horsley, Leatherhead, Surrey. He was the husband of Mrs C. E. Izzard of Mill Lane, Sheet, Petersfield, Hants.

In 1901 George was a groom in Wonersh and later moved to become employed as a stud groom for Colonel Stephenson R. Clarke, C.B. of Borde Hill. He and his wife then lived at Naldred Cottages, Cuckfield.

George enlisted in Cuckfield into the 37th Battalion, Royal Fusiliers (City of London Regiment) Service number 40814.

He saw action in France and Flanders and died of wounds during the Somme offensive at Dernancourt on 5th August 1916 aged 38 years.

Shirley Bond

He is remembered with honour in Dernancourt Communal Cemetery ref J.22.

His name appears on the war memorial in the churchyard of Holy Trinity Church, Cuckfield, on the marble memorial inside the Church and on the memorial board in the Queen's Hall, Cuckfield.

K

LANCE - CORPORAL ALBERT KEEP

Albert was born in 1885 in Letcombe Regis, Wantage, Berkshire, son of Mr and Mrs J. Keep and husband of Mrs M. E. Keep of 'Durnford House', Cuckfield, Sussex.

Albert was the eldest son in a large family and at the age of 15 on the 1901 census he was a groom. Brother William was born in 1888 and was an agricultural labourer. Ann was born in 1889, Ruth in 1893, Henry in 1895, Fred in 1898 and Margaret born in 1899.

Albert enlisted in 1914 in Haywards Heath into the 2nd Battalion, Royal Sussex Regiment, 1st Regular Division, Service number G/1286.

Mid-Sussex Times - 15th August 1916
MISSING
We regret to have to state that Mrs Keep, of Whitemans Green, has been

officially notified that her husband Lance-Corporal Albert Keep, Royal Sussex Regiment, was posted as missing after an engagement in France on the 23rd July.

He joined up on 1st September 1914, and had been in France for nine months. Prior to being a soldier he was employed in the stables at 'Mill Hall', Cuckfield.

He had several brothers in the Army, one being killed in action last May. This brother does not appear on any of the Cuckfield war memorials. Inclusion of any name was at the discretion of the family.

Mid-Sussex Times - 14th November 1916
LANCE - CORPORAL A. KEEP
The unofficial news has reached Cuckfield that Lance-Corporal A. Keep of the Royal Sussex regiment, who has been missing for some months, was killed on July 23rd. He was formerly employed at 'Mill Hall'.

He is commemorated on the Thiepval Memorial, Ref Pier and Face 7C.

His name appears on the war memorial in the churchyard of Holy Trinity Church, Cuckfield, on the marble memorial inside the Church and on the memorial board in the Queen's Hall, Cuckfield.

CAPTAIN ARCHIBALD EDWARD KENNEDY

Archibald was born on 7th September 1878, the eldest son of Sir John Gordon Kennedy, K.C.M.G. and Evelyn Adela Kennedy of 'Burnthouse', Cuckfield. He was a Captain in the 93rd Battalion, Argyll and Sutherland Highlanders and was killed at Le Cateau on 26th August 1914 aged 35.

He is buried in Le Cateau Military Cemetry ref 111.C.1

CAPTAIN JOHN PATRICK FRANCIS KENNEDY

John was born in 1892, the youngest son of Sir John Gordon Kennedy, K.C.M.G. and Evelyn Adela Kennedy of 'Burnthouse' Cuckfield. They formerly lived at 50, Cranley Gardens, South Kensington, London. John was a Captain in the 5th Battalion attd. 2nd Battalion of the Rifle Brigade and was killed at Villiers Bretonneux on 24th April 1918 aged 26.

He is buried in Crucifix Corner Cemetry, Villers-Bretonneux ref 111.D.3

CAPTAIN PAUL ADRIAN KENNEDY

Paul was born on 11th December 1886 the third son of Sir John Gordon Kennedy, K.C.M.G. and Evelyn Adela Kennedy of 'Burnthouse' Cuckfield. They formerly lived at 50, Cranley Gardens, South Kensington, London.

Paul was a Captain in the 4th Battalion attd. 2nd Battalion Rifle Brigade and was killed on 9th May 1915 at Fronelles.

He is remembered on the Ploegsteert Memorial, Panel 10

All three of the sons of Lord and Lady Kennedy are remembered on the 'Kennedy Memorial' situated on the south wall in the belfry in Holy Trinity Church , Cuckfield.

PRIVATE WILFRED RALPH KERISTON

Wilfred was born in Cuckfield in 1883, the son of Mark and Sarah Lelliott of Cuckfield. At the beginning of the war when he enlisted as Keriston (not Lelliott) he was residing at Palmers Green, Middlesex.

He enlisted in Canterbury into the 1st Battalion Duke of Cambridgeshire's Own, Middlesex Regiment, 33rd New Army Division. Service number 207772.

Wilfred saw action in France and Flanders and was killed in action on 29th September 1918 aged 35 years.

He is remembered with honour at Villers Hill British Cemetery. Villers-Guislain ref.1.B.8 as Wilfred Keriston.

His name, William R. Lelliott appears on the war memorial in the churchyard of Holy Trinity Church, Cuckfield, on the marble memorial inside the Church and on the memorial board in the Queen's Hall, Cuckfield as William Ralph Lelliott.

Cuckfield Parish Magazine - November 1918
WILLIAM LELLIOTT
William was the son of the late Mark Lelliott and he was born and brought up in Cuckfield. Although he had not lived there during recent years he was well remembered and had many friends, by whom his death is regretted.

PRIVATE HENRY THOMAS KNAPP

Henry was born in Staplefield in 1873, the son of Mr W. G. Knapp of 60, School House, Borde hill, Cuckfield.

He enlisted in Haywards Heath into the 1st/4th battalion of the Royal Sussex Regiment, 34th New Army Division, Service number 200853.

Henry was part of the British Expeditionary Force, served in Egypt and Palestine and was twice wounded.

Mid-Sussex Times - 13th August 1918
Death of Private H. T. Knapp
We regret to have to record the death of this soldier, whose parents live at 60, School House, Borde Hill. He was killed in action on 23rd July. Prior to enlisting in November 1914 he worked at Borde Hill.

His parents and friends may well be proud of his good record while they lament his loss.

Henry is buried in Raperie British Cemetery, Villemontoire ref. IVA. E. 7

His name appears on the war memorial in the churchyard of Holy Trinity Church, Cuckfield, on the marble memorial inside the Church and on the memorial board in the Queen's Hall, Cuckfield.

L

GUNNER ERNEST JOHN LANDER

Ernest was born in Horley, Surrey in 1892, the son of Walter John and Lucy A. Lander who lived in Whitemans Green. Ernest's father was a whitesmith. Ernest had an older sister Mary J. born in 1880, a brother Walter born in 1887, and a brother Harry born in 1891.

Ernest was the grandson of Mrs L. A. Lander of 1, Woodcroft Villas, Whitemans Green, Cuckfield.

He enlisted in Brighton, Sussex into 'D' Battalion, 74th Brigade Royal Field Artillery, Service number 227032 and served in France and Flanders.

Mid-Sussex Times - 11th June 1918
KILLED IN ACTION

On Saturday last, Mr and Mrs. John Lander, of 1, Woodcroft Villas, Whitemans Green, received the sad news that their youngest son, Gunner Ernest Lander, R.F.A., was killed in action on the previous Sunday, 2nd June. The news was sent by a Sergeant of the Battery to which the deceased soldier was attached as a Signaller, and he wrote that death was instantaneous and that the body was brought back and buried on the following day in a pretty cemetery behind the lines. Two of his chums who were killed at the same time were buried with him.

Gunner Lander was employed by Messrs S. Knight & Co before he joined up, and he was described by his Sergeant as a cheery, good fellow and an efficient soldier whose death was much regretted by all his comrades. Ernest was 30 years old.

He was buried in Bienvillers Military Cemetery, Ref XIX.C.12

His name appears on the war memorial in the churchyard of Holy Trinity Church, Cuckfield, on the marble memorial inside the Church and on the memorial board in the Queen's Hall, Cuckfield.

PRIVATE MARK LONGHURST

Mark was born in Cuckfield in 1884, the second son in the large family of Jesse and Ann M. Longhurst. Jesse was a farm labourer living at 10, Highlands Cottages, Cuckfield. Son David was born in1881, Eva G. was born in 1887, Hilda J. was born in 1890, Frank was born in 1892, Dorothy was born in 1896, Mary L. was born in 1898 and Ruby A. was born in 1900.

Mark enlisted in Haywards Heath into the 13th Battalion, Royal Sussex Regiment, 39th New Army Division. Service number SD/2958.

Mid-Sussex Times - 25th July 1916
MARK LONGHURST - DIED OF WOUNDS
Mrs Longhurst, of 10 Highlands, received the sad news on Thursday, from one of his mates, that her son, Private Mark Longhurst, Royal Sussex Regiment, has succumbed to wounds received in action. No official news has yet been received.

Mid-Sussex Times - 15th August 1916
DEATH OF PRIVATE MARK LONGHURST

Lieutenant F. A. Fabian of the Royal Sussex Regiment, has written to Mrs Longhurst, of 10, Highlands, Cuckfield, as follows:-

'Dear Madam,

I deeply regret to tell you that the news you have received of your son is true. He was wounded in action on 30th June, and died in hospital a few days later. He was a good steady soldier and much respected by all. I assure you of sincerest sympathy in your great loss'.

The deceased soldier was 31 years of age and was educated at Cuckfield Church School. For several years he was in the employ of Mr Pratt. He joined the Colours in 1914 and went to France in March 1916. To those who now mourn his loss he will be honourably remembered as 'a soldier and a man.'

He served in the British Expeditionary Force and died of his wounds suffered on the Rue de Bois on 1st July 1916

He is buried in Merville Communal Cemetery ref V.A.3

Mark is Remembered with Honour on the war memorial in the churchyard of Holy Trinity Church, Cuckfield, on the marble memorial inside the Church and on the memorial board in the Queen's Hall, Cuckfield.

TROOPER EDWARD WHITAKER LOWNDES

Edward was born in Cainscross, Stroud, Gloucestershire in 1885, the second son of Robert Baxter Lowndes and his wife Marian. Edward had an elder sister called Eva Marian born in1881, a brother Robert born in 1882, another sister called Margaret born in 1882 and after Edward there was born another brother, Ashley Gordon.

Father Robert was a solicitor who was born in Liverpool. His wife was born in London as were most of their children. His parents had moved to Cuckfield by the start of the war and were living at 'Waverley', Cuckfield.

Edward enlisted as a trooper with the 3rd Australian Light Horse Regiment, Service number 80.

He died of wounds received in the Dardanelles on May 28th 1915 aged 30 years and is buried in Beach Cemetery, Anzac ref 1.C.1.

Edward's name appears on the war memorial in the churchyard of Holy Trinity Church, Cuckfield, on the marble memorial inside the Church and on the memorial board in the Queen's Hall, Cuckfield.

The Commonwealth War Graves Commission give Edward's nationality as Australian but it is not known when this change in his position occurred.

MAJOR EDWARD LYCETT LYON

Edward was born in Valpariso, Peru, South America in 1877. He was the son of Emma Lyon who was born in Monte Video in 1851.

The 1901 census shows him living with his mother at 161, Cromwell Road, South Kensington, London. His mother was not a widow at that time but there is no mention of Edward's father. He may have been away serving in the army but this is not known.

In 1891 Edward was a boarder at Grove Lodge School in Upton-cum-Chatrey in Buckinghamshire. He joined the 18th (Queen Mary's Own) Hussars, attached to the Somerset Light Infantry and served in the South Africa Campaign.

Mid-Sussex Times - 26th September 1916

Cuckfieldians will learn with deep regret that Major Edward Lycett Lyon, Queen Mary's Own Hussars, attached to the Somerset Light Infantry, died on 17th September from wounds received in action at Flers Courcelette. He was 39 years of age and the husband of the Hon. Mrs Lyon of 'Copyhold Cottage'.

He is remembered with honour at Corbie Communal Cemetery Extension.

His name also appears on the war memorial in the churchyard of Holy Trinity Church, Cuckfield, on the marble memorial inside the Church and on the memorial board in the Queen's Hall, Cuckfield.

M

PRIVATE JOSEPH WILLIAM MARKWICK

Joseph was born in Cuckfield in 1899, the son of Alfred and Elizabeth Annie Markwick of Jubilee Cottages, Broad Street. At the time of Joseph's death they were living at 'Provident Cottage', Brainsmead, Cuckfield and Alfred was a horse carter on a farm.

Joseph had two older brothers, Edward G. born in 1888 and Fred born in 1890. Then two sisters were born, Edith K. in 1892 and Nellie in 1897.

Joseph enlisted in Haywards Heath into the Royal Sussex Regiment, Service number 1852 and later transferred to the Royal Warwickshire Regiment and then to the 8th Battalion, Queen's Own (Royal West Kent Regiment) 24th New Army Division, Service number 202801.

He served in France and Flanders and died of multiple gunshot wounds suffered at Cambrai on 8th December 1917. He was aged 19 years.

PRIVATE MARKWICK

Mrs Markwick of 'Gravelye Cottage' has received the following communication from the Officer Commanding her son's Company :

"B.E.F. 24th December 1917 -
I have just heard that your son, Private Markwick, has died of wounds, and am writing to tell you how very sorry I am. He was one of the best soldiers in the Company, and had been already marked out for promotion. Everything possible was done for him at the time. I was with him when he was hit, and afterwards saw him in the dressing station, where he was very cheerful and bearing the pain like the splendid soldier he was. The other officers, with the men of the Company, wish me to convey their condolences to you and your family in your great loss."

Cuckfield Parish Magazine - January 1918
Joseph was the third son of Mr and Mrs Alfred Markwick of 'Gravelye Cottage'. As a lad - and he was not much more than that when he died - he worked at Borde Hill and he was in the 4th Sussex when the war broke out. After a time he was transferred to the Royal Warwickshire Regiment and then to the Royal West Kents. He went to the front in 1916 and he was wounded on 5th August 1917. Having made a good recovery he rejoined his unit and was soon called upon to make the supreme sacrifice. He was a lad well liked by all who knew him, and we offer our sincere sympathy to his father and mother and to other members of his family in their sorrow.

Joseph is buried in Tincourt New British Cemetery ref 1V. B. 3.

His name also appears on the war memorial in the churchyard of Holy Trinity Church, Cuckfield, on the marble memorial inside the Church and on the memorial board in the Queen's Hall, Cuckfield.

LANCE-CORPORAL JAMES MATTHEWS

James was born in Cuckfield in 1895, the son of James and Margaret Elizabeth Matthews who, in the 1901 census were living at 'The Martin's Nest', Blo'Norton Banks, Diss, Norfolk.

James had four older sisters, Minnie born in 1888, Lottie born in 1890, Lillie born in 1891 and Annie born in 1892. His father was a platelayer on the railway.

James enlisted in 1914 in Haywards Heath into the 9th Battalion, Royal Sussex Regiment, 24th New Army Division. Service number G/3587.

Mid-Sussex Times - 16th March 1915
LANCE-CORPORAL J. MATTHEWS

Another Cuckfield lad has to be added to the Roll of Honour as having died for his country. Lance-Corporal J. Matthews, only son of Mr James Matthews, of Hodshrove Farm, Ansty, Cuckfield succumbed at the 2nd Eastern General Hospital, Brighton on Sunday, March 17th, from pneumonia. He was on duty at the beginning of last week, but a bad cold developed into pneumonia and his death took place at half-past twelve on

Sunday in the presence of his father and sister who had just arrived to see him.

The young soldier was twenty years of age and joined the 9th Sussex with several Ansty chums in September of last year. He was attached to 'B' Company and his interest in his military duties soon won him his first stripe.

Lance-Corporal Matthews received his education at the British School and later at the Church Schools and on leaving, worked on the farm with his father until the war broke out.

A CUCKFIELD SOLDIER LAID TO REST
LANCE-CORPORAL JAMES MATTHEWS

Cuckfield mourned for another of its soldier sons on Friday afternoon. In the short period of a few weeks, two of its lads who joined the Army at the end of last summer have been laid to rest in the quiet local cemetery, and the whole town has gone out in sympathy for the bereaved ones.

Friday's ceremony followed on the death, the previous Sunday, of Lance- Corporal James Matthews of the 9th (Service) Battalion Royal Sussex Regiment, who succumbed to pneumonia in the 2nd Eastern General Hospital at Brighton. The funeral took place from the deceased's home at Ansty, and the little hamlet showed the upmost respect as the sad procession passed through on its way to Cuckfield Congregational Church. Nearing the town the cortege dropped into a slow march, whilst the fife and drums band of the 9th Sussex, under Drum Major Ware, which had played the hymns, 'Abide with Me', and 'Safe in the Arms of Jesus', while passing through Ansty, played a favourite hymn of the deceased, 'Jesu, Lover of my Soul', as the procession passed through the streets. It was led by the firing party, with arms reversed, under Sergeant Laing, and the band. Next came the hearse bearing the coffin covered with the Union Jack and many beautiful wreaths, among them being two large tributes, tied with the regimental colours, from the officers and men of his own Company.

The family mourners followed, and then came the escort of his Company, under Sergeant Rist, with Lieutenants Collingbourne and Marks following. Sergeant Boyd and six men of the Post Office Rifles, and Assistant Scout Master Rapley and Patrols of the Cuckfield Boy Scouts brought up the rear. Large numbers of people lined the High Street, the shops of which were temporarily closed, whilst at the top of

Church Street the school children were lined up under Mr. W. Herrington and the teachers. The school flag was also lowered to half mast during the funeral.

On arriving at the Congregational Church six Lance-Corporals bore the coffin into the building, where the Rev. S. Maddock, conducted the service. The Pastor spoke a few touching words to the assembled mourners, and a hymn for the men at the front, entitled, 'Lord God of Hosts, Whose Mighty Hand', was sung, Miss Payne being at the organ.

As the cortege left the church, the organist played, 'O Rest in the Lord', whilst on the journey from the church to the cemetery the band played the Dead March in 'Saul'.

At the graveside a large crowd of people had gathered. Here the Rev. S. Maddock read the committal prayers, the bearer party lowered their dead comrade to his last rest and the sad service concluded with the firing of the usual three volleys and the sounding of the 'Last Post'.

The coffin, which was of polished elm, with brass fittings bore the inscription:

LANCE-CORPORAL JAMES MATTHEWS
DIED 7th MARCH 1915
AGED 20 YEARS

The chief mourners were Mr James Matthews (father), Lance-Corporal and Mrs P.J. Channon (brother in law and sister), Miss L. Matthews and Miss A. Matthews (sisters), Mr Smith (grandfather), Mr and Mrs Matthews (grandfather and grandmother), Mr. A. Matthews (uncle), Mrs Tidy (aunt), Mrs A Newham and Mrs W Newham (cousins), Miss May Fox, Miss Beale, Miss Payne, and Mr and Mrs Funnell (Portslade), with whom deceased was billeted.

James is buried in Cuckfield Cemetery Ref H.8.

His name appears on the war memorial in the churchyard of Holy Trinity Church, Cuckfield, on the marble memorial inside the Church and on the memorial board in the Queen's Hall, Cuckfield.

PRIVATE HUGH GRIER MERTENS

Hugh was born in Ardingly in 1882 to Frederick M. and Gertrude Mertens. Frederick was a clergyman in the Church of England.

The family consisted of Bertha M. born in1875, Reginald H. born in 1879 and Bernard M. born in 1881.

On the 1901 census, Hugh was listed as a student at Lancing College, Sussex.

He enlisted in Brighton although he was living in St Pancras at the time. He enlisted into the 13th (County of London) Battalion (Princess Louise's Kensington Battalion) 56th London Regiment Service number 495707.

Mid-Sussex Times - 1st October 1918
DIED FOR HIS COUNTRY

The official notification has been received of the death of Private Hugh Greir Mertens, London Regiment, and it is stated that he was killed in action on August 9th.

The deceased was the youngest son of Mrs Mertens, of 'Whitmore', Cuckfield, and of the late Rev. F. M. D. Mertens, Headmaster of Ardingly

College. He joined up about two years ago and previous to that he was engaged in the Newcastle-on-Tyne branch of the Bank of England.

He saw action in France and Flanders and died of wounds suffered at Amiens on 9th August 1918. He was 36 years of age. He had been missing for some while before that date.

He is buried in Beacon Cemetery, Sailly-Laurette ref 111.1.5

His name appears on the war memorial in the churchyard of Holy Trinity Church, Cuckfield, on the marble memorial inside the Church and on the memorial board in the Queen's Hall, Cuckfield.

PRIVATE THOMAS MITCHELL

Thomas was born in 1896, a son of Frederick and Rose Mitchell of Brainesmead, Cuckfield. Frederick was a bricklayer. The eldest son was Arthur born in1891, then Henry born in 1894, Wilfred in 1897, Lucy in 1899 and William born in 1900.

Thomas enlisted into the 3rd Battalion Coldstream Guards, 2nd Regular Division in Exeter, Service number, 9989 as at that time he was living with his father at 'The Danes', Killerton, Broad Clyst, Exeter.

Mid-Sussex Times - 9th March 1915
PRIVATE THOMAS MITCHELL

Mr and Mrs F Mitchell, of Brains Mead, Cuckfield, received the sad news last Tuesday that their son, Private T. Mitchell, of the Coldstream Guards, had succumbed to his wounds at No 1 Clearing Hospital in France.

As was stated in this column a fortnight ago, Private Mitchell had a leg amputated through being hit by a German shell, and reports spoke of him as progressing favourably. It came as a severe shock to his mother therefore, when she opened the letter from the War Office, telling of his death on February 14th, for only a few days previously she had received a post card from her son - written as it transpired, on the day he died, saying:

'Dear Mother,

Just to say my wound is going on fine. I think I am on my way to England today or tomorrow. I had to have my leg off, but I am receiving every attention.'

Surely this lad, who could write such a cheery message to his mother a few hours before death, was a typical example of the best tradition of the British soldier, and without a doubt that postcard will remain a cherished possession of his parents.

Private Mitchell, who was nineteen and a half years old, was educated at the Cuckfield National Schools, and after leaving he worked for Mr Bunting for some time. He then went to relatives at a farm in Devonshire, and later joined that counties Regiment. He was only connected with it for four months, when he then joined the Coldstream Guards, with whom he had been connected for about two years at the time of his death. He went to France on 8th September 1914 and died from wounds received in action on 14th February 1915, aged 20 years.

He is buried in Choques Military Cemetery, Ref 1.A.25.

His name appears on the war memorial in the churchyard of Holy Trinity Church, Cuckfield, on the marble memorial inside the Church and on the memorial board in the Queen's Hall, Cuckfield.

LIEUTENANT WILLIAM HOLFORD MITCHELL

William Holford Mitchell was born in 1898, the son of Edward Albert Mitchell an electrical engineer who was born in Cuckfield. His wife Elizabeth was a school teacher. Edward was one of the sidesmen at Holy Trinity Church. William's elder brother Harold was born in 1894 and sister Ethel Mary was born in 1895.

When war broke out, the family were living at 'The Grange', South Park, Reigate, Surrey but at the time of William's death they had moved to 'The Mount', Broad Street, Cuckfield.

William enlisted into the 4th Battalion, East Surrey Regiment attached to the 2nd Battalion with the 28th Division in Salonika, Greece.

Mid-Sussex Times - 7th September 1915
PRIVATE W. H. MITCHELL

A Commission as a probationary Second Lieutenant in the East Surrey Regiment has been given to Private W. H. Mitchell, of the Inns of Court O.T.C. He is a son of Mr E. A. Mitchell, of 'The Mount', Broad Street, Cuckfield.

His ship the 'Arcadian' was torpedoed on the voyage home and William was drowned, lost at sea on 15th April 1917 aged 19 years.

He is remembered with honour on the Mikra Memorial.

His name appears on the war memorial in the churchyard of Holy Trinity Church, Cuckfield, on the marble memorial inside the Church and on the memorial board in the Queen's Hall, Cuckfield.

PRIVATE WILLIAM JAMES MITCHELL

William was born in 1898 in Bognor, the son of George and Annie Mitchell of 37, Clifford Road, South Norwood, London.

He enlisted in Bognor into the 'D' Company, 11th Battalion, Royal Sussex Regiment Service number SD/820.

The 1901 census shows that his mother was not widowed but his father was not at home on that day. William had an elder brother Edward George, born in 1888, a sister Clara born in 1889, Mabel born in 1893, a brother Arthur born in 1896 and a younger sister Alice born in 1900.

By the time her sons were fighting in the war Mrs Mitchell had moved to live at 'Albany Villas', Cuckfield. The Cuckfield Parish magazine offers its sympathy to Mrs Mitchell especially as it states he is the second son she has lost in the war. However, only William James is listed on the Cuckfield memorials.

William was killed in action with the British Expeditionary Force on 18th September 1917 aged 19 years.

He is buried in La Clytte Military Cemetery ref 111.A.8

His name appears on the war memorial in the churchyard of Holy Trinity Church, Cuckfield, on the marble memorial inside the Church and on the memorial board in the Queen's Hall, Cuckfield.

LIEUTENANT DAVID HENRY CARMICHAEL MONRO

David Munro was born in 1885, the son of David Carmichael Monro and Elizabeth Josephine Monro of 'The Chestnuts', Lindfield, Sussex and later of 'Burnt House', Cuckfield.

He was serving in the 29th Battalion, Canadian Infantry (British Columbia Regiment).

The Mid-Sussex Times - 16th May 1916
DEATH OF LIEUTENANT D. H. C. MUNRO

Deep sympathy has been extended to Mr and Mrs Munro of 'Burnt House', on the death of their son, Lieutenant David Henry Carmichael Monro, Canadian Light Infantry, he dying of wounds on 4th May. He was 31 years of age and a barrister.

At one time he was in the Nigerian Civil Service, but on account of ill-health left and went to Canada. He joined the Canadian Army early in

September 1914, came to England in May 1915 with his Regiment, and went with it to the front on 17th September in the same year.

He was killed in action on 4th May 1916 aged 31 years and is Remembered with Honour in Reninghelst New Military Cemetery Ref. 1 B.18

His name appears on the war memorial in the churchyard of Holy Trinity Church, Cuckfield, on the marble memorial inside the Church and on the memorial boards in the Queen's Hall, Cuckfield.

Shirley Bond

ABLE SEAMAN PERCIVAL EDWARD MORFEE

Percival was born in Bridport, Dorset in 1879. His father Edward Morfee was a school master and his mother Elizabeth A. was a school mistress. Both were born in Hastings, Sussex. Their eldest son was Edward born in Wotton, Surrey in 1870, then Ernest born in 1874, Evelyn in 1875, then Percival, They were all born in Bridport. Sister Beatrice was born in Cuckfield in 1878.

In 1901 Percival was living in 16 York Street, Southampton where he was working as a solicitors clerk. He married Adeline who lived in Wivelsfield.

Percival joined the Royal Naval Volunteer Reserve, Nelson Battalion, Royal Naval Division. Service number R/25

Cuckfield Parish Magazine - January 1917
The sad news has been received that Percy E. Morfee died on January 25th in hospital in France. He was 39 years old. The cause of death was peritonitis. He had many friends in Cuckfield, where he spent all his early

life. As a boy he was a member of the Parish Church Choir and he was also later on a Bell Ringer. On the outbreak of the war he was living at Southampton and he joined the Royal Naval Division. He was home on leave last summer and his friends were pleased to see him so well and cheerful. Much sympathy is felt for his mother who is also well known and respected, and also for his widow and two little children.

He is buried in Varennes Military Cemetery, grave ref.1.H.2

His name appears on the war memorial in the churchyard of Holy Trinity Church, Cuckfield, on the marble memorial inside the Church and on the memorial board in the Queen's Hall, Cuckfield.

PRIVATE GEORGE HENRY MURRELL

George was born in Cuckfield in1887, the son of George and Elizabeth Mary Murrell of Brainsmead, Cuckfield. He had an elder brother James born in 1884, a sister Mabel born in 1886 and a younger brother Bertie born in 1889. George senior was a general labourer born in Ardingly.

George junior, enlisted in Haywards Heath into the Royal Sussex Regiment, Service number 9724.

He transferred to the 7th Battalion Queen's Royal West Surrey Regiment, 18th Eastern Division Service number G/24536.

Mid-Sussex Times - 9th December 1916
PRIVATE G. H. MURRELL - MISSING
Mr and Mrs George Murrell, of Brainsmead, have received official information that their son, Private G. H. Murrell, Queen's Royal West Surrey Regiment, has been missing since November 18th 1916. He joined up in March and went to the front in July.

Previous to joining the Forces he was employed by Mr Webber, coal merchant, of London Lane, Cuckfield.

Cuckfield Parish Magazine - January 1917
Mr and Mrs George Murrell, of Brainsmead, who have been in a state of great anxiety about their son, Private George Murrell, The Queen's Royal West Surrey Regiment, who was reported missing since November 18th, have received a field service card from him dated November 23rd and stating that he was quite well and a prisoner of war in Germany. We are glad that their anxiety has been allayed and we hope that they will continue to have good reports from him.

Mid-Sussex Times - 3rd July 1917

PRIVATE GEORGE MURRELL - Died a prisoner of war

Mrs George Murrell of Brainsmead, Cuckfield, received official notification on June 30th that her son Private George Murrell died a prisoner of war in Germany on January 7th 1917. The cause of death is unknown. Private Murrell was captured in November 1916. Mrs Murrell had a card from him dated 27th November and has since been anxiously awaiting news of him.

When George died in captivitiy he was aged 30 years.

He is buried in Ronssoy Communal Cemetery Ref Row F

His name appears on the war memorial in the churchyard of Holy Trinity Church, Cuckfield, on the marble memorial inside the Church and on the memorial board in the Queen's Hall, Cuckfield.

P

GUNNER SAMUEL ERNEST PATEMAN

Samuel Ernest was born in Cuckfield in 1885. He was the son of Samuel Lewis Pateman who was a coachman born in Denham, Bucks and Eliza Pateman. In 1901 they were living in London Road, Cuckfield. Ernest had an elder brother called Arthur born in 1883 and a younger sister Alice born in 1888.

In 1901, Ernest, aged 17, was a butcher.

He enlisted first with the 9th Lancers and then moved into the Royal Garrison Artillery, 104th Heavy Battery as a Gunner, Service number 26494. He was later in the 9th (Queen's Royal Lancers).

He died in Mesopotamia on 24th July 1917 aged 32 years and is buried in Basra War Cemetery, Iraq.

His name appears on the war memorial in the churchyard of Holy Trinity Church, Cuckfield as Ernest S. Pateman, on the marble memorial inside the Church and on the memorial board in the Queen's Hall, Cuckfield.

Records show that he served at times under the name Merton instead of Pateman.

PRIVATE FREDERICK JAMES PEARCE

Frederick was born in 1890 in Hambledon, Hants, the son of Frederick and Jane Annie Pearce of 'Stroods' Brook Street, Cuckfield. Frederick senior was a cattleman on a farm.

Frederick had an older sister, Ellen M. born in 1889 and a younger sister Flora born in 1898.

He enlisted in Brighton into the 9th Battalion Royal Sussex Regiment, Service number G/3009.

He served in the British Expeditionary Force and was killed in action on 25th September 1915 aged 25 years.

He is Remembered with Honour on the Loos Memorial, reference panel 69 to 73.

Although Frederick's photograph appears with all the other photographs of men from Cuckfield who gave their lives, his name does not appear on any of the Cuckfield War Memorials.

PRIVATE JESSE PELLING

Jesse was born in 1877 in Saddlescombe, Nr Hassocks. Sussex. He was the son of Hannah, born in Balcombe in 1840 and Frederick Pelling.

By 1881 Hannah was a widow and living in Balcombe with her children, George born in 1864, Flora in 1873, Harry in 1875 and Jesse born in 1877.

Hannah married again to John Edwards, and by 1891 the family, including Jesse, had moved back to Saddlescombe to live with their stepfather. Jesse now aged 14 years was a milk boy and had two step sisters Lottie Edwards born in 1879 and Grace Edwards born in 1884.

Before enlisting, Jesse worked for the Urban District Council.

Jesse moved to Cuckfield and enlisted in Brighton into the 14th Battalion, Royal Sussex Regiment, Service number 3657.

He was transferred to the Eastern Command Labour Centre, Service number LC/74702.

He died at Woking, Berks, of pneumonia, consequent on a chill caught when coming home on leave on 14th August 1918.

He was aged 41 years old and is remembered with honour at Brookwood Military Cemetery, Surrey ref X111 C.8.

His name appears on the war memorial in the churchyard of Holy Trinity Church, Cuckfield, on the marble memorial inside the Church and on the memorial board in the Queen's Hall, Cuckfield.

RIFLEMAN ALFRED UWINS PENNIFOLD

Alfred was born in Hurstpierpoint in 1895, the son of John and Hannah Pennifold of ? 'Wapress Farm', Twineham. His father John was born in Cuckfield and was an agricultural foreman on the farm. The family later moved to Cuckfield. Alfred was one of five children, John born in 1885, Emily born in 1889, William born in 1891 and Rhoda born in 1897.

He enlisted in Cuckfield into the 2nd/8th Battalion (The Post Office Rifles) The London Regiment, 58th Division, Service number 371123.

Mid-Sussex Times - 18th September 1917
ALFRED PENNIFOLD

We regret to state that the sad news has been officially communicated to Mrs Pennifold of 2, New Road Cottages, Chatfield Road, Cuckfield that her third son Private Alfred Unwins Pennifold, London Regiment, has made the supreme sacrifice, he being killed in action on 16th June. He was twenty two years of age and prior to joining up two years ago last February was employed in the garden at 'Copyhold' by Mr Drake.

Mrs Pennifold who is a widow, has two other sons in khaki and one son at home aged twelve years. A second son is still in hospital in London having been taken there from France where he was for eight months suffering from pneumonia.

Sympathetic Letter
Mrs Pennifold of Chatfield Road, Cuckfield whose son Alfred Unwins was killed in action in France in June aged 22 years, has received the following letter from Major Ash of the London Regiment --

Dear Mrs Pennifold,

'I am afraid the news of your boy's death must have been a sad blow to you and I am very sorry that it has not been possible to write to you earlier about it. He was a most stout hearted fellow and had excellent spirits and will be much missed in 'C' Company. If one has to suffer a loss such as yours it is at least some consolation to know that his death was painless and that he was doing his duty nobly and manfully and I only wish he were with us still. Please accept my sincere sympathy'.

He is Remembered with Honour on the Arras Memorial ref Bay 10.

His name appears on the war memorial in the churchyard of Holy Trinity Church, Cuckfield, on the marble memorial inside the Church and on the memorial board in the Queen's Hall, Cuckfield.

Q

SERGEANT STANLEY QUAIFE

Stanley was born in St Leonard's on Sea, Hastings, Sussex in 1880, the son of Mary R. Quaife and James Quaife who was an assistant in an ironmongers shop. Stanley was the youngest in a large family. Brother James was born in 1867, Alfred in 1871, Harold in 1874 and Ada R. born in 1876.

Before the war Stanley worked for Colonel Stephenson Clarke at Borde Hill, as a gardener. He was married and had a child.

He enlisted in Haywards Heath into the 9th Battalion Royal Sussex Regiment, Service number G/3335.

Stanley was killed in action with the British Expeditionary Force on 28th September 1915.

Mid-Sussex Times - 5th October 1915
SERGEANT QUAIFE

In a letter received by a local resident this morning (Tuesday) the news was conveyed that Sergeant Stanley Quaife of the 9th (Service) Battalion Royal Sussex Regiment was killed in the last great battle in France.

Sergeant Quaife was employed by Colonel Stephenson R. Clarke, C.B. at Borde Hill, Cuckfield as a gardener, and was a highly esteemed employee. He was a very capable vocalist and a good 'Buff', and at charity concerts in aid of distressed brethren he willingly gave his services. In the letter above referred to, it is stated, 'Stanley Quaife was a good soldier, and he died like a soldier. His death is regretted by all'.

He leaves a widow and a young son.

He is Remembered with Honour on Loos memorial, panel 69 to 73

He is remembered in Cuckfield, and his photgraph is included with others who gave their lives because his work at Borde Hill made him a resident of the town. However his name does not appear on any of the memorials in Cuckfield.

R

PETTY OFFICER 1st CLASS CHARLES WESLEY RANDALL

Charles was the son of Austin James Randall and his wife Margaret of Hassocks, Sussex. He was married to Celia of 113, Waldegrave Road, Brighton. He was brought up by the late Mrs King, at 'Vine Cottage', Cuckfield, and received his education at the Cuckfield Church Schools. He entered the Navy on leaving school, and was on board H.M.S. 'Terrible' when she visited Natal during the South African war, being one of the party landed with naval guns to assist in the relief of Ladysmith. For this he received the South African medal with one clasp. His name is inscribed on the schools honours board of the old boys who served in that war. When Ladysmith had been relieved the 'Terrible' went to China, to help put down the Boxer rising, and Randall received the China medal for this exploit.

He then joined the Royal Navy H.M.S.'Good Hope', Service number 196243.

Mid-Sussex Times - 17th November 1914
LOSS OF THE 'GOOD HOPE'
The Admiralty have given notice that Charles Wesley Randall, First Class Petty Officer, was on board the 'H.M.S. Good Hope' when it went down with all hands on 1st November 1914. He was a married man, and his wife and one child are living in Portsmouth.

He is commemorated on the Portsmouth Naval Memorial ref. 1

Because all his young life was spent in Cuckfield, Charles is remembered on the war memorial in the churchyard of Holy Trinity Church, Cuckfield, on the marble memorial inside the Church and on the memorial board in the Queen's Hall, Cuckfield.

CAPTAIN STUART KEPPELL REID MC

Stuart was born in 1888, the son of Florence Reid and the late Percy T. Reid of 'Mill Hall', Cuckfield. Percy Reid was a retired marine underwriter. Stuart was educated at Eton.

He was in the 1st/4th Battalion (Territorial) Royal Sussex Regiment, 34th New Army Division.

Mid-Sussex Times - 8th June 1915
LIEUTENANT STUART K. REID
Lieutenant Stuart K Reid of the 4th Battalion Royal Sussex Regiment, T.F. son of Mrs Reid of Mill Hall, has been gazetted to the rank of Captain.

Mid-Sussex Times - 17th October 1916
WELCOME HOME
Within the past few days Mrs Reid, of Mill Hall, has had the pleasure of welcoming home on leave her two sons - Lieutenant -Colonel P.L.Reid, Irish Guards (from France) and Captain Stuart Reid, 4th Royal Sussex

Regiment (from Egypt). The latter had been absent from England for fifteen months.

Cuckfield Parish Magazine - September 1916
We wish to congratulate Major Reid who has been promoted to the rank of Lieutenant Colonel and given command of one of the Battalions of the Irish Guards. Unfortunately he is at present in hospital suffering from trench fever, but we hope that he may soon be convalescent.

Mid-Sussex Times - 5th December 1916
HONOURS FOR CAPTAIN S. K. REID
Cuckfieldians will learn with no little pleasure that Captain S. K. Reid, Royal Sussex Regiment, third son of Mrs Reid, of Mill Hall, has received from the Khedive of Egypt, the Order of the Nile, 4th Class. Prior to going to Egypt, Captain Reid was at the Dardanelles

Cuckfield Parish Magazine - June 1917
Captain Reid has been awarded the Military Cross, an award announced in the London Gazette. The terms of the announcement stated that it was conferred on him and well deserved, 'For conspicuous gallantry and devotion to duty. He led his Company with great judgement and coolness under heavy fire. By his skilful use of his Lewis gun he prevented a counter attack on his exposed flank, having appreciated the danger at the right moment.'

He is now serving with the British Force in Palestine and has taken part in all the terrible fighting near Gaza.

Captain Reid died of wounds suffered at Grand Rozoy on 29th July 1918. He was aged 30 years.

He is remembered with honour at Vauxbuin French National Cemetery, Ref 11.A.1

He is also listed on Eton College Memorial and the Scottish National Memorial in Edinburgh.

His name appears on the war memorial in the churchyard of Holy Trinity Church, Cuckfield, on the marble memorial inside the Church and on the memorial board in the Queen's Hall, Cuckfield.

The white marble war memorial inside Cuckfield church was a gift from Stuart's mother Mrs Reid.

PRIVATE WILLIAM RHODES

William was born in 1879 in Bitteswell, Leicestershire. He was the son of William Rhodes, who was born in Bolney in 1837, and his wife Harriet, born in 1847 in Cuckfield. William Junior had an older sister Harriet born in Bolney in 1871.

William Senior was a gardener and domestic servant for Charles Sergison at 'Cuckfield Park' and the family lived in Gardeners Cottages. The 1891 census shows William was twelve years old and a scholar, and Harriet was a parlourmaid. The family later moved to live at 'Oakroyd', Broad Street.

William went to school in Cuckfield and sang in the Parish Church choir.

He enlisted in Bedford into the 2nd Battalion, The Bedfordshire Regiment, 30th New Army Division on 27th March 1915, Service number 27864.

He was reported missing on 2nd August 1917 and is now assumed to have died on that date or since.

He is remembered with honour on the Ypres (Menin Gate) Memorial ref panel 31 and 33.

His name appears on the war memorial in the churchyard of Holy Trinity Church, Cuckfield, on the marble memorial inside the Church and on the memorial board in the Queen's Hall, Cuckfield.

PRIVATE JAMES FRANK RIDLEY

James was born in 1890, in East Chiltington, Sussex, the son of James and Hannah Ridley. James was a carter on a farm at the time of the 1901 census.

James junior had an elder brother Thomas born in 1885, a younger sister Beatrice born in 1893 and two younger brothers, Albert born in 1895 and Arthur Stanley born in 1900.

At the time James enlisted for service he was living at Hapstead Farm, Ardingly with his wife Margaret Ethel Ridley (later Yeat).

He enlisted in Lewes into the 7th Battalion, Royal Sussex Regiment, 12th Eastern Division. Service number G18154.

James served in the British Expeditionary Force and was killed in action at Arras on 9th April 1917 aged 27 years.

He is remembered with honour on the Arras Memorial ref Bay 6.

His name appears on the war memorial in the churchyard of Holy Trinity Church, Cuckfield, on the marble memorial inside the Church and on the memorial board in the Queen's Hall, Cuckfield.

LANCE-CORPORAL ARTHUR WILLIAM ROBINSON

Arthur was born in Papworth, Everard, Cambridgeshire in 1896, the son of John Robinson a green-keeper at a golf club at that time, and Ellen Robinson. By the start of the war the family lived at 5, Albany Villas, Broad Street, Cuckfield.

Arthur was educated at the village school, and was formerly a member of the Church Lads' Brigade. He will be remembered, too, by the members of the West Park Golf Club, as for eight years his parents acted as caretakers at the Club House, during which time young Robinson showed rare ability at the game for a boy, and could hold his own with many of the gentry of the district.

Before enlisting, Arthur volunteered as a Marine on 'HMS Triumph' in China from 5th to 25th August 1914.

He then enlisted in Chichester into the 2nd Battalion, Duke of Cornwall's Light Infantry. 27th Regular Division, Service number 9561.

Mid-Sussex Times - 20th October 1914
NEWS FROM THE FAR EAST

Mrs Robinson, of Albany Villas, Hatchgate Lane, has received news from her son, Private A. Robinson (Duke of Cornwall's Light Infantry) who is stationed at Whitfield Barracks, Kowloon, Hong Kong. Along with others of his regiment, young Robinson, who is not yet twenty, has been serving as a marine on 'H.M.S, Triumph' which has been bombarding the forts of Tsing Tau.

Mid-Sussex Times - 4th May 1915
LANCE-CORPORAL ROBINSON

Mr and Mrs J. Robinson, of 'Albany Villas', Broad Street, Cuckfield, have received unofficially, the sad intelligence that their only son, Lance-corporal Arthur Robinson, Duke of Cornwall's Light Infantry, was killed in action on April 20th aged 20 years. The news was received through Mrs Robinson's sister who had recently forwarded her nephew a parcel from the address of her employer, Lady Holford, of Dorchester House, Park Lane, London. The latter received the following letter from the Front at the beginning of last week -

'Lady Holford - I take the liberty in writing to you in reference to a parcel received here for Lance-Corporal Robinson, having your address on the box containing cake, cigarettes etc. We surmise that it has come from someone in your employ or otherwise known to you. Hoping this note will find satisfaction, I would ask you to forward enclosed message to same.

Thanking you in anticipation, I remain yours truly

Lance-Corporal E. Hughes.'

The enclosed message ran -

'To the persons known to the late Lance-Corporal Robinson'.

I pen lines of regret to you to state that Lance-Corporal Robinson was killed on the 20th April; he was struck by shrapnel. I have shared contents of parcel amongst his comrades. We are very much upset about losing such a good chap, as he was well liked by his comrades. We all send our sympathy to you.

Lance-Corporal E. Hughes'.

Had he lived, young Robinson would have celebrated his 20th birthday on 22nd April and much sympathy will be felt for his parents, as he was their only child. When war broke out he was stationed with his regiment in Hong Kong and volunteered as a Royal Marine for duty on 'H.M.S. Triumph' in the storming of Tsing Tau.

Afterwards the regiment came to England, when he paid a brief visit home before leaving for France. He then experienced several weeks in hospital with frost-bitten feet, but returned to duty, and had since been in several big engagements. After Neuve Chapelle he wrote home saying he had come safely through a big battle, although it was very sad to know that forty-two of his comrades who were with him at Hong Kong had been killed.

The Duke of Cornwall's Light Infantry was warmly praised for their gallantry by Sir John French in his report on the battle.

Arthur is remembered with honour at Bedford House Cemetery, Zillebeke ref Enclosure No 2 V.A.4

His name appears on the war memorial in the churchyard of Holy Trinity Church, Cuckfield, on the marble memorial inside the Church and on the memorial board in the Queen's Hall, Cuckfield.

RIFLEMAN FRANK SIDNEY ROWLAND

Frank was born in Cuckfield in 1882, the son of Edmund Rowland, a bricklayer and his wife Elizabeth who lived in 'Maltmans', High Street. Their eldest daughter Ada was born in 1877, Alfred in 1879, and after Frank were born Albert in 1888 and Emily in 1891.

In the 1901 census Frank is shown working as a fishmonger for Ellmer's fish shop in Haywards Heath and living with the owners as a boarder.

At the beginning of the war he was living in Battersea, London and that is where he enlisted into the 4th Battalion, Rifle Brigade (The Prince Consort's Own) Service number 1490.

Frank served in many places around the world and during his tour of duty sent an interesting letter home relating his experiences.

It is interesting to note that he was present at the Service of Intercession for our Soldiers and Sailors on the morning of the second Sunday in January.

Mid-Sussex Times - 6th July 1915

RIFLEMAN FRANK ROWLAND - FROM SOMEWHERE IN FRANCE

Rifleman Frank Rowland of the 4th Battalion Rifle Brigade, son of Mr Edmund Rowland of South Street, summarises his war experiences thus -

'I left England for abroad in 1906 and after being stationed at Malta, Egypt, Khartoum and India I was called home for active service in November 1914. After a short stay in England I left for the front in December.

We have had a hard task, owing to the winter and our coming from a hot climate. What with the rain and mud up to our knees, it began to tell within a few days. Many men suffering from frostbitten feet were sent to England. We kept struggling and having small attacks and a few casualties, till the 14th and 15th of March, and then came the battle of St Eloi, which lasted two days. We had many casualties in officers and men who fought well for their country.

Our next move was in support to Hill 60, which was known as 'Little Hell', and that place will always be remembered. From there we went to Ypres, where we came in the thick of it. The bombardment was a great sight. Houses were blown clean down by one 17 inch shell. It was a big battle there and lasted from 22nd April to the 14th May. Casualties were very heavy.

On the 15th the Brigade came out for a rest, and were visited by Sir John French, who complimented the men on the most magnificent manner in which they had held on to their trenches under a more severe artillery bombardment than has ever been known. We also received a message of congratulation from the general officer commanding our Division'.

While serving in France, Frank was killed in a railway accident at Versailles, near Paris on 17th January 1917. He had been home on leave and was returning to duty when he was killed.

He is buried in Les Gonards Cemetery, Versailles ref 4.20.

His name appears on the war memorial in the churchyard of Holy Trinity Church, Cuckfield, on the marble memorial inside the Church and on the memorial board in the Queen's Hall, Cuckfield.

PRIVATE JAMES ROWLAND

James was born in Cuckfield in 1891, the eldest son of Ernest Rowland, a bricklayer's labourer and his wife Maria, of South Street. James had several brothers and sisters - a brother born in 1894, Dorothy born in 1895, Elizabeth in 1897, Olive in 1899 and Clifford born in 1900.

He enlisted in Haywards Heath into the 13th Battalion, The Royal Sussex Regiment, 39th New Army Division. Service number G/1463

Mid-Sussex Times - 31st September 1915
PRIVATE J. ROWLAND
Private James Rowland, 2nd Battalion Royal Sussex Regiment, eldest son of Mr and Mrs Ernest Rowland of South Street, Cuckfield, has sent home the brief intimation contained on a postcard that he has been wounded and admitted to hospital. He adds he is going on well. The card was written on Saturday.

Mid-Sussex Times - 2nd November 1915
PRIVATE J. ROWLAND HOME ON LEAVE
On Friday afternoon, Private J. Rowland of the 2nd Sussex , had the

pleasure of returning to 'home sweet home'. He was looking remarkably well, and naturally his kith and kin were delighted to greet him once again.

His home is in 28, South Street and he is the eldest son of Mr and Mrs E. Rowland. He was wounded in the thigh by a bullet on September 25th, at Vermelles. He returned to Cuckfield from a military hospital at Leicester, and at the expiration of ten days leave will proceed to the Depot at Chichester.

He has had more than one narrow escape from death in France. On one occasion he was getting over a trench when a shell exploded and a fragment blew away his water bottle from its sling; and another time he was with others in a reserve trench when a German aeroplane passed over and spotted them.

Shortly afterwards the enemy commenced shelling. The first shell having exploded, the trench was forsaken, but the Germans continued their deadly fire. When it ceased, Private Rowland returned to the spot, and found everything completely destroyed. Had the Sussex men remained in the trench, their days work, he says, would have been done.

Private Rowland speaks highly of the Sussex boys. He considers them 'good sports' and they always try to do their best

Mid-Sussex Times - 16th October 1917
On Wednesday morning Mr and Mrs E. Rowland 28, South Street, received the sad news that their eldest son Private James Rowland, Royal Sussex Regiment was killed in action on 26th September.

The Officer commanding the platoon, in conveying the news to the parents, said that Private Rowland died very soon after being hit so that he did not suffer much pain and he added, 'He did his duty to the very last and set a fine example to his comrades'.

The deceased soldier who was 26 years of age was formerly a gardener at 'Ditton Place' and joined up at the commencement of the war. He had been twice invalided through severe wounds.

James served in the British Expeditionary Force and was killed in action at Ypres on 26th September 1917 aged 26 years. He is buried in Perth Cemetery, (China Wall), Belgium. Ref V.G.8

His name appears on the war memorial in the churchyard of Holy Trinity Church, Cuckfield, on the marble memorial inside the Church and on the memorial board in the Queen's Hall, Cuckfield.

S

PRIVATE SYDNEY SCOTT

Sydney was born in 1900 in Uckfield, Sussex, the son of Spencer Scott an agricultural labourer and his wife Harriett.

Daisy was their eldest child born in 1890, then Edith born in 1892, Walter in 1895 and Frank who was born in 1898. All the children were born in Maresfield.

Sydney enlisted in Haywards Heath into the 8th Battalion (Pioneer Battalion) Royal Sussex Regiment, 18th Eastern Division. Service number G/2429.

He served in the British Expeditionary Force but died on 6th June 1918 aged 18 years.

He is buried in Annois Communal Cemetery ref I.C. 16

His name appears on the war memorial in the churchyard of Holy Trinity Church, Cuckfield, on the marble memorial inside the Church and on the memorial board in the Queen's Hall, Cuckfield.

Note -
Sydney's father was born in Maresfield and his mother was born in Buxted. There is no indication on any of the censuses, or other records I obtained, of any direct connection with Cuckfield to explain why his name is commemorated on the memorials there. However Sydney may have been working in Cuckfield before enlisting.

SERGEANT ALBERT EDWARD SELBY MM

Albert was born in Cuckfield in 1894, the son of Edward Selby and his wife Caroline of 'Longacre', Cuckfield.

He enlisted in Haywards Heath into 'A' Coy, 7th Battalion, Royal Sussex Regiment. 12th Eastern Division. Service number G/111.

Mid-Sussex Times - 9th May 1916
Lance Corporal Albert Edward Selby, 7th Royal Sussex Regiment has been promoted to Corporal.

Mid-Sussex Times - 19th September 1916
A SOLDIER'S BRAVERY
Corporal Albert Edward Selby, of the Royal Sussex regiment, has been promoted to Sergeant and awarded the Military Medal for gallantry and bravery in the field and for meritorious services in carrying dispatches. His mother, Mrs Selby, of 'Longacre', Cuckfield, received from him an illuminated card, signed by the Brigadier General, worded thus -

'Presented to Sergeant A. E. Selby for his gallant conduct on the 4th and 6th August 1916, at - (name given) -when he went out on patrol on three occasions and returned under heavy fire with valuable information.'

While with the British Expeditionary Force, Albert was killed in action on 8th August 1918 age 24 years. August 4th was his birthday. The plucky soldier was a grandson of the late Mr William Vincent, of West Street, Cuckfield.

Albert is buried in Beacon Cemetery, Sailly Laurette ref 11.G.9

His name appears on the war memorial in the churchyard of Holy Trinity Church, Cuckfield, on the marble memorial inside the Church and on the memorial board in the Queen's Hall, Cuckfield.

PRIVATE CHARLES SELBY

Charles was born in Cuckfield in 1891, the son of Henry and Susannah Selby who lived in Brook Street. Henry was a bricklayer and labourer. The 1891 census shows that their first child was Edith born in 1883, followed by Ellen in 1884, Percy in 1887, George in 1889, followed by Charles in 1891, Arthur in 1893 and Sidney born in1900.

In fact they were such a large family that on each census there are several in the family not included as they had left home. The family later moved to Ansty.

Charles enlisted in Cuckfield into the 7th I.W. Company, Royal Fusiliers, Service number 31452.

He was later transferred to the (68066) 114th Company Labour Corps.

The Cuckfield Parish Magazine of September 1918, records that he was home on leave in the middle of 1918 but shortly after returning to the war area he was killed by a shell in France.

Charles is buried in Wood Cemetery, Marcelcave ref B. 20.

His name appears on the war memorial in the churchyard of Holy Trinity Church, Cuckfield, on the marble memorial inside the Church and on the memorial board in the Queen's Hall, Cuckfield.
Charles's brother William George was also killed in the war in October 1914. Another brother Percy Harold was killed in the war in October 1917.

LANCE-CORPORAL PERCY HAROLD SELBY

Percy was born in Cuckfield in 1897, the son of Henry Selby a bricklayer and his wife Susannah who lived in Brook Street, Cuckfield. He had an elder brother George W. born in 1889, a brother Arthur E. born in 1893, Claude F. born in1896 and another brother Sidney F. born in1900.

Percy enlisted in Haywards Heath into the Royal Sussex Regiment, Service number 2169. He was transferred to the 1/6th Battalion - Territorial, Royal Warwickshire Regiment, 48th South Midland Division. Service number 241868.

He served in France and Flanders and was killed in action on 4th October 1917 aged 20 years.

Mid-Sussex Times - 26th October 1917
KILLED IN ACTION

On Friday last, the sad news was received that Lance Corporal Percy Harold Selby, Royal Warwickshire Regiment, was killed in action on 4th October. The deceased soldier, who was only 20 years of age, was formerly a cowman at Sidney Farm. He joined up at the outbreak of the war and having been wounded in 1916 was in hospital in England for some months, returning to the Front on January 7th this year. He was the fourth son of Mr and Mrs H. Selby of Brook Street with whom much sympathy is felt, as this is the second son whom they have given to the Great Cause, their eldest son William, Royal Sussex Regiment having been killed in October 1914.

Cuckfield Parish Magazine - January 1918
Mr and Mrs Selby have received details of the death of their son Lance-Corporal Percy Selby who was killed in action on 4th October.

The Officer in command of his Company writes -

'He was shot in the head and died at once, just as he was about to jump into the German front line trench. He was in charge of a Lewis gun team. He was a jolly fine fellow. All his friends miss him very much and speak so well of him in the show. His cheery presence was a great help to team men.' This is a good record and Mr and Mrs Selby may well be proud of their son, who so bravely gave his life to defend us.

He is remembered with honour on the Tyne Cot Memorial Panel 23 to 28 and 163A.

His name appears on the war memorial in the churchyard of Holy Trinity Church, Cuckfield, on the marble memorial inside the Church and on the memorial board in the Queen's Hall, Cuckfield.

Percy's brother Charles died in the war in mid 1918 and brother William was killed in October 1914.

PRIVATE WILLIAM GEORGE SELBY

William was born in Cuckfield, in 1888, the eldest son of Henry, a bricklayer and Susanna Selby of Brook Street, Cuckfield. William, or George W as he appears on the census, had two older sisters, Edith A. born in1883 and Ellen S. born in 1884. Brother Arthur was born in1893, Claude was born in 1896, Percy Harold was born in 1897 and Sidney was born in 1900.

William was the husband of Sarah Selby of 45, Sixth Street, Shankhill Road, Belfast.

He enlisted in Chichester into the 2nd Battalion, Royal Sussex Regiment, Service number L/8311 and served in the British Expeditionary Force.

Mid-Sussex Times - 17th November 1914
ROYAL SUSSEX REGIMENT LIVING LIKE RABBITS
Cuckfieldians cheery letter
In a letter to his mother, Mrs Selby, of Brook Street, Cuckfield, Private William George Selby of the Royal Sussex Regiment, describes how the regiment are living. He says he is still quite well, and adds-

'We are well off now for different things; everybody is sending things, and we receive them with the best wish to everybody from those who send them. We are having good weather here, but very cold at nights. However we have very good clothes, and we cannot grumble.

One of our chaps receives the Mid-Sussex Times out here so I see all the little things that happen round that way. Young **Knight** is out here with me, and I hear that **Albert Jennings** is home on furlough, so I suppose he must have got wounded. We are like the rabbits here: we dig holes in the bank, and come out to fry a piece of bacon, hear a bang and in we pop. In fact I think we are quicker than the rabbits, for we don't prick our ears up first to see what noise it is. We are as sharp as razors. Save me a piece of Christmas pudding'.

Mid-Sussex Times - 15th December 1914
PRIVATE W. G. SELBY

News was received on Thursday by Mr and Mrs Henry Selby, of Brook Street, that their eldest son, Private William George Selby, of the 2nd Battalion Royal Sussex Regiment, had been the first Cuckfield soldier to lay down his life for his country.

He was killed in action at Ypres on October 30th. Six days previously he had written a jovial letter to his mother comparing their life out in France with that of the rabbits at home. Private Selby as a boy was educated at Cuckfield School, was in the local Church Lads Brigade, and for several years in the Brook Street Mission Church Choir. On leaving school he worked for Mr Richard Worsley of 'Broxmead' and at the age of seventeen he joined the Royal Sussex Regiment. After leaving the army he worked in Messrs Hall's ship building yard at Belfast and rejoined his regiment at the beginning of the war as a reservist.

He was 26 years of age, a married man, and leaves a widow and three children, the two eldest being twins aged three years and the youngest a baby of eighteen months. Their home is in Belfast, Northern Ireland.

William is remembered with Honour on the Ypres (Menin Gate) Memorial ref Panel 20 and also on the Irish National Memorial.

His name appears on the war memorial in the churchyard of Holy Trinity Church, Cuckfield, on the marble memorial inside the Church and on the memorial board in the Queen's Hall, Cuckfield.

William's brother Percy Harold was also killed in the war, on 4th October 1917, and brother Charles in mid 1918.

PRIVATE ALFRED ERNEST SMITH

Alfred was born in Slaugham in 1873, the son of Frederick and Mary Smith who by 1901 were living at 9, Highlands, Cuckfield. In 1881 when Alfred was 8 years old the family lived at Middle Pilstye (Farm) Staplefield, where Frederick was an agricultural labourer. Alfred had a younger sister Alice born in 1878.

Alfred enlisted in Haywards Heath into the 2nd Battalion Royal Sussex Regiment 1st Regular Division, Service number GS/297.

He served for many years in the Royal Garrison Artillery in India, West Africa and China.

Mid-Sussex Times - 24th August 1915
PRIVATE A. E. SMITH
After having been officially informed that he was wounded, and later missing, Mr and Mrs Frederick Smith, of Lower Highlands, Cuckfield, have now been notified that their second son, Private Alfred Ernest Smith, 2nd Battalion Royal Sussex Regiment, has been killed in action.

The official intimation from the Record Office, which was received last Thursday, states that he fell at Richebourg l'Avoué on 9th May 1915.

At the outbreak of war, Private Smith was a pensioner of the Royal Garrison Artillery, in which he had served seventeen years, and during that time he saw service in China, India and in South Africa during the last war. He was a first class gunner on his retirement. He bravely responded to his country's call and joined the 2nd Battalion, Royal Sussex Regiment last August, and was not too old at forty two to fight again for his country, and for which he has now died. He was born at Slaugham, Handcross, educated at Staplefield School and was unmarried.

He joined the British Expeditionary Force and when killed in action was aged 42 years.

He is remembered with honour on Le Touret Memorial ref Panel 20 and 21.

His name appears on the war memorial in the churchyard of Holy Trinity Church, Cuckfield, on the marble memorial inside the Church and on the memorial board in the Queen's Hall, Cuckfield.

He was the uncle of Cyril Ralph Smith who died in May 1915.

PRIVATE CYRIL RALPH SMITH

Cyril was born in Cuckfield in 1890, the son of Samuel Lewis Smith a general labourer and his wife Mary. He was the eldest grandson of Frederick Smith and Mary Smith of 9, Highlands, Cuckfield.

He was educated at the National Schools and was employed by Mr F. H. Beeny nearly three years previous to joining up in September 1914.

Cyril enlisted in Cuckfield into the 8th Battalion, Royal Sussex Regiment, 18th Division. Service number G/2663.

He went to France on 24th July 1915 and was killed on May 16th last when he was 26 years of age and just one year after his uncle, Private A. E. Smith.

Mid-Sussex Times - 23rd May 1916
DEATH OF PRIVATE CYRIL SMITH

The sad news has been received at Cuckfield that Private Cyril Smith, of the Royal Sussex Regiment, has been killed. He had been out digging a trench and was just preparing to come back when he was hit, the bullet lodging in his back.

'His death' says his Captain, writing to Mrs F. Smith, 'was perfectly peaceful. I need hardly add that his death will be a great loss to his platoon, and consequently to my Company, as he was a very good worker and always cheerful. Words I am afraid are not of much consolation at a time like this, but you must be proud of him. He has given his life doing his bit.'

Cyril is buried in Carnoy Military Cemetery ref U.16

His name appears on the war memorial in the churchyard of Holy Trinity Church, Cuckfield, on the marble memorial inside the Church and on the memorial board in the Queen's Hall, Cuckfield.

ABLE SEAMAN HENRY FREDERICK SMITH

Henry was born in Cuckfield in 1897, the youngest son of Henry James Smith, a chimney sweep. His mother Mary Ann was born in Brucklands ? Buckinghamshire.

Henry had several brothers and sisters who were all born in Cuckfield. The eldest was Clara, born in 1884, then George born in 1891, Sophia in 1893, Flora in 1892, Jane in 1896, and after Henry, Alice born in 1899. They all lived in Brook Street.

Henry was educated at Cuckfield Church School and entered the Navy at the age of sixteen; he had been on the reserve about ten years. Previous to the war he carried on the trade of a chimney sweep at High Street, Cuckfield where his widow, Matilda and only child, a little girl now reside. The 1901 census shows Henry aged 23, as an Able Seaman crew member on board the 'H.M.S Majestic'.

Mid-Sussex Times - 5th October 1915
ABLE SEAMAN HARRY SMITH

We stated in these columns last week that Able Seaman Henry Smith who was serving on H.M.S 'Glory' was in hospital with dysentery, the information being conveyed in a letter to his wife at High Street, Cuckfield. The latter received the sad intelligence on Friday morning that her husband had succumbed to enteric fever on board the H.M. hospital ship 'Aquitania' on September 18th 1915.

He had been fighting in the trenches at the Dardanelles and in his last letter home he stated he was in a stationary hospital, but expected to be moved to Alexandria shortly, so it is presumed he died on the voyage. He was thirty seven years of age at the time of his death.

Henry is remembered on the Portsmouth Naval Memorial Ref 8.

His name appears on the war memorial in the churchyard of Holy Trinity Church, Cuckfield, on the marble memorial inside the Church and on the memorial board in the Queen's Hall, Cuckfield.

BOY - 1ST CLASS BERNARD SMYTH

Bernard was born in 1898 in Erith, Kent, the son of Reginald and Emily Smyth. Reginald was born in Guernsey and when his sons were born he was living on his own means in Linden Cottage, Ifield near Horsham, West Sussex.

Reginald, junior, was the couple's first son, born in 1894 and after Bernard they had another son called William born in 1900.

As a boy Bernard lived in Bolney Road, Ansty and was for many years a choir boy in Holy Trinity Church, Cuckfield and also in Ansty.

He joined the crew of H.M.S. 'Formidable' as a Boy 1st Class.

When the ship was hit on New Years Day 1915 and it began to sink, Bernard was saved into an open boat. It was therefore extra sad that after surviving many hours in the boat he collapsed and died immediately on landing. He was aged 17 years.

He is remembered in Lyme Regis Cemetery ref D. 14/17

Although his name does not appear on any of the three memorials in Cuckfield he is listed in the Church Roll of Honour and his name was included in the Intercession Services for those who had given their lives during the war.

Cuckfield Church Magazine - February 1915
In May 1915 a brass tablet was presented and fixed on the wall above the choir stalls with the following inscription -

'In memory of Bernard Smyth, sometime choir boy of Ansty, who gave his life for his country in the loss of H.M.S. 'Formidable', January 1st 1915, aged 17.

PRIVATE GEORGE ERIC STEVENS

George was born in Preston Park, Brighton in 1888, the son of William and Grace Stevens of 'Garnolds', Cuckfield and before that of 'Beechfields', Bolnore Road. William was a solicitor and Public Notary. George had a brother Frank G. born in 1890 and a brother William B. born in 1897.

He enlisted in Brighton into 'D' Company, the 20th Battalion Royal Fusiliers (City of London Regiment) Service number PS/5691.

He saw action in France and Flanders and was killed in action near Cambrin on 13th March 1916 aged 27 years.

Mid-Sussex Times - 21st March 1916
PRIVATE ERIC GEORGE STEVENS

A well known young townsman of Cuckfield, Private Eric George Stevens, third and youngest son of Mr William Stevens J.P. and Mrs Stevens, of 'Garnolds', lost his life on Sunday, 12th March. A telegram to his father last Thursday conveyed the sad news that he had been shot through the head.

The deceased enlisted in August 1914, immediately on the outbreak of the hostilities, his regiment being the 20th Royal Fusiliers (3rd Public Schools Battalion) and he was serving as a stretcher bearer in the western theatre of war. Before going out in November 1915 he had successively been in camps stationed at Epsom, Mansfield and Tidworth.

Like his father - the head of the old established firm of Messrs Stevens and Son, solicitors of 26, Marlborough Place, Brighton - Mr Eric Stevens belonged to the legal profession and was admitted a solicitor in 1912.

He obtained honours in his final examination in October 1911 and the Law Society awarded the Mellersh Prize for that year as a result of his success. This is open for competition among candidates who have been articled in the counties of Surrey or Sussex, or who are the sons of solicitors who have resided and practised in either of these counties, and is awarded to the candidate who shows himself best acquainted with the law of real property and the practice of conveyancing.

The deceased, who was 27 years of age, was a Bachelor of Laws of London University and acted as managing clerk to his father. He had been prominently associated with Liberal politics, and was a frequent speaker at meetings in Mid-Sussex and elsewhere. At Cuckfield he was Hon. Secretary of the local Association, and he was a former Treasurer of the Association and Club at Haywards Heath, besides being interested in other movements of the day. His father, who is a member of the Brighton Town Council and well known in the Borough, and mother have received an overwhelming number of sympathetic letters.

19th March 1916
Letter from the Chaplain of the 20th Royal Fusiliers, 3rd Public Schools Battalion

'It was my sad duty as Chaplain to the 20th Royal Fusiliers to take the burial service for your son, who was killed in action on March 13th. We buried him in Cambrin Churchyard, just behind the trenches, just after 6.00 p.m. on March 15th. A simple white cross, made and put up by the Battalion, marks the spot where his body rests, beside those of some of his comrades who fell at about the same time.

If you should care to have a photograph, I think that I might be able to get one for you, though there might be some delay as the Churchyard is frequently shelled. In Peace time it must be a pretty little spot and to us it will always be sacred, for several of our best officers and men lie there. Others will have written to tell you how your son fell and how proud we all are of him.

I trust that you may find some comfort in the thought that he gave his life to try and help a fallen comrade, the fairest sacrifice that a man can make and a most gallant act. Of course we realise that war must take its toll of some, but that does not lessen our sorrow at the loss of such men as was your son, nor our sympathy for those who mourn their loss at home'.

2nd April 1916

Letter from the Officer Commanding 'D' Company (to which Eric was attached as a stretcher bearer) of the 20th Royal Fusiliers, 3rd Public Schools Battalion:-

'The fact that I have myself been ill and on leave is my only excuse for not having written to you before to express my sympathy with you in the loss of your son.

I had known him ever since he joined, and had learned to appreciate his genuine worth. In a Company full of unusually fine fellows he took a place of which his relations may well be proud. He was a good soldier, cheerful and willing. I never knew him to complain even when things were hard: he commanded the respect and esteem of all who knew him, whether they were his superiors in rank or no. In writing this letter I can assure you that I write not only on my own behalf, but that I voice the feeling of the whole Company who all miss a good fellow and a brave soldier'.

Mid-Sussex Times - 21st March 1916
THE LATE PRIVATE G. E. STEVENS

On Sunday morning the service at the Congregational Church was 'In Memoriam' to Private G. Eric Stevens, whose widely lamented death, while on active service in France, is referred to elsewhere in this issue. Under the pulpit hung a laurel wreath with the words 'Victory' upon it in white letters.

There was a large congregation and during the service the Choir sang, very feelingly, Stainer's anthem, 'What are These'. The Rev. S. Maddock took his text from John XV, 13, 'Greater love hath no man than this, that a man lay down his life for his friends'.

During the course of his sermon the preacher spoke of his knowledge of Private G. E. Stevens and mentioned that it was the sight of the first batch of the wounded coming into Brighton that decided him to enlist. He hated the military regime as such, with every fibre of his soul. It was hard to imagine him lifting a rifle to kill a fellow man, even a German, and it was much more in keeping with his character when he found a chance for service in the 'Stretcher Bearer' Section of the Public University Corps, which he had joined.

'I can conceive', Mr Maddock proceeded, 'no greater loss to our country than that of such manhood as his - that type of man whom England will most need in the days of reconstruction that lie ahead of us. Inheriting as he did the fine traditions of a family in the truest sense ennobled by sacrificial deeds and lives with his educational advantages and his splendid natural gifts, his chief aim was to serve his generation in the highest things. He could not brook a narrow patriotism. I have heard him say that he considered a Sunday School teacher as truly a patriot as a military officer, and few know the time, the thought, the money, the energy, the prayer he spent on the lads of Cuckfield, and more than one will carry his memory as an inspiration and a beacon star to his dying day. He was one of the noblest men I ever met: whole-souled, selfless, humble, deeply earnest, with high ideals, and sparing no pains to achieve them - knowing no barriers of caste to hinder him. He freely gave to all. England can ill spare such lives as these. Sacred indeed is the ground of Flanders where blood like his is shed. Sacred indeed will be that possession of national liberty that has cost such priceless lives. England that has received so richly will have a debt to pay to those brave heroes that can only be discharged by building around us an England worthy of them. He is recruited for higher service above', said the preacher in closing.

Miss Cleare, who presided at the organ, opened the service with, 'I know that my Redeemer liveth' and closed it with the voluntary, 'O Rest in the Lord'.

George was buried in Cambrin Churchyard Extension ref L1.10D

He is also listed on Brighton War Memorial.

His name appears on the war memorial in the churchyard of Holy Trinity Church, Cuckfield, on the marble memorial inside the Church and on the memorial board in the Queen's Hall, Cuckfield.

T

LIEUTENANT HARCOURT CHARLES TURNER

Harcourt Charles was born in 1886, the son of Montague and Augusta Turner of 'Hortons', Cuckfield. Montague Turner was a solicitor. In 1891 the family lived in 'Milton House', Lindfield. Their eldest child was Ivy born in 1880 and then they had five sons, Montague born in 1882, George in1884, Harcourt in 1886, Clive in 1889 and Lionel born in 1890.

Harcourt was in the 3rd Battalion of the Duke of Cornwall's Light Infantry and later in the 6th Battalion of the Duke of Cornwall's Light Infantry.

Mid-Sussex Times - 7th December 1915
A COMMISSION
Mr Harcourt C. Turner, son of Mrs A. Montague Turner has been

gazetted as Second Lieutenant in the 3rd Battalion of the Duke of Cornwall's Light infantry.

Mid-Sussex Times - 4th September 1917
LIEUTENANT HARCOURT TURNER

The sad news was received last week that Second Lieutenant Harcourt. C. Turner of the Duke of Cornwall's Light Infantry had met his death in France while gallantly leading his platoon in resisting a German counter attack on a trench which our troops had taken.

He was the third son of the late Mr Montague Turner and Mrs Montague Turner of 'Hortons', Cuckfield and grandson of the late Sir Charles Lennox Peel, KCB., Clerk to the Privy Council. He took up farming in Canada for a time but returned to England before the war. When war broke out he joined the ranks and in 1915 was given his commission. In France he performed good work and was liked by all who had associations with him. He was a true Britisher, fearless and cheerful, and as he spent his dear life for England will ever cause his name to be honoured by the family to which he belonged.

He was well known in Cuckfield where he had many friends, to whom his death has come as a real grief, and much sympathy is felt for Mrs Montagu Turner and the members of her family in their sorrow.

He was killed in action at Langemark near Ypres on 23rd August 1917 aged 32 years and is remembered with honour on the Tyne Cot Memorial panel ref 80 - 82 and 163A.

His name appears on the war memorial in the churchyard of Holy Trinity Church, Cuckfield, on the marble memorial inside the Church and on the memorial board in the Queen's Hall, Cuckfield.

U

RIFLEMAN HORACE WILLIAM UPTON

Horace was born in Balcombe, Sussex in 1888, the son of William and Mary Upton. His father William was born in Cuckfield and was an agricultural labourer. Horace had an elder sister Ellen C. born in 1886 and a brother Arthur B. born in 1887.

He enlisted in Brighton into the 2nd Battalion, Kings Royal Rifle Corps 1st Regular Division, Service number 7250.

He served in France and Flanders and died of wounds on 31st October 1914 aged 26 years.

Mid-Sussex Times - 8th February 1916
PRIVATE HORACE UPTON

Official notification has just been received by the relatives of Private Horace Upton, 6th Battalion Kings Royal Rifles, that he was killed in action on or about the 31st October 1914. At that time he was reported wounded and missing, since when nothing further had been heard of him.

He had served several years with his regiment and on the outbreak of war he was recalled to the Colours, and he fell in action soon afterwards, the exact date and place of his death being unknown.

His father with whom we wish to express our sincere sympathy, used to live at Iron Pear Tree Cottages and has now moved to a house near Burgess Hill.

Horace is remembered with honour on the Ypres (Menin Gate) Memorial ref Panel 51 and 53

His name appears on the war memorial in the churchyard of Holy Trinity Church, Cuckfield, on the marble memorial inside the Church and on the memorial board in the Queen's Hall, Cuckfield.

LANCE-CORPORAL LAWRENCE UPTON

Lawrence was born in Cuckfield in 1892, the son of Mr Charles Upton, a coachman and groom, and Mrs Esther Upton of 43 Hatchgate Cottages, Cuckfield.

The eldest son was Joseph, born in 1879, Isaac born in 1886, Charles born in 1888, Nathan born in 1890 and then a younger sister Miriam born in 1895. Lawrence was well known in Cuckfield Sunday School.

Lawence enlisted in Woolwich as he was living in Plumstead at the time. He enlisted first into the London Regiment, Service number 6473 and was then transferred to the 97th Company Machine Gun Corps (Infantry) No 63055 when he became Lance Corporal.

He served in France and Flanders.

Mid-Sussex Times - 25th September 1917
LANCE-CORPORAL LAWENCE UPTON -
Died of Wounds

The sad news was received on Sunday morning, of the death of Lance Corporal Lawence Upton, Machine Gun Corps, GC London Regiment. The deceased was the younger son of Mr and Mrs Charles Upton of

Hatchgate Lane, Cuckfield. He was wounded in action in Ypres on the morning of 18th September being hit by a machine gun bullet. He died the same evening and was buried on the following day in the British Cemetery. He was 25 years of age. The officer commanding the section to which Lance Corporal Upton belonged, speaks of him as an excellent soldier and very popular with all ranks.

Mid-Sussex Times - 16th October 1917
LANCE-CORPORAL L. UPTON'S DEATH
Further information as to the manner in which Private Lawrence Upton, Machine Gun Corps, son of Mr and Mrs Charles Upton, of 48, Hatchgate Lane met with his death which was recently recorded under this heading, is to hand, the Rev S. Maddock having been instrumental in getting it forwarded. It seems that the deceased was in the act of relieving sentries and appeared to fall at the first shot fired on the party. This was on 18th September and death ensued about three quarters of an hour after Upton received the wound. His left lung was probably penetrated.

Much sympathy is felt with Mr and Mrs Upton who lost an elder son Nathan, killed in action in the autumn of 1915.

Mr and Mrs Upton have had many expressions of sympathy in their great loss including that of the King and Queen, and for them they desire to tender their heartfelt thanks.

Lawrence is remembered in Coxyde Military Cemetery Belgium ref 111.J.7

His name also appears on the war memorial in the churchyard of Holy Trinity Church, Cuckfield, on the marble memorial inside the Church and on the memorial board in the Queen's Hall, Cuckfield.

PRIVATE NATHAN UPTON

Nathan was born in Cuckfield in 1890. He was the son of Charles Upton, a coachman and groom and Esther his wife who lived at 48, Hatchgate Lane, Cuckfield and before that in Cuckfield High Street. He was an elder brother of Lawrence Upton who was also killed during the war.

Private Nathan Upton was born in Cuckfield twenty five years ago last April, and received his education at the British School. Before the war broke out he was a gardener by occupation, in service at Ascot, Berkskhire, and previously he was in the employ of Mr. R. A. Bevan, J.P., of 'Horsegate', Cuckfield.

Nathan enlisted in Reading, although living in Cuckfield at the time, into the 8th Battalion, Princess Charlotte of Wales (Royal Berkshire Regiment) Service number 13121.

Mid-Sussex Times - 12th October 1915
PRIVATE NATHAN UPTON
Unofficial but trustworthy information reached Mr and Mrs C. Upton, of 'Maltmans', High Street, Cuckfield, on Saturday morning, that their fifth son, Private Nathan Upton, No 13121, 'A' Company, 8th Battalion Royal Berkshire Regiment, had been killed in action. The dead soldier's fiancée received some photos, on the back of which was her address, from Private D. A. Jeffreys, 2nd Battalion Welsh Regiment, and he broke the news of Private Upton's death in the following letter:-

'You may be surprised to receive this short note from me, but seeing that I picked up the enclosed photos on the battlefield during the recent big advance we have made, I feel it my duty to return the same to you, because the address was on the photos. They were in the pocket case of No 13121, Private Nathan Upton, of the 8th Royal Berks Regiment, and thinking he might be some relation of yours it would be best for you to have them.

I am very sorry as a comrade, to inform you that he has been killed up against the German barbed wire in front of their trenches, but he died a noble hero in a great charge. I trust you will hear the sad news bravely, because I can assure you he died a hero, as he was among the first line of men to advance in the same danger as we have all got to face in this war.'

Mid-Sussex Times - 16th November 1915
PRIVATE NATHAN UPTON
Mr and Mrs C. Upton of Maltmans Cottages, High Street, Cuckfield, have received from the War Office a notification that their son, Private N. Upton No 13121, Royal Berkshire Regiment, was killed in action with the British Expeditionary Force on September 25th. Mrs Upton has received the following sympathetic letter from Lance-Corporal F.H. Kemp, Post Orderly, 8th Berkshires, B.E.F -

'Madam -

I have made the necessary enquiries, and, while I loath the idea, I have to inform you that the result of the said enquires is I have to report that your brave son has lost his life fighting for his country. A better man, both in camp life and on active service, could not be wished for, but the fortunes of war is that 'men must fight and women must weep'.

You cannot think what an effort it requires for me to write such a letter, but I have one consolation: I am doing what your son would wish me to do could he speak - that is lesson the suspense, which is to my idea, worse than the thing itself.

Well Madam, please accept my deepest sympathy, and console yourself in the fact that he did his duty nobly.

P.S. I received a letter addressed to your son this morning, which I destroyed.'

Nathan served in France and Flanders, and when killed in action at Loos on 25th September 1915 he was aged 25 years.

He is remembered with honour on the Loos Memorial ref panel 93 to 95.

His name appears on the war memorial in the churchyard of Holy Trinity Church, Cuckfield, on the marble memorial inside the Church and on the memorial board in the Queen's Hall, Cuckfield.

V

PRIVATE GEORGE WILLIAM VICKERS

George William was born in Cuckfield in 1891. He was the son of William Bampton Vickers and Rebecca Vickers of 'Myton House Stables', Warwick.

He enlisted in Bury St Edmunds although he was living in Haywards Heath at the time. He served in the 19th Ammunition Sub Park, Royal Army Service Corps, Service number M2/035363.

Mid-Sussex Times - 21st March 1916
PRIVATE G. W. VICKERS
Yet another name has to be added to the Cuckfield Roll of Honour.

The news came as a great shock to Mrs Vickers of 2, Briar Cottages,

Cuckfield to hear that her son, Private George W. Vickers, Motor Transport, A.S.C had died in a hospital in France of pneumonia. She had heard nothing of his illness until Tuesday last, when the Chaplain of the hospital wrote saying he had been admitted. Nothing more was heard till Friday, when she received the sad intelligence that he has passed away on Tuesday evening. He was 24 years of age. The father is in the Blue Cross (A.V.C) and is in France and a brother, who is also in the Mechanical Transport, was with the deceased when he died.

George served in France and Flanders and died on 14th March 1916.

He is buried in St. Venant Communal Cemetery Ref 11.G.6

His name appears on the war memorial in the churchyard of Holy Trinity Church, Cuckfield, on the marble memorial inside the Church and on the memorial board in the Queen's Hall, Cuckfield.

W

ABLE SEAMAN CHARLES HENRY WEBBER

Charles was born in Balcombe in 1881, the third child and second son of James John Webber a wheelwright and blacksmith born in Balcombe in 1854.

His mother was Agnes Emily Webber born in Burgess Hill in 1857. They had a large family, Louisa Fanny born in 1877, John Alfred born in 1879, and after Charles, Rose Ann born in 1882, Lillian Lucy in 1884, James George in 1886, Mark William in 1887, Nellie Maud in 1891, Horace in 1895, Kate in1896, Daisy also born in 1896 ? twins, Percy born in 1899 and Grace born in 1900.

They lived in 'Rose Cottage', Balcombe, but by 1901 the family had moved to live at Whitemans Green, Cuckfield and James was still a wheelwright.

On the census taken in 1901, Charles is shown as an ordinary seaman crew member of a ship, so he had made the sea his career. He joined the Royal Navy H.M.S. 'Good Hope', number 197166 with the rank of Able Seaman.

Mid-Sussex Times - 10th November 1914
LOCAL MAN ON THE 'GOOD HOPE'

The feared loss of H.M.S. 'Good Hope', in the Pacific battle has a close interest for Cuckfieldians, for a local man forms one of the crew. He is Charles Henry Webber, Able Seaman, second son of the late Mr and Mrs J. J. Webber of Whitemans Green.

A single man, he made his home with his brothers and sisters at the above address, and as a member of the Royal Fleet Reserve he went to Portsmouth and joined the 'Good Hope' for his months annual training on 13th July and has not been seen since.

On the eve of hostilities he wrote and said they were all ready and waiting for the warning. On the outbreak of war the ship journeyed to the West Indies, and about a month ago he wrote and said they were leaving there for South America. This is the last communication his family have had from him and they are anxiously awaiting news of his fate.

Mid-Sussex Times - 5th January 1915

Charles Henry Webber, Able Seaman. H.M.S 'Good Hope' died by drowning off the Chilean Coast on November 1st 1914

At sea our fleet is carrying on its useful work of safeguarding our transports and our food. On November 1st a naval battle took place off the coast of Chilli in which our ships had to fight a superior force. H.M.S 'Monmouth' and H.M.S 'Good Hope' were sunk with total loss of lives on board. On the latter vessel was Charles Webber, of Whiteman's Green, the first Cuckfield man to lay down his life for his country in the present war.

He is remembered on the Portsmouth Naval Memorial ref 2.

His name appears on the war memorial in the churchyard of Holy Trinity Church, Cuckfield, on the marble memorial inside the Church and on the memorial board in the Queen's Hall, Cuckfield.

PRIVATE HENRY EDWARD WILLIAMS

Edward was born in 1899 in Cuckfield, the son of Henry and Ellen Williams of 'Old Thatch Cottage', Whiteman's Green. Henry was a general labourer.

Edward enlisted, aged 18, in Haywards Heath into the 'C' Company, 2nd Battalion, Royal Sussex Regiment, Service number L/10320.

He was a Cuckfield lad by birth, and was educated at the local Church Schools and was also at one time a member of the troop of Boy Scouts. Before enlisting in the Army he worked in the gardens at 'Knowle Lodge', the residence of Mrs Knott.

He had seen considerable fighting during the present campaign.

Mid-Sussex Times - 19th October 1915
Through the agency of a letter written home by Private H. Knight, son of Mr and Mrs G. Knight, of 'Hanlye', Mr and Mrs H. Williams, of Whitemans Green, Cuckfield, learned last week that their only son had

been killed in action at Loos on 25th September 1915. He was 19 years of age last April.

Edward is remembered on the Loos Memorial Ref panel 69 to 73.

His name appears on the war memorial in the churchyard of Holy Trinity Church, Cuckfield, on the marble memorial inside the Church and on the memorial board in the Queen's Hall, Cuckfield.

GUNNER RICHARD E. WOODHAMS

Richard E. Woodhams was born in Hastings in 1885, the fifth child of James and Agnes Woodhams. His older sister Ada was born in 1872, then Emily born in 1876, Alice in 1881, James in 1883 and after Richard, Stuart was born in 1886, Margaret in 1888 and Irene born in 1890.

Father James was an auctioneer, valuer and land agent.

In the 1901 census Richard is shown as a boarder at Fosters School, Sherborne, Dorset.

He served in the Royal Garrison Artillery, 41st Siege Battery Service number 154083.

Before joining up he was foreman gardener at Peachey's nurseries Balcombe and the family lived in Chatfield Road, Cuckfield. He was married to Alice, who, when he was killed, was left with four children, the eldest being ten years and the youngest 18 months.

Mid-Sussex Times - 11th November 1917
On Saturday, Mrs Woodhams, of Chatfield Road, Cuckfield, received the following letter from an officer in the R.G.A.

'It is my sad duty to inform you that your husband was seriously wounded and succumbed to his injuries in the field ambulance some little time after. He formed one of a party of four men who were carrying stores up to the forward guns on the 11th inst when a shell pitched close by and seriously wounded three, of whom your husband was one. Some RFA men nearby, carried them on stretchers to the nearest dressing station.

Yesterday we received a letter from the medical officer in charge of the dressing station to the effect that your husband died of wounds on the 11th inst.

This war is terrible enough at any time. It is when casualties occur that one realises the full horror. I had known your husband as a man who could always be depended upon to carry out any task given him with cheerfulness and without hesitation. More than that it is impossible to expect of any man'.

Richard was 32 years of age.

He was buried in Bard Cottage Cemetery ref V1.B.32

Sadly, although Richard was a resident of Cuckfield he is not remembered on any of the war memorials.

Y

FIRST AIR MECHANIC - ALBERT FRANKLIN YOUNG

Albert was born in 1899 in Marylebone, London, the son of Albert and Kathleen Young who by the time of the First World War had moved to live in the 'Studio', Cuckfield.

Albert was the eldest child and he had a sister Dorothy K. born in 1900. His parents had a step-child called Gerald Edward born in 1889. Father Albert was a photographer.

Albert was in the Wireless School, Royal Air Force, number 9177

The account of Albert's death in the Mid-Sussex Times describes how he sadly met his death on 9th June 1918.

Mid-Sussex Times - 11th June 1918

DIED OF WOUNDS

On Sunday morning Mrs Young, of 'The 'Studio', Cuckfield, learnt that her only son, Franklin Young, had passed away during the night. Although only 19 years of age, he had been promoted 1st Air Mechanic and he was a promising and efficient member of the Royal Air Force. In March, the aerodrome in France in which he was stationed was bombed by the enemy and he received a severe wound in the head. After a time he was brought to the 2nd General Hospital in London, where he was twice operated upon, and after a long period of alternating hopes and fears he has succumbed to his wounds.

Mrs and Miss Young wish to thank all who have given them kind sympathy in their loss. The funeral will take place on Wednesday next 12th June.

Mid-Sussex Times - 18th June 1918

HONOURED IN DEATH
IMPRESSIVE MILITARY FUNERAL AT CUCKFIELD

Day by day in Mid-Sussex the chord of human sympathy is being touched by the loss of gallant sons in the war. 'Died of wounds' is a significant phrase - indicative of the suffering and 'the greatest gift of all' for the Empire's cause - and patriotic Cuckfield has shown that it honours the memory and mourns the death of its young heroes.

First Air Mechanic Albert Franklin Young, Royal Air Force, of 'The Studio', Cuckfield was wounded in France last March, when an aerodrome was bombed by the enemy, and he was brought to hospital in London, underwent operations, and passed away on the 9th inst.

He was given a military funeral at Cuckfield on Wednesday afternoon. The 'D' Company, 8th Battalion Sussex Volunteer Regiment, met at the old Drill Hall, Second Lieutenant F. H. Bocquet being present, with members from Cuckfield, Haywards Heath and Lindfield. Platoon Sergeant Ferguson had control of a firing party, with Platoon Sergeant Green as Acting Corporal, and the bearers comprised Corporal Carter (in charge), Lance- Sergeant Purvey, and Privates Willsman, Boniface, Godsmark and Slatter.

The Company marched to The Studio, presented arms when the coffin, which was covered with the Union Jack, was brought out, and as they approached the grand old Parish Church it was seen that three Union Jacks in the locality were flying at half mast. The Volunteers came on with slow and measured tread and arms reversed, and at the lych gate the order was given, 'Firing party, rest on your arms reversed'.

Here Canon Wilson (Vicar of Cuckfield), the Rev. J H. Layton and the choir met the funeral cortege, and the opening sentences of the burial service were uttered. Mr W. Herrington carried the processional cross. In addition to the three family mourners, we noticed, Mrs C. H. Waugh, Mrs Stewart, Mrs Wilson, the Misses Wilson, Mrs Neate, Mr W. E. Mitchell, Mr and Mrs H. Stevens, Mr Askew, Mr and Mrs A. Burtenshaw, Mrs Avery, Miss Avery, Mrs Bowell, Mrs Murrell, Mrs Biggs, Mr R. T. Anscombe, Mr A. Robinson, Mrs Glyde, Mrs Purkiss, (Brighton), Miss F. Mitchell, Miss Wells, Mrs Butcher, Mrs Bartlett, Gunner Stevens R.M.A., Mr F. Hounsell, 2nd Air Mechanic N. V. Bransden, Royal Air Force, and many others.

Canon Wilson very impressively conducted the service, and the Rev J. H. Layton read the lesson. Mr T. E. P. Attewell was at the organ. The hymns, 'Brief life is here our portion', 'Abide with me', and 'Jesus lives' were sung, also a Psalm and the Nunc Dimittis. At intervals the Volunteers stood at the 'present' on either side of the pathway, and the cortege emerged from the church and passed between the lines.

The scene in Cuckfield's famous churchyard was very solemn and pathetic, yet beautiful and effective, and as all moved forward to the grave, and viewed the fair expanse of the Sussex Weald, the sweet melody of the choir and the emphatic words of the favourite hymn were ringing in our ears, - 'I triumph still, if thou abide with me'. The vicar having concluded the committal portion of the service, the Volunteers paid their final respects to the deceased. Volley firing with blank cartridges - load - present - fire. Three fine volleys were got off. Then the men fixed bayonets and presented arms, and Sergeant-Bugler F. Hounsell sounded with wonderful clearness, 'The Last Post'.

A peep into the grave revealed the following inscription on the coffin, on which were deposited the family wreaths.

1st Air Mechanic.
Albert Franklin Young, R.A.F
Died 9th June 1918
Aged 18

Floral tributes were sent by Father and Mother, Kath, Mr and Mrs Constable and Family, Rev Cannon and Mrs Wilson, Mr and Mrs C. Gibbs, Mrs C. H. Waugh, Mrs and Walter Pinder, Mrs Manvell, Douglas and Leslie Black and Mrs and Miss Butcher.

Albert's name appears on the war memorial in the churchyard of Holy Trinity Church, Cuckfield, on the marble memorial inside the Church and on the memorial board in the Queen's Hall, Cuckfield.

CHAPTER 7

THE WOUNDED MUST BE REMEMBERED TOO

THE WOUNDED MUST BE

REMEMBERED TOO

Those men who were wounded while serving their country also played a very valuable part in the success of the war. Their names do not appear on any war memorials. While they could be called the lucky ones because they were able to return home and attend the welcome home dinners described, many were seriously hurt, many lost limbs and many suffered various nervous complaints or mental breakdowns and had to be discharged from service.

The following accounts of the wounded men from Cuckfield indicate the problems encountered. There are undoubtedly many more who suffered for whom we have no record.

Those residents of Cuckfield, past and present, who are interested in their family history may well find their ancestors mentioned here.

A

Mid-Sussex Times - 18th July 1916
SERGEANT M. ANSCOMBE - Wounded
Many Cuckfieldians will be very sorry to learn that Sergeant M. Anscombe, whose cheery letters in the Mid-Sussex Times have always been read with pleasure, has been wounded in France and sent down to a field hospital. The postcard was addressed by himself to his parents, and was received this Tuesday morning.

LETTERS FROM SERGEANT M. ANSCOMBE
Writing home a few days later from France, Sergeant M. Anscombe of Cuckfield, said:

'Just a few lines to let you know I have been wounded in the left leg and right foot by shrapnel. I am glad to say the wounds are not serious. I am in the base hospital at present, but expect to go to 'Blighty' in a day or so. Our division got called up again after a few days rest, and on the night of 14th (July) we went up to a wood where a lot of fighting had been going on. Our lot drove the Germans clean out of it. We were supposed to dig a trench and wire it in to stop the enemy's counter attack, but we got shelled so heavily that it was net to an impossible job, so we took what cover we could in shell holes and waited. It was then that I got hit. There were five of my section in this shell hole when another shell dropped straight in. We all got wounded, but not seriously. **Frank Elphick** and **Harry Chatfield,** who used to work at Denman's, were two out of the five. I haven't heard yet how the other Cuckfield boys got on, as they are in different Companies. **Bill Fox** fell out on the way up through exhaustion. We are treated jolly well here. It is a bit different sleeping in a bed to lying on the ground - the same as we have been doing'.

Writing on 26th July, Sergeant Anscombe said:
'Glad to tell you I am going on famously. I was operated on two days ago, and everything went off well. The doctor gave me a fine piece of shrapnel

which he took out of my foot. It will make a decent souvenir. I do not know how long I shall be kept here, but I don't fancy it will be very long. Do not send me any more parcels until I let you know, as they will only get 'lost'.

The weather is not much class out here now. But, of course that doesn't worry me much, as I haven't to go out in it, but I feel sorry for the Boys up the line who have. There is no need to worry about me at all. I am having a proper rest. Hope the war will be over before I go up the line again. If things go on as well as at present the Kaiser will soon chuck up the game'.

Mid-Sussex Times - 10th September 1918
PRIVATE HARRY ASKEW
Private Harry Askew, younger son of Mr H. Askew, of Church Street, is in hospital in Italy suffering from dysentery. The latest news is that he is making satisfactory progress though lately he has had a slight relapse.

Mid-Sussex Times - 20th November 1917
CORPORAL T. A. AVERY R.G.A - In Hospital
Mr and Mrs A. Avery of Broad Street have heard that their son Corporal Thomas A. Avery R.G.A is in hospital abroad owing to shell shock.

Mid-Sussex Times - 2nd July 1918
Corporal T. A. Avery R.G.A who is still being treated for shell shock, has been removed to another hospital at Plymouth, the surroundings of which, he says, are extremely pleasant. It was in November last that Corporal Avery who is 20 years of age, had his breakdown. The latest report is that he is making progress, although slowly, towards recovery.

Mid-Sussex Times - 5th November 1918
IN CIVIL LIFE AGAIN
T. Avery son of Mr and Mrs Arthur Avery, of Broad Street, has received his discharge from the Army, being certified medically unfit for further service. He joined up two and a half years ago, and served in the R.G.A. Shell shock caused his breakdown in health.

B

Cuckfield Parish Magazine - July 1917
PRIVATE F. BACKSHALL
Private F. Backshall has been invalided home suffering from trench fever and is now in hospital in Chichester.

Mid-Sussex Times - 12th October 1915
PRIVATE H. A. BARNETT
Private Harold A Barnett, No 2638 B Company, 9th Battalion, Royal Sussex Regiment, has written home to his mother at Brook Street, Cuckfield, informing her that he has been wounded and is in hospital, but is going on well. A later card says he has arrived in Dublin Red Cross Hospital, Ireland.

Mid-Sussex Times - 5th October 1915
LANCE-CORPORAL F. G. BEARD
Lance-Corporal Frederick George Beard, 4th Battalion Royal Sussex Regiment, son of Mr and Mrs G. H. Beard of Oak Cottage, Whiteman's Green, Cuckfield, is reported to be suffering from dysentery. His parents received the news in a communication from a friend on Saturday morning.

Mid-Sussex Times - 2nd October 1916
LANCE CORPORAL W. BENNETT
Lance-Corporal W. Bennett, son of Mr and Mrs Bennett of Brains Mead has been wounded in the shoulder and is in hospital in London.

Cuckfield Parish Magazine - July 1919
Mr and Mrs Bennett have been notified that their younger son, **PRIVATE J. W. BENNETT,** West Yorkshire Regiment, is in hospital in France.

Cuckfield Parish Magazine - September 1917
COLONEL BERLY
It was noted that Colonel Berly is making good progress towards recovery, though, unfortunately it is not very speedy

Mid-Sussex Times - 3rd September 1918
GUNNER WALTER BLAKE
Mrs Walter Blake, High Street, has received official news that her husband Gunner Walter Blake, R. G. A., is in hospital suffering from malaria and is dangerously ill.

Mid-Sussex Times - 5th June 1917
PRIVATE J. BONE
Private J. Bone who has been serving with the British Force in Egypt, is in hospital suffering from a fracture of his left leg and injuries to his head, the results of an accident.

Mid-Sussex Times - 19th June 1917
Local Man injured in Egypt
The many friends of **Private Jack Bone**, Army Ordnance Corps, son of Mr J. Bone formerly chauffeur at 'Ockenden' and now at Kelvendon, Essex, will be sorry to learn that he has met with a serious accident while on active service at Port Said. He was run over by a motor lorry and is now in hospital with his left leg broken and his right leg and head badly bruised. We are glad to say that he is making favourable progress. Private Bone is an old boy of the Cuckfield Church School and an ex chorister of Holy Trinity Parish Church. In a letter to his brother Eddie, he said,

'I am running against a few of the Sussex boys here just now. The chap in the next bed to me is the postman from Hurstpierpoint - **Pavey** by name. He is pretty lively just now'.

On May 16th I was reading in bed when I heard someone say. 'Hello Boney, what are you doing here and bless me if it wasn't **Fred Beard** from Whitemans Green. Needless to say we had a long chat - he had a bullet through the face but the wound is now well and he has gone back to his Regiment. I got a lot of news from him about boys up the line. **Joe Jupp** had been wounded but he is not here. **Wilfred Mitchell**, **Steve Knight**, **Lt Pearce** and his brother, and **Captain Reid** from Mill Hall are all well at present. The doctor has just been round and dressed my leg and I feel like a sardine in a tin now. He says the bone is healing up nicely it is very pleasant to be in a nice bed once more with sheets and a spring mattress. I hope to be able to get up very shortly. I could do with a stick of rhubarb to keep the flies and other animals away.'

September 1917
Mr John Bone reports that his son Jack who met with a very serious accident some time ago is now quite well again. He has now returned to Port Said, after having six days at Alexandria where he met **George Perry** of Cuckfield.

Mid-Sussex Times - September 1918
PRIVATE F. BOTTING
Private F. Botting has been discharged from the Army owing to wounds and illness.

Mid-Sussex Times - 10th December 1918
GUNNER SIDNEY BOURNE
Mrs and Mr F. Bourne, 1, Khama Cottages, Cuckfield, have received official news that their eldest son, Gunner Sidney Bourne R.G.A is lying dangerously ill in a hospital in France. He is suffering from influenza and the latest report is that his condition is very serious.

By **January 1919** Sidney had also contracted pneumonia and his condition caused grave anxiety but he is now on the way to convalescence.

Mid-Sussex Times - 18th May 1915
PRIVATE A. E. BROOKSHAW
Notification has been received by Mr J. Brookshaw of Ansty, that his elder son, Private Arthur E. Brookshaw who is in the King's Royal Rifles, has been wounded.

Mid-Sussex Times - 12th January 1915
ACCIDENT TO A TERRITORIAL - NORMAN BOWELL
A startling accident occurred at Newhaven at the beginning of last week, as the result of which a Cuckfield territorial is lying in the 2nd Eastern Hospital at Kemp Town with a bullet in the upper part of a leg. He is

Private Norman Bowell of the 4th Battalion Royal Sussex Regiment and a son of Mr and Mrs Bowell, of 'Woodcroft Villas', Whitemans Green. It seems that young Bowell was in a hut near the Workhouse and a corporal was outside with a loaded rifle, and by some means it discharged, the bullet passing through the side of the hut before entering Bowell's leg.

The unfortunate youth is going on quite well and it is stated there is no danger. In a letter home he makes the comment, 'It's rather hot in the firing line'.

Mid-Sussex Times - 14th September 1915
PRIVATE SIDNEY BURT - WOUNDED

Mr and Mrs H. H. Burt, of 'Barnsnape', Cuckfield, have received an intimation that their son, Private Sydney Burt, 14th Battalion, Royal Sussex Regiment was wounded at Gallipoli and is now in Netley Hospital very seriously wounded and it is feared it will be several months before he is fit to be moved. He is an old and respected member of the Church Choir.

15th March 1916

Sydney Burt, 4th Royal Sussex Regiment, who was severely wounded in the back at the Dardanelles and taken last September to Netley Hospital, still remains there. At one time he was completely paralysed but he is now able to walk a little.

Mid-Sussex Times - 26th September 1916
PRIVATE T. D. BUTLER

Private T. D. Butler, Royal Sussex Regiment, son of Mr and Mrs F Butler of Whiteman's Green, is in hospital at Stonebridge, and being treated there for a bullet wound in his elbow. He is progressing satisfactorily.

C

Mid-Sussex Times - 18th July 1916
PRIVATE J. CHAPMAN
J. Chapman of the Royal Sussex Regiment was reported as wounded in one of last weeks casualty lists.

Mid-Sussex Times - 25th May 1915
LANCE-CORPORAL F. CHATFIELD
News has been received by Mr and Mrs Chatfield, of Pickwell Lane Cuckfield, that their son, Lance-Corporal Frank Chatfield of the 2nd Battalion Royal Sussex Regiment is wounded and missing. Lance-corporal Chatfield, who joined the army soon after the outbreak of war was formerly an attendant at the Brighton County Borough Asylum at Haywards Heath.

Mid-Sussex Times - 3rd September 1918
PRIVATE R. CHINNERY - WOUNDED
Mr T. Chinnery, High Street Cuckfield has received the news that his son, Private Reggie Chinnery, Northamptonshire Regiment, was severely wounded on 22nd August. He has been brought to England and is now in the Lord Derby War Hospital at Warrington. He is quite comfortable, and the wound, which is a clean one, is doing well. Before joining up Private Chinnery was in the employment of Mr B. Y. Bevan of 'Woodcroft'.

Mid-Sussex Times - 26th September 1916
SERGEANT F. H. B. CLEAVER
of the Royal Sussex Regiment, has been wounded, his name appearing in the official lists last week.

Mid-Sussex Times - September 1918
Gunner Cleaver has been discharged from the army owing to wounds and illness.

Mid-Sussex Times - 7th September 1915
PRIVATE G. COX
From an unofficial source we learn that Private G. Cox, 4th Battalion Royal Sussex Regiment, whose name appears in the Cuckfield list in our Roll of Honour, has been wounded. Previous to the war he was employed in the gardens at 'Broxmead'.

D

Mid-Sussex Times - 26th September 1916
PRIVATE T. H. DANCE - 'Gassed'
Mrs Dance, of Barracks Cottages, Brook Street, received news on Friday that her third son, Private T. H. Dance, Machine Gun Corps, has been gassed and is in the First Australian General Hospital. Nothing has been heard as to his condition.

Mid-Sussex Times - 18th April 1916
PRIVATE F. J. DANCY - In Hospital
News has been received that Private J. Dancy, Signal Section East Surrey Regiment, fourth son of Mr and Mrs W. Dancy of Whitemans Green, Cuckfield is lying in hospital in France suffering from pneumonia and pleurisy. A later report states that he is making a steady, satisfactory progress.

Mid-Sussex Times - 3rd September 1918
GUNNER H. J. DAVIS - News from a far country
Mrs Davis of 'Maltmans', has received reassuring news with regard to her husband, Gunner H. J. Davis R. F. A. He has been dangerously ill, suffering from dysentery in hospital in Salonika, but the latest report is that he is now out of danger.

Cuckfield Parish Magazine - September 1918
LIEUTENANT GILBERT DENMAN spent a long time in
hospital in Brighton suffering with his eyes as a result of being gassed.

E

Cuckfield Parish Magazine - 5th November 1918
PRIVATE W. EDE
Mr and Mrs Ede, of 'Longacre' have received the good news that their son, Private W. Ede who has been for a long time a prisoner of war in Germany, has been sent back to England. He landed at Boston on 24th October and is now in hospital in London. He has unfortunately lost his right arm, but he is otherwise quite well, though he has apparently suffered a good deal from insufficient food. He is certainly very thankful to be out of the hands of the enemy whose treatment of the prisoners has been so peculiarly brutal.

Mid-Sussex Times - 3rd December 1918
BUGLER H. F. ELLMER
We are sorry to learn that that Bugler H. F. Ellmer has received his Army discharge, owing to paralysis, due to shock. He was well known in Haywards Heath as well as Cuckfield. Prior to the war he was in the Volunteers and acted as Band Instructor to the Boy Scouts.

Mid-Sussex Times - 21st December 1915
PRIVATE REG ELLMER
The friends in Haywards Heath and Cuckfield of Private Reg Ellmer, 2nd Battalion Royal Fusiliers, will regret to learn that he is in hospital at Malta, having been wounded at the Dardanelles. The latest news is that he is on the mend.

Mid-Sussex Times - 25th July 1916
PRIVATE FRANK ELPHICK
whose father used to drive the Cuckfield bus is in hospital in Westmorland. He has had a piece of shrapnel taken from his shoulder blade. He also received other wounds. Happily he is going on well.

F

Mid-Sussex Times - 31st September 1915
PRIVATE W. FOX
Private William Fox, 8th Royal Sussex Pioneers, son of Mr and Mrs W. Fox of Brainsmead, Cuckfield is an inmate of the Denmark Hill Hospital London. He is suffering from a nervous breakdown.

Cuckfield Parish Magazine - August 1916
PRIVATE W. FOX
It was stated in the magazine that this soldier was still in hospital suffering from shell shock.

G

Mid-Sussex Times - 25th January 1916
NEWS FROM PRIVATE P. GANDER
Mr and Mrs Peter Gander of 6, Glebe Road, Cuckfield have received the following letter, dated 10th January, from their son, who is in hospital in Rouen -

'Just a few lines to let you know I have been wounded, and from the address you can see I am in hospital a few miles from the firing line. I cannot say yet whether I shall get to England. This is how I got wounded. My platoon was attached to 'C' Company, and we were digging a new reserve trench when the enemy commenced shelling us. I was almost lying on the bottom of the trench when I was hit in the neck by a piece of ground shrapnel. I started to find the stretcher bearers, and as I was walking down the trench one of our officers stopped me and asked me what was up. I told him, so he bandaged me up and gave me a drink of rum as I was feeling a bit run down, having lost so much blood. He took me to the dressing station, and later I had to walk to the field ambulance - a distance of some four miles. There I had a nice pot of tea and was put to bed, for which I was very thankful, as we had been up in the trenches three days. Later I was sent where I now am. I have to undergo an operation to get a bullet extracted from my throat. It will not be serious, as it is only between the skin and wind-pipe. I was hit on the left side, and the doctor said I had had a narrow escape. Something seemed to tell me when we shifted that I would get hit or damaged in the trenches'.

On the 13th inst Private Gander wrote another letter home stating, 'I have got through my operation all right, and am feeling A1 now I have lost the bullet from my throat. I have the bullet, and if I cannot get home I will send it on to you to keep, and a few more as well. When you see it you will have some idea of the kind of things we have to dodge all day and night, and you never know where they are going to settle. The doctors and nurses said it was a marvellous escape. If it had been a rifle bullet instead of shrapnel I should have been 'pushing up the daisies' by now!'

Mid-Sussex Times - 11th July 1916
WOUNDED
Information has been received that **Private Peter Gander,** Royal Sussex Regiment, has been again seriously wounded and is in hospital in Scotland.

Mid-Sussex Times - 14th May 1918
PRIVATE GLADMAN - WOUNDED
On Saturday Mr and Mrs Gladman, of 'Bedlam Cottage', learnt that their only son, Private H. L. Gladman of the Royal Fusiliers, was in hospital at Rouen, he having been wounded in the right arm by a shell as he was passing along a road to the trenches.

H

Mid-Sussex Times - 11th July 1916
PRIVATE J. HAYWARD

In the latest casualty lists the name of Private J. Hayward appears as being wounded.

Mid-Sussex Times - 5th November 1918
PRIVATE WILLIAM HAZELGROVE

Private William Hazelgrove of the East Surrey Regiment, son of Mr Hazelgrove, of Brook Street, has been severely wounded and sustained the loss of a leg. He is now in hospital in Birmingham.

Cuckfield Parish Magazine - August 1916
PRIVATE HUGH HUCKETT

Hugh Huckett, son of the Rev. Walter Huckett of 'Meadfoot', Cuckfield has been wounded in the hand and is in hospital near Norwich.

J

Mid-Sussex Times - 29th September 1914
PRIVATE A. JENNINGS

Private Albert Jennings of the 2nd Battalion Royal Sussex Regiment, has sent an intimation to his people that 'he is coming home with many others, he having received a tap on his right hand'. He managed to write these lines with his left hand. Private Jennings is the eldest son of Mr and Mrs Laban Jennings of Hatchgate Cottages, Broad Street, Cuckfield.

K

Cuckfield Parish Magazine - November 1918
CADET HENRY KLEINWORT
Cadet Henry Kleinwort has been lying dangerously ill at the Royal Navy Hospital in Plymouth, but is now we are glad to say, well on the way to recovery. However he later had two severe attacks of pneumonia and died and was buried in Cuckfield in May 1921.

Mid-Sussex Times - 8th January 1918
Septic poisoning has brought **CHARLES KNIGHT** back to England. On being fit again for duty he was sent to Egypt and has been there ten months. Altogether he has served nine years in the Royal Sussex Regiment and has now been transferred to the Sussex Yeomanry. His parents who live at 'Hanlye Cottage' have five sons serving their king and Country:-

Private A. Knight, Royal Sussex Regiment (over twelve years service)
Sergeant A. C. Knight
Private H. Knight (over seven years service)
Gunner Knight, RFA, slightly wounded twice and two years and four months in France
Private E. Knight, Royal Sussex Regiment (seven years service) has been to France three times and wounded twice. He is now in Italy.
Not a bad family record.

Mid-Sussex Times - 11th July 1916
PRIVATE E. KNIGHT - WOUNDED
Mr and Mrs G. Knight, of 'Hanlye Cottage', received the sad news on July 5th that their youngest son, Private E. Knight, of the Royal Sussex Regiment, who had been in fierce fighting in France, had been wounded through the muscle of his left arm. At present he is in hospital in Scotland and is going on fairly well.

Mid-Sussex Times - 12th October 1915
SERGEANT STEPHEN KNIGHT
Sergeant Stephen H. Knight, 4th Battalion Royal Sussex Regiment, who for several weeks has been in hospital at Malta with a poisoned hand, is, we learn, progressing favourably. He is the elder son of Mr S. Knight, builder, of Cuckfield and the popular captain of the Cuckfield Football Club.

Mid-Sussex Times - 13th November 1917
SECOND LIEUTENANT S. H. KNIGHT eldest son of Mr Steven Knight came home last Tuesday on three weeks leave. He is in the Royal Sussex Regiment and when he left the boys in Palestine they were all in jolly good health and spirits. Mr Knight has another son in Palestine and he is with the Engineers as a Wireless telegraphist.

Mid-Sussex Times - 5th February 1918
SECOND LIEUT. S. H. KNIGHT of the Royal Sussex Regiment, son of Mr Stephen Knight, of Cuckfield, was one of those saved from the torpedoed transport 'Aragon' and it is gratifying to learn that he is safe and well. All his personal belongings as well as parcels he was taking out to brother officers in Egypt, went down with the transport and are now at the bottom of the sea. In a letter home he said the behaviour of the men after the boat was struck was splendid.

Mid-Sussex Times - August 20th 1918
LIEUTENANT S. H. KNIGHT, eldest son of Mr Stephen Knight J. P., of Cuckfield, is now in hospital at Fratton. His general health is good, but it is questionable whether his left arm will have to be amputated. The shell that injured him killed a man on each side of him. The gunshot wounded his left arm; both bones were fractured resulting in him spending some time in a hospital at Rouen.

Mid-Sussex Times - 24th September 1918
LIEUTENANT S. H. KNIGHT of the Royal Sussex Regiment, eldest son of Mr Stephen Knight J. P. of Cuckfield, is now in hospital at Brighton, and we are pleased to be able to add that there is every hope of saving his left arm. His general health is excellent.

M

Mid-Sussex Times - 10th October 1916
SECOND LIEUTENANT HENRY. C. S. MAINE

Second Lieutenant H.S.C. Maine, Grenadier Guards, younger son of Mrs Maxwell Campbell of 'Henmead Hall', Cuckfield was wounded on 24th September 1916. A bullet lodged in his ankle but it was extracted a few days later.

Mid-Sussex Times - July 2nd 1918
CAPTAIN J. MCCONNEL D.S.O

Captain J. McConnel, D.S.O. who was recently home on leave, is now in hospital with trench fever.

Mid-Sussex Times - 3rd September 1918
PRIVATE C. MEANING - WOUNDED A SECOND TIME

On Wednesday, Mr and Mrs Meaning of 'Glendale', received officially the news that their second son, Private C. Meaning, Essex Regiment had been severely wounded in both thighs and right wrist. This makes the second time within ten months that he has been wounded. On the first occasion he received a bullet wound, when in Egypt, on the left side. He has now been removed from France to a hospital in Orpington. We are pleased to be able to add that he is progressing satisfactorily.

Mid-Sussex Times - 18th May 1915
PRIVATE F. MOCKETT

A former Cuckfield boy, who came back to England with the Canadian contingent, is now lying at the Redress Hospital in Dublin Castle. He was wounded during the Canadians grim struggle near Ypres a few weeks ago, being shot through the thigh during a charge against the Prussian Guards on April 23rd. News has been received that he is slowly mending.

Mid-Sussex Times - 12th September 1916
PRIVATE W. F. MILES
Private W. F. Miles, Royal Fusiliers, has been admitted to the Military Hospital at Manchester from overseas.

Mid-Sussex Times - 9th March 1915
PRIVATE HARRY MITCHELL - IN HOSPITAL
Another son of Mr and Mrs F. Mitchell of Braines Mead, Cuckfield, is making excellent progress after being dangerously ill in St. Omer Hospital with cerebro-spinal meningitis. He is Private Henry Mitchell of the 2nd Battalion Royal Sussex Regiment, and it will be remembered he was invalided home with foot trouble early in the war. His present indisposition was brought about by a German shell exploding in front of him and burying him with earth. His mother received much better news from him in a letter last week. He says -

'Just a few lines to let you know I am a lot better. I can just manage to write you a few lines, but I am a bit shaky. I don't know who let you know I was in hospital, for I don't seem to remember much for two or three days. I have never felt so bad in all my life before. I had to be carried to hospital on a stretcher, for I couldn't walk. You must look forward to seeing me soon, for I think I have a furlough to come after this. It will do me good too, for it has taken all my strength away'.

Cuckfield Parish Magazine - August 1916
We are glad to welcome Private Harry Mitchell home and to see that he has made a good recovery of his wounds, though he has unfortunately lost his left hand. He will shortly go to Roehampton to have an artificial hand fitted on.

Mid-Sussex Times - 18th January 1916
CORPORAL E. McGEORGE MITCHELL
Last week Mr. W. E. Mitchell, of 'Annandale', Cuckfield, received the distressing news that his son, Corporal E. McGeorge Mitchell, who only returned to the Front on the 10th inst, had been wounded in the thigh by a high explosive shell and would be probably sent to England. We have from time to time published some deeply interesting letters from

Corporal Mitchell, and, with us, our readers, we feel sure will wish him a speedy and complete recovery.

25th January 1916
HOW CORPORAL E.M.MITCHELL WAS WOUNDED

Corporal Edward McG. Mitchell, R.E. writes as follows from the Australian Hospital in France, to his father, Mr W.E.Mitchell, of 'Annandale', Broad Street,

'Thanks very much for the parcel and letters received yesterday. I am still progressing all right, though it will be a bit longer than was first expected. The piece of shell made a bit of a mess inside, and made one or two splinters. They have bored a hole right through the leg and put a rubber tube in to keep it open. The most awkward part is I can only lie on my left side and partly on my back. It is a bit painful at times, and also when they dress it. The nurses and doctors are awfully nice here. The food is very fine, only at present I can't eat much, so please don't put in anything to eat in my parcels. The Hospital is beautifully situated on the cliffs. They say you can see England on a clear day. Boulogne is about four miles south.

By the bye, I don't think I told you how I was wounded. I was patrolling one of the lines with another chap. We had just got there, and he went inside. I went back about a dozen yards to look at something when I heard a 'whiz-bang' and something struck me in the leg. I fell like a log. The other chap came out then and helped me into a dug out. Some Artillery chaps bandaged me up, put me on a stretcher, and took me to a dressing station. I was taken from there to another clearing hospital by motor ambulance, and I was glad when it was over: the roads were awful. I stopped there the night, and was put on a hospital train the next day at 3.00 p.m. and arrived at Boulogne at 10.00 p.m. The train went awfully slowly but it did not bump a bit. It was very comfortable. Most of the patients here go to England for convalescence, so quite possibly I may go too. I am afraid it is very doubtful if I shall get back to the 24th Company. Please don't bother to send me any daily papers, as we get plenty.

Mr **Thrupp,** formerly of Haywards Heath is here wounded.

Mid-Sussex Times - 15th February 1916
CORPORAL E. McG. MITCHELL R.E., son of Mr W.E.Mitchell of Cuckfield who was recently wounded in the fighting near Ypres, is now in Reading Hospital and is going on very nicely. He hopes soon to be able to get about on crutches.

Mid-Sussex Times - 21st March 1916
CORPORAL E. McG MITCHELL R.E. son of Mr W. E. Mitchell of Cuckfield is, we are pleased to be able to state, on the mend and able to walk a little. It will be remembered that he was wounded in the thigh in France last January. He is still in hospital in Reading.

Mid-Sussex Times - 30th May 1918
SERVED ON THREE FRONTS
Corporal E. McG. Mitchell second son of Mr W. E. Mitchell of Cuckfield who has seen service in France and Mesopotamia, is now in Egypt, and in a letter home last week he said he was in the best of health. Two years ago last January he was severely wounded in France and was laid up for ten months. For a young man of 22 he has certainly 'seen life'.

Cuckfield Parish Magazine - June 1917
CORPORAL W. E. MITCHELL
Corporal W. E. Mitchell, London Scottish, has been invalided home suffering from enteric. He is now in hospital at Birmingham and is getting on fairly well.

Mid-Sussex Times - 15th February 1916
CORPORAL R. MYRAM - WOUNDED
Corporal R. Myram, Sussex Yeomanry, whose name appeared in a recent casualty list as being wounded whilst serving with the Mediterranean Expeditionary Force, is a son of Mr W. Myram, of Pondlye Farm, Cuckfield. In a letter home he says he is in hospital.

N

Mid-Sussex Times - 8th October 1918
PRIVATE WALTER NASH - WOUNDED
The many friends of this well-known soldier will be sorry to learn that he was wounded in the left leg by shrapnel on 18th September.

After being operated upon at an American hospital he was subsequently sent to England and is now in Nottingham General Hospital. He went to France with the Royal Sussex Regiment last January. Prior to joining up he was in the employ of Messrs John Denman & Co.

Mid-Sussex Times - 25th July 1916
SECOND LIEUTENANT H. K. NEWMAN - SLIGHTLY WOUNDED
Mr and Mrs H Newman, of Hanlye Farm, Cuckfield, have received a letter from their son, Second Lieutenant H. K. Newman of the Buffs, stating he has been slightly wounded in the left shoulder, by shrapnel. He is still able, he is pleased to be able to add, to keep with the Battalion.

Mid-Sussex Times - 26th September 1916
PRIVATE R. NEWNHAM
Private R Newnham, Royal Sussex Regiment, husband of Mrs Newnham, of Whiteman's Green, is in hospital in France, having been wounded in the right leg by shrapnel. We are glad to be able to add he is doing well.

Mid-Sussex Times - 5th October 1915
PRIVATE WILLIAM NYE
Mrs Nye, of Bolney Road, Ansty, Cuckfield received a postcard on Thursday from No 6 Stationary Hospital, France, informing her that her eldest son, Private William Nye, 9th Battalion Royal Sussex Regiment, was an inmate, having been wounded in action. He has sustained injuries to his shoulder and knee.

Mid-Sussex Times - September 1918
It is reported that **William Nye** has received a severe gunshot wound and has been sent to hospital in Rouen.

P

Mid-Sussex Times - 18th June 1918
SERGEANT LEONARD ADOLPHUS PALMER D.C.M.
who is in the Royal Field Artillery and is the only son of Mr and Mrs Palmer of Lodge Farm, has, we regret to learn, been seriously wounded in the abdomen on 2nd June. He is in hospital in France, but is going on as well as can be expected.

Cuckfield Parish Magazine - September 1918
SERGEANT LEONARD PALMER
Sergeant Leonard A. Palmer R.F.A. elder son of Mr and Mrs Palmer of 'The Lodge Farm' has now been invalided out of the army on account of severe wounds received in action on June 2nd. He has left the army with an excellent character, and with a good record of meritorious service, which earned for him the D.C.M. We hope that he will be quickly restored to good health.

Mid-Sussex Times - 26th June 1916
HENRY FRANK PATTENDEN - IN HOSPITAL
Mr and Mrs Frank Pattenden, of Brook Street, have heard from the officer in charge of Infantry Records, that their son, Henry Frank Pattenden, Royal Sussex Regiment, is in hospital suffering from simple flesh contusion and wounds. A postcard from him states that he is in Wharncliffe War Hospital, Sheffield.

Mid-Sussex Times - 31st August 1915
LANCE-CORPORAL A. R. PIERCE
Lance- Corporal A. R. Pierce of New Zealand, son of Mr and Mrs S. Pierce of Penland Farm, Cuckfield, has been wounded in the left arm by

a sniper at the Dardanelles. In addition to the wound he is also suffering from scarlet fever, and is in hospital at Alexandria. His brother **Sapper E. Pierce**, who joined up from the Haywards Heath Post Office, is in hospital in Malta, suffering from dysentery.

Mid-Sussex Times - 14th September 1915
PRIVATE J. T. PORTWAY

Information has been conveyed to Mr and Mrs T. Portway of High Street, Cuckfield by the London Record Office of the New Zealand Expeditionary Force, that their elder son, Private J. T. Portway, of the Wellington Infantry, was wounded in action in the Gallipoli Peninsula on August 8th. Private Portway sent a card home a few days after this date to say he was in hospital, but the place was not mentioned. His parents have reason to believe his wound is not of a serious character, but they are anxiously awaiting further news.

Private Portway emigrated to Australia a few years ago with a friend, and went to the Wellington Infantry at the beginning of the war.

A later letter received yesterday (Monday) says:-

'I suppose you will be anxious to know how I am getting on after the heavy fighting at the _____ and perhaps you have heard by now that I have been wounded. I am in a hospital on an island not far from the Dardenalles; it is only a slight wound on the head, so I shall be all right in a few days, and back at the front again before long. I think I am one of the luckiest men in the Peninsula to be alive today; we made an advance a few day ago, and it was like hell upon earth for a while, with shrapnel, bombs and bullets dropping like hail all round us, and after we had got dug in all the men about where I was were either killed or wounded; and when reinforcements came up they made another firing line behind us, so that left me and a few more chaps, who were also wounded, between our trenches and the Turks, so we had a hot time of it that day. I think I was the only one out of about six to be able to crawl back to our lines at night.'

R

PRIVATE P. REEVE

Mrs Reeve, Cuckfield's lady shaver, tells me that her husband Private P. Reeve MGC, after seven months in France is now back in hospital in England where he is being treated for rheumatic fever. It is just possible he may get his discharge from the army.

Mrs Reeve has pluckily carried on the shop and shaving part of the business during her husbands fourteen months absence, and I was glad to learn that she still has those of her husband's customers left in Cuckfield. Asked on whom she first practised shaving she replied, 'my hubby and never once cut him'.

Mid-Sussex Times - 1st June 1915
MAJOR P. L. REID

The name of Major Percy L. Reid, Irish Guards, appeared amongst the wounded in casualty lists issued last Wednesday night. He is a son of Mrs Reid, of 'Mill Hall', Cuckfield and received his wound from a shell which burst near him during an attack near La Bassée on May 18th. He was first taken to a hospital at Rouen and is now in a nursing home in London.
Major Reid joined his regiment in 1902 and became adjutant in 1908. Afterwards, as a captain, he was brigade major of the 5th London Infantry Brigade and he held this appointment in August last when his units, the Poplar, Woolwich and St Pancras Battalions and the London Irish Rifles were mobilised. Soon after the commencement of hostilities he was gazetted a brigade major in the regular forces for the period of the war, but rejoined his regiment on attaining field rank.

Cuckfield Parish Magazine - August 1916
PRIVATE W. J. ROBINSON

We understand that Private W. J. Robinson of the Royal Sussex Pioneers is in hospital in England suffering from shell shock.

Mid-Sussex Times - 31st September 1915
PRIVATE J. ROWLAND

Private James Rowland, 2nd Battalion, Royal Sussex Regiment, eldest son of Mr and Mrs Ernest Rowland of South Street, Cuckfield has sent home the brief intimation contained on a postcard that he has been wounded and admitted to hospital. He adds he is going on well. The card was written on Saturday.

Mid-Sussex Times - 25th July 1916
PRIVATE JAMES ROWLAND - WOUNDED

Private James Rowland (Royal Sussex Regiment) son of Mr Ernest Rowland of 28, South Street, Cuckfield, has been wounded in the left hand, with the first two fingers cut deeply, and he is now in the 2nd Western General Hospital at Stretford, Manchester.

In a letter home he states that his wound is healing nicely and it will not be long before he visits Cuckfield again. He describes the bombardment of the German lines and the work leading up to the attack, also the reply of the enemy with machine guns and shells, and he states that he was hit by shrapnel. 'As soon as we got into hospital at Manchester' he says 'we had the pleasure of jumping into a bath, which we all appreciated very much. Shower baths had been very common at the front - but they were not the right sort'.

Mid-Sussex Times - 22nd August 1916
PRIVATE J. ROWLAND

of the Royal Sussex Regiment, is in hospital at Manchester. On Thursday he wrote to his mother, who lives in South Street, as follows: -

'Just a line to let you know I am still improving. The doctor examined the hand this morning, and he said the dressings were to be continued again. There is not much life in the finger yet. The hand is also very shaky. I've got some gold stripes for my tunic and great coat. They are quite swanky.'

S

Mid-Sussex Times - 7th September 1915
PRIVATE CLAUD SELBY
Private Claud Selby, 4th Battalion Royal Sussex Regiment, a son of Mr and Mrs H. Selby, of Brook Street, Cuckfield has written home from the Dardanelles to say he has been slightly wounded. He writes -

'Just a few lines, hoping they will find you well. I am quite well except that I have just got a hit in the knee with a bullet. Don't worry, as I am well looked after and hope to see you soon.'

The official notice from the War Office conveying the information that Private Selby had been wounded was received on Saturday evening, but the nature of the wound was not stated.

Mid-Sussex Times - 9th April 1918
BRIGADIER GENERAL B.N. SERGISON-BROOKE
D.S.O we regret to learn has been wounded.

Mid-Sussex Times - 31st September 1915
ABLE SEAMAN B. H. SMITH
Mrs Smith, of High Street, Cuckfield has received a letter from her husband, Able Seaman Harry Smith, in which he says he is suffering from dysentery and is in the 1st Australian Stationary Hospital. He expects shortly to be moved to Alexandria.

Able Seaman Smith was called up as a naval reservist on the mobilisation of the Navy just before the outbreak of war, and was attached to H.M.S. 'Glory' which proceeded on duty to guard the Atlantic trade routes. Latterly, however, Smith has been in the trenches at the Dardanelles.

Mid-Sussex Times - 2nd October 1916
PRIVATE A. J. STEVENS
On Sunday morning, Mr H. Stevens, of Ockenden Gardens, received the news that his son, Private A.J.Stevens, Middlesex regiment, had been wounded. He sustained a gunshot wound in the left shoulder, the bullet passing right through. He also sustained a slight injury to his left elbow.

He is now in hospital at Hove, and his condition is satisfactory.

Cuckfield Parish Magazine - April 1916
JOHN HENRY STEVENS who recently joined the Royal Marine
Artillery has been dangerously ill in hospital in Haslar but is making good progress.

Mid-Sussex Times - 29th August 1916
SERGEANT T. STONER - WOUNDED
Last week Mrs Stoner, of Longacre Farm, received the news that their eldest son, Sergeant T. Stoner, Royal Sussex Regiment, had been wounded in the right arm, and was now in the Red Cross Hospital at Gloucester. Mrs Stoner has another son in the Army and he is in France.

T

Mid-Sussex Times - 2nd October 1917
PRIVATE ARTHUR TREE
News has been received that Private Arthur Tree, Royal Scots, son of Mr George Tree of Highbridge Mill, has been wounded and is now in hospital.

W

Mid-Sussex Times - 14th September 1915
PRIVATE FRANK WEBBER

Private Frank Webber, son of the late Mr and Mrs J. Webber, has written home to his sister at Whitemans Green to say he has been slightly wounded. In his letter he says,

'It has been like hell out here, and one would have to be like a puff of wind if one did not want to get hit. I have got a slight wound in the head just above the left eye. I am on a hospital boat at present, but don't quite know what I am going to do. I may stop here at the base until I get better and then go out again, or may get to England, but I don't suppose so. Poor old Bill **(Private William Dancy)** went out like a puff of a candle and **Jonas Wall**, from Lindfield, he was a special chum of mine; they were put in the same grave. All my special chums are wounded'.

Mid-Sussex Times - 22nd August 1916
INVALIDED OUT OF THE ARMY

Private J. Webber, Royal Sussex Regiment, son of the late Mr and Mrs J. Webber of Whiteman's Green, has been granted his discharge from the Army owing to heart trouble. He enlisted two years ago. His occupation is that of a gardner and he will be glad to find an opening.

Mid-Sussex Times - 28th August 1917
LIEUTENANT DOUGLAS WOOD - WOUNDED

Mrs James Wood of 'Sunnybank', Broad Street, has received the news that her younger son, Second Lieutenant Douglas Wood, Royal Berkshire Regiment is in hospital in France. He was wounded on August 16th in 'going over the top', the bullet striking him in the thigh. He has been able to write a few lines to his mother and it is hoped that he is going on well.

Cuckfield Parish Magazine - September 1917
SECOND LIEUTENANT STANLEY WOODS
Stanley Woods is in hospital at Rouen having been seriously injured by a gunshot wound to the head.

Cuckfield Parish Magazine - August 1916
LIEUTENANT WILLIAM PHILIP WOOD
It is reported that Lieutenant William Wood of the Hants Regiment has been invalided from Mesopotamia and is in hospital at Simla where he is doing well.

Y

Mid-Sussex Times - 4th April 1916
PRIVATE YORK
News has been received by Mrs York of 'Chatfield Cottage', London Lane, Cuckfield, that her husband, of the Royal Sussex Regiment has been wounded. Second Lieutenant Cassells, in conveying this information by letter, says -

'Private York was always willing and ready to do his share - and more than his share - of any work that came along. He was a very good soldier and he hopes he may have a good recovery after he is sent to England'.

Cuckfield Parish Magazine - August 1917
PRIVATE JOHN YOUNG
Private John Young, Royal Sussex Regiment, has been wounded in both legs by shrapnel and is now in hospital in Leeds.

CHAPTER 8

WORK CARRIED OUT BY WOMEN IN CUCKFIELD DURING THE WAR

WORK CARRIED OUT BY WOMEN IN CUCKFIELD DURING THE WAR

Cuckfield Parish Magazine - November 1914
BELGIAN REFUGEES

A meeting was held, by invitation, at the Vicarage on Monday October 19th at 3.00 p.m. to consider what could be done for the Belgian refugees. After the Vicar had given all the information he had gathered as to the various funds and the possibility of obtaining houses for the refugees, a strong feeling was manifested that some local effort of housing should be made. About fifty were present and the following expressed their willingness to serve as a committee...

Mrs Fisher
Mrs Stevens
Mrs Maddock
Miss Bevan
Miss Gray
Miss Huckett
Miss Wrightson

...with power to act and power to add to their number. The thanks of the meeting were expressed to Miss Rilands for placing 'Landcroft' at their disposal and to Miss Bunting for offering two houses free of rent until Christmas and at a reduced rent after that date.

The Committee acted at once and energetically, viewed 'Landcroft', got promises of furniture, communicated with the War Refugees Committee. Alas for high hopes. The Committee, while thanking them for their kind offers of hospitality, replied that they had received instructions from the Home Office not to send refugees to Sussex, amongst other counties.

What then was to be done. The plan of giving hospitality could not be carried out, so the Vicar with the acquiescence of the Committee, decided to ask that the collection at the Public Meeting called for Friday, October 23rd to support their plan for housing, should be sent up to the Central War Refugees Committee as a sympathetic offering from Cuckfield for the refugees.

Cuckfield Parish Magazine - November 1914
FACILITIES FOR WOUNDED BELGIANS

A hospital for wounded Belgians was set up in the Queen's Hall, the work being done by members of the V.A.D. Several Belgian refugees were sheltered in Cuckfield and were housed in Mrs Schlisinger's cottage at Slough Place and also at a house called 'The Haven' in Broad Street.

Mid-Sussex Times - 30th November 1915

The way in which the women of England have come forward to do work of a real helpful nature in connection with the war is really splendid. Our men are doing their bit to keep the home fires burning, and they can face whatever befalls them much more cheerfully when they know that the women in the old country are thinking of them and working for them. While the men of Cuckfield were away fighting, the women left behind were not idle. As soon as help of any kind was required they would work to get something organised. Some of the work was knitting various items, packing bandages and so on.

At Cuckfield there has been established for some time now a branch of the Hove War Hospital Supply Depot, and at 'Ockenden', by kind permission of the Misses Wrightson, the workers meet on Mondays, Wednesdays and Fridays, afternoon and evenings, to make such things as bandages, dressing towels, hospital bags, mufflers, operation stockings, swabs, day and night shirts, pillow cases, ward shoes, slings, pyjamas, bed rests, bed jackets and socks.

Since June no fewer than 8,559 articles have been sent from Cuckfield to the Hove depot and the whole of the money so far required to meet the cost of materials, amounting to £111, has been found by the workers. The articles are made under hygienic conditions, and on several occasions great satisfaction has been given to headquarters by the prompt way in which an urgent demand for certain things has been met. The Secretarial work in connection with the Branch is very kindly done by Mrs Lampson.

Mid-Sussex Times - 30th March 1915
SERVING HER COUNTRY

We hear that a Cuckfield nurse had volunteered her services for the sick and wounded soldiers in France. Nurse A. M. Mitchell daughter of Mr and Mrs J. Mitchell of 'Percy Cottage' has joined the nursing staff of the Duchess of Westminster's War Hospital at Le Touquet. Writing home she says she was very busy and that the hospital is quite a modern one with 270 beds.

THE V.A.D. HOSPITAL

An account which appeared in the
Cuckfield Parish Magazine in June 1919

The following account, which we are very pleased to publish, is a very interesting record of the work which was done at the Queen's Hall during the war, and we may well be grateful to all those who, by their self-denying and untiring efforts, did so much to restore our wounded soldiers to health and strength.

On 28th April some fifty of those who had worked for the Hospital during the past four years met together for tea in the Parish Room and were most kindly entertained with music etc by friends from Haywards Heath. Since 1913 there has been a Detachment of the Red Cross in Cuckfield, and so in November 1914 (when the English Military Hospitals were filled to overflowing by the influx of Belgian as well as English patients), the C.O. of the 2nd Eastern General Hospital at Brighton accepted the offer of a Red Cross Hospital here.

The Queen's Hall was placed at the disposal of the local Branch by the Urban Council and on November 3rd twelve Belgian patients were received, followed a few days later by four more. By the end of the year, however, the majority of these sixteen had either been discharged cured or else required special treatment in other hospitals, and no fresh patients had been admitted.

The Queen's Hall was urgently required for the use of the P.O. Rifles then billeted in the town, and so the hospital was closed down on January

2nd 1915 and the furniture, all of which had been lent, was stored away in the building, so that it was ready for use whenever the time came to re-open again.

In July 1915, the troops having left, the Hall was prepared to receive patients once more and on the 16th it re-opened with twenty beds. From that date till December 18th 1918 it was never closed for a single day. 1,295 patients have been received, the great majority of whom went away far better than when they arrived. The number of beds was increased gradually to forty-five.

After the hospital was closed, a letter was received from the A.D.M.S of the Sussex District, in which he says -

'On the occasion of the closing of the Cuckfield V.A.D. Hospital, I should like to express my appreciation of all the good work that has been done in the Hospital since it was opened....'

The Hospital was always most satisfactorily administered and the patients received every care and attention. I should be glad if you would kindly convey to the members of the Staff of the Hospital my most sincere thanks for all they have done, often, no doubt, at considerable personal sacrifice.'

The Cuckfield Urban District Council passed the following resolution:

'As representing the inhabitants of Cuckfield, we desire to place on record our gratitude to the ladies forming the staff of the V. A. D at Cuckfield for their untiring and valuable service in connection with the Hospital for wounded during the war.'

CHAPTER 9

1919

CELEBRATIONS FOR THOSE WHO RETURNED HOME

Cuckfield Vicarage,

14th April, 1919.

DEAR SIR,

I have much pleasure in inviting you to attend a WELCOME HOME SERVICE which will be held at the Parish Church *on Sunday, April 27th, at 6.30 p.m.*, and at which we shall return thanks to Almighty God for the safety of those who have been on service during the War. It is proposed that the men shall assemble at 6 p.m. opposite the " Rose and Crown," and come to Church in a body preceded by the Scouts' bugle band. Major Bridgman and Col.-Sergeant C. Newnham have kindly consented to organize the procession, and I hope you will be able to attend.

Yours very faithfully,

C. W. G. WILSON.

CELEBRATIONS FOR THOSE WHO

RETURNED HOME

Mid-Sussex Times - 27th April 1919

CUCKFIELD'S GALLANT SONS

WELCOME HOME SERVICE AT THE PARISH CHURCH

When hostilities ceased there was a feeling of intense relief in Cuckfield as everywhere else. The little town has always been noted for its intense patriotism, and all the vicars of the parish within living memory have encouraged the people to be true to their Sovereign and dear old England. When Germany upset the peace of the world and the call was sounded for men to rally to the defence of the Empire, Cuckfield performed her part nobly and well. The young men readily 'followed the drum' and older men, despite family ties, also joined up, feeling that their country had first claim upon their services.

A number of those who crossed the water have passed through the Valley of Shadows and on the field of battle gained their Heavenly crowns. For them, memorial services have been held in Cuckfield Church and in fond remembrance the townspeople hold them still.

Those who have been permitted to return to their homes, to parents, to wives, to children and to friends, how delighted all of us have been to greet them. With a zeal well becoming a Vicar of a parish, the Rev Canon Wilson has kept himself in touch with Cuckfield's gallant sons and that he should have arranged a Welcome Home Service will stand to his lasting credit. It was held last Sunday evening and a magnificent service it was.

Major Bridgeman and Colour Sergeant C. Newnham superintended the assembling of the ex-servicemen at the 'Rose and Crown', and in procession - headed by the Union Jack, the Scout's flag and the Scout's Bugle Band - they marched to the Parish Church. Joyful was the sound made by the band and joyful too, must have been the men's feelings as they marched along, despite the wintry conditions - joyful because they had played a man's part and had been spared to see the war through.

There were 73 men in the procession, and 47 officers and men came direct to the service. Special seats were reserved for them, and also for Cuckfield Urban Councillors and their wives. The churchwardens (Mr B. Y. Bevan, J.P. and Mr W. E. Mitchell) and the sidesmen, merit a word of appreciation for the way in which they looked after the seating. Daffodils adorned the chancel screen and the choir stalls, and wreaths of laurel topped the Union Jack and the flag of St George - carried by Christopher Monks and William Clarke. The processional cross was borne by Mr W. Herrington.

The processional hymn was 'Onward Christian Soldiers', and when the drums joined in, the effect was thrilling. The drummers were Sergeant-Drummer M. Auger (Royal Scots), Sergeant M. Anscombe and Mr Alfred Murrell.

The flag bearers stood on either side of the altar until the hymn was sung through. Canon Wilson then said 'Let us return thanks to Almightly God for the safe return of so many of our Cuckfield men from the Great War' and at once the congregation got upon its knees.

Next remembered in prayer were 'our brothers who are still on service on the different Fronts', and finally, prayer was offered up for the Empire.

The preacher was Canon Wilson who has the happy gift of finding the fitting word for the occasion.

'My friends', was how the Vicar addressed those in the pews. 'He found it very difficult', he said, 'to express all the thoughts that came into his mind, and which must arise in their minds, on that occasion. That night was a great event in the lives of all of them, and the service one which would not quickly fade away from their memories. During the last four years they had had in that church many services that would be long remembered - memorial services, intercession services and thanksgiving services. We at home have passed through dark days during the war, and our hearts, at times, sank very low. But we trusted you men on sea, land and air. We felt that you would never fail us, and that, with the help of

God, you would carry out the work to which you had put your hands. I should like you to know that week after week and Sunday after Sunday we offered up earnest prayers on your behalf. We felt that was one thing we could do - and we did it.

This service tonight is a fitting sequel to those that have gone before - a service of welcome home to dear old Cuckfield, where so many of you were born, in the old parish church which has so many associations for you. In the nature of things it was impossible to welcome you home individually. We might have said but little on your return. We English people do not wear our hearts upon our sleeve. But our feeling of gratitude for all you have done for us is real and our appreciation is sincere. When we saw you giving up khaki and putting on civilian attire the thought arose - Let us have a welcome home service.

Since you responded to the call, 'Your King and Country need you', what terrible experiences you have had. On many fronts you have jeopardised your lives, you have seen awful sights, death and destruction in most terrible forms, sights you will never forget, sights which will make you different men to what you were before. Some went away lads and have come back men.

And now once more you are home! You have fought a good fight, and you have done nobly in the war and we welcome you home!

In solemn tones, the vicar then said. 'We do not forget those who will not return home - those whose bodies lie at rest in many parts of the world. They have answered the Call, they have given up their lives in the most righteous war that this country has ever engaged in. Amid all our happiness our hearts go out in sympathy to those who are sorrowing for the loss of those who were so dear to them.'

In his hands Canon Wilson said he held a copy of the service at Cuckfield at the conclusion of the war in South Africa, and comparing the figures he found that four Cuckfield men died in South Africa and nine returned to Cuckfield.

In the war just ended, 82 Cuckfield men had made the supreme sacrifice, and so far about 180 had returned home. So they could see how great and terrible and wonderful had this last war been. This service tonight is one of thanksgiving for victory and safe return'.

In concluding, Canon Wilson emphasised the privilege and responsibility of service, and urged the men to live good, honest, pure, useful and

Christ-like lives. In that way they could shew their thankfulness to God for bringing them safely through the war.

As the final notes of the hymns died away the Vicar, with uplifted hands, pronounced the Benediction - and we all felt it was good to have been present. Such a service - as Canon Wilson said - will not readily be forgotten. It will ever stand out prominently in the history of Cuckfield.

Mid-Sussex Times - 6th May 1919

CUCKFIELD AND THE WAR

THE MEN WHO 'GOT THROUGH' ENTERTAINED TO DINNER

A MEMORABLE GATHERING

It did ones heart good to be in the Queen's Hall, Cuckfield last Wednesday evening. Seated at the flower-bedecked tables from end to end of the room were rows of men - 160 in all - who had fought for the British Empire in Belgium, in Italy, in Egypt, in Palestine, in Mesopotamia, and at Salonika, Gallipoli and other distant parts. And although many had had thrilling and, at times, awful experiences as soldiers in trenches, and in deserts, and as naval men, upon the sea, yet all carried their heads high - as became heroes - and bore expressions giving little indication of what they had passed through. Fine indeed, is British pluck. To be the parents of brave sons is something to be proud of, and we wish it had been possible for the mothers and fathers of the men at the Welcome Home Dinner to have taken stock of them, and to have seen what splendid fellows went from Cuckfield to serve their King and Country in the Great War.

We have mentioned that the tables were made attractive with flowers, and overhead were gaily coloured pennons and also the flags dear to the heart of every patriot.

'Welcome Home' was the motto at one end of the room, and at the other end 'God bless our saviours - the Army, Navy and Air Force'. Simple words maybe, but they got home!

At seven o'clock Cuckfield's esteemed vicar, Canon Wilson, took the chair, and his supporters were -

Major Colin King, R.A.M.C.
Captain E. B. Woollan. M.C.
Captain Ralph S. Clarke
Lieutenant R. Worsley
Lieutenant Gilbert Denman
Lieutenant S. H. Knight
Lieutenant Stanley Wood

Other guests were -

Lieutenant H. M. Wells
H. Hobbs
L. Rhodes
J. Grant
A. Henley
J. Young
A. Pix
Ben Newnham
H. Barrow
E. Rowland
E. Barnes
P. Conn
J. Webber
E. Mays
W. Murdoch
R. Chinnery
W. G. Mitchell
W. B. Vickers
P. Cox
W. Mewlett
C. Moore
F. Rhodes

F. Brooks
F. Berry
O. Whappam
C. Newman
F. Blackshall
W. Nye
A. Urban
Peter Gander., Jun,
C. Selby
L. Murrell
A. W. Farrow
G. Osbourne
L. A. Palmer
? Green
W. F. Voller
N. Newham
W. A. Brookshaw
T. Batchelor
C. H. Mascall
A. T. Sayer
A. Brown
J. P. Jenner

R. Hillman
F. Parker
A. J. Stevens
H. Rowland
A. Hillman
G. Scovell
J. Webb
E. J. Hooker
F. Henley
C. Cook
G. Apps
W. Haynes
D. E. King
J. Gasson
F. Webber, Jun.
F. Beard
A. Harding
J. Dance
G. E. Thompsett
P. Reeve
C. A. Tyrrell
J. Page
E. Tidey
J. Godsmark
F. Quin
E. H. Bleach
F. Mitchell
W. J. Jones
W. P. Nash
N. Bowell
L. Riches
J. W. Stoner
F. Fuller
C. Wells
F. Markwick
F. Leaney
C. Knight
F. Cleaver

H. Mansbridge
J. H. Stevens
C. A. Elsworth
T. Wells
W. Leaney
W. Graham
W. Miles
S. Burt
C. Stoner
M. Upstone
F. Knapp
E. Quickenden
W. Whitton
W. Robinson
J. Cartner
A. Croucher
F. Simmons
W. Hazelgrove
C. Rowland
C. Marchant
J. Woodland
H. Tidey
H. Blackburn
C. Webber
M. Auger
T. Haylor
W. Scovell
C. T. Stoner
F. Knight
? Gillett
S. Bourne
E. Morfee
A. Webb
F. Field
P. Stenning
G. Hall
E. Hillman
G. Scovell. Sen

H. Whymark
P. Bist
A. Murrell
S. Revel
A. W. Dancy
H. Upton
C. Mitchell
T. Smith
M. Anscombe
N. Bransden
J. Jupp
J. Mascall
A. Turner
Ernest G. Hayden

J. Watson
F. Simmons
A. Wilkins
J. Mascall
W. Simmons
F. Pattenden
A. Morgan
F. Bleach
W. Hammond
P. Gander. Sen
J. Clayton
J. Budgen
W. Horn?

There were 195 invitations issued but 35 officers and men, to their deep regret, found themselves unable to attend.

The inhabitants of the town contributed about £115 to meet the expenses.

C. W. G. Wilson

A

FORM OF THANKSGIVING AND PRAYER

TO BE USED

In all Churches and Chapels in England and Wales, and in the
Town of Berwick-upon-Tweed

On SUNDAY, JULY 6, 1919

Being the Day appointed for Thanksgiving to
Almighty GOD on the occasion of the signing of the

TREATY OF PEACE.

By His Majesty's Special Command.

LONDON
Printed by EYRE and SPOTTISWOODE, LTD.
Printers to the King's most Excellent Majesty.

1919

CUCKFIELD PARISH CHURCH.

Thanksgiving for Victory and Peace,

SUNDAY, 6th JULY, 1919.

A

SPECIAL SERVICE of PRAISE and PRAYER

Will be held at 3.30 p.m.

PREACHER—

Rev. C. W. C. WILSON, M.A.

Vicar of Cuckfield, Canon and Prebendary of Chichester.

The Offerings at this Service will be given to Lord Roberts' Memorial Workshops for Disabled Sailors, Soldiers and Airmen.

THE OTHER SERVICES WILL BE:

7 a.m., 8 a.m. and 12.15 p.m.   -   Celebration of Holy Communion.
11 a.m.   -   Morning Prayer, Thanksgivings and Sermon.
6.30 p.m.   -   Evensong, Thanksgivings and Sermon.

Copies of the Official Forms of Service will be provided if they can be obtained.

Cuckfield Church Log Book - 6th July 1919

SPECIAL SERVICE OF PRAISE AND PRAYER THANKSGIVING SUNDAY AT THE PARISH CHURCH

These services will long be remembered. They began with a celebration of Holy Communion at 7.00 a.m. followed by another at 8.00 a.m. and a third after matins. The only addition to the decorating of the Church was an effective display of the flags of the Allies, which was placed on the chancel screen. The official form of service was used at all the services, and there were crowded congregations, especially at the afternoon service, when the Church was filled to overflowing, although additional accommodation had been provided. Special seats were reserved for the Urban Council.

After the processional hymn at Matins, the Vicar (Canon Wilson) who conducted the services all day, came forward and read the King's Proclamation, which was followed by the singing of the National Anthem. The lessons in the morning and afternoon were read by Mr B. Y. Bevan, J.P.

The afternoon service was opened by the singing, in procession, of the hymn 'Onward Christian Soldiers'. Mr Herrington carried the cross and was followed by two choir boys - W. Clarke and Christopher Marks - bearing the Union Jack and the Standard of St George. Mr Young presided at the organ, and was accompanied in some of the music by the drums - played with great effect by Messrs M. Angel and M. Anscombe and Patrol Leader A. Murrell. The service, in which the large congregation joined very heartily, followed the order as laid down in Part 111 of the official form, the hymns being 'Praise my Soul, the King of Heaven', and 'Peace, Perfect Peace'.

Canon Wilson took as his text the concluding lines of the lesson appointed for the service - 'So the Lord God will cause righteousness and praise to spring forth before all the nations' (Isaiah 1x1- x1). The reverend gentleman pointed out that this was a great and glorious promise of God, which was a source of strength and encouragement to his people who trusted in his love. We had consciously, or unconsciously, taken this promise to ourselves during the five years of war, and the assurance that in the end God would give us the victory had never failed. The day of praise had now come, for the victory had been gained and Peace had been signed. In speaking of the price that had been paid, the preacher made a touching allusion to those who had died, emphasising the fact that those who had passed within the veil were conscious of our rejoicings and were joining their thanks with ours that they did not die in vain. They were among the crowd of witnesses by who we were surrounded. The Sunday previous, the preacher went on to say, they had as a congregation offered their thanks, but today in accordance with the proclamation of the King, they were taking part in the great national act. Surely they had much to be thankful for. There was no need to remind them of the past, which was stamped indelibly on their mind, but he would refer them to the Treaty, severe but just, the result of which would be, as they all hoped, to make impossible such a war as that which had just been brought to an end. Meanwhile they must see to it that god's righteousness should be made supreme - a far off Divine event which seemed, indeed, so distant. But as Christian men and women they must, if only out of gratitude for what God had done for them, help forward the movement and establish the rule of Christ over the hearts of men. At the conclusion of the service the National Anthem was sung in full.

The collection, which amounted to £11.14s.10d. was given to Lord Robert's Memorial Workshops for Disabled Sailors, Soldiers and Airmen. The collections at the other services were given to the Sick and Poor Fund, and amounted to £12. 16s. 6d. After evensong Mr Young played a selection of national airs, much to the pleasure of a large number who stayed to listen.

Cuckfield Parish Magazine July - 1919
PEACE WITH GERMANY

The greatest war in history was brought to a conclusion on Saturday, June 28th, after having lasted 4 years and 328 days, and it was with feelings of great thankfulness and relief that we received the news of the signing of the Treaty of Peace.

SUNDAY JULY 6TH will always be remembered as Thanksgiving Day in Cuckfield and we in Cuckfield took our part in the great national chorus of thanksgiving and praise. There were crowded congregations at all the services, which were of a very hearty nature and at which the official forms of service were used, and particular mention may be made of the special service held in the afternoon, when the Church was crowded almost to its utmost extent, although extra seats had been provided. Before the service a quarter peal was rung on the Church bells with very pleasing effect. The service itself was in every respect worthy of the occasion, the Cross and the flags being carried in procession, the organ was supplemented by three drums and the music and singing were excellent.

The services on Sunday were of a special character, and were a great act of thanksgiving on the part of the people of Cuckfield. It was a memorable day and we hope it will never be forgotten.

A word of special recognition is due to the Organist and Choir, who did so much to make the services worthy of the occasion, as well as to those who played the drums and gave valuable and effective help. The Ringers also did their part in the rejoicings, both by the peal of Saturday night and Sunday and by the closing peal after Evensong on Sunday night.

It is now officially notified that Sunday next is to be observed as the day of Thanksgiving. The form of service which has been issued will be used and we must consider how far we can repeat the services of last Sunday.

CUCKFIELD
PEACE CELEBRATION.

July 19th, 1919.

CHAIRMAN—THE REV. CANON WILSON.

———————•———————

At a Public Meeting held in the Queen's
Hall on the 4th inst. a Committee was elected
to carry out the following suggestions as a Peace
Celebration :—

1.—Tea and Sports for the Children.
2.—Tea for Old People.
3.—Dancing in the Park.
4.—Carnival and Torchlight Procession.
5.—Fireworks and Bonfire of old Tar Barrels
given to the Committee.

It is not generally considered advisable that
a large sum of money be spent, but to be worthy
of the occasion and to be remembered by the
children, at least £75 will be required.

Donations may be sent to
A. T. RAPLEY,
"Sidbury,"
Hon. Secretary ;
G. VAUGHAN,
Hon. Treasurer ;
or the Official Collector,
A. BROWN,
42 Hatchgate Lane.

CUCKFIELD PEACE CELEBRATIONS.

July 19th, 1919.

CHAIRMAN—THE REV. CANON WILSON.

TEA for **CHILDREN** between the ages of 4 years and 14 years, and for **CUCKFIELD BOY SCOUTS**, at the **QUEEN'S HALL**, at 3.45 p.m.

TEA for **OLD AGE PENSIONERS** and for those eligible for Old Age Pensions, at the **PARISH ROOM**, at 4 p.m.

> (Invitations may be obtained from the Vicar).

At 5.0 p.m. —Procession from Queen's Hall to Cuckfield Park.
> It is hoped that those with Fancy Dresses, Decorated Cars, &c., will join in this Procession.

At 5.30 p.m.—Sports for School Children and Adults.
> The latter will include a Tug-of-War for Teams of Six, Events for Service and Ex-Service Men, and for Veterans—Ladies and Gents.

At 7.30 p.m.—Selection of National Songs, Morris Dances, &c.

DANCING.   BRASS BAND.   Conductor—Mr. J. GASSON.

At 9.0 p.m. —Carnival and Torchlight Procession through the Town.
> Cuckfield Boy Scouts' Bugle Band.   Prizes are offered for the Best Fancy Dresses—Adults and Children ; Best Decorated Bicycle ; Decorated Trolleys or Wagons, with Tableau ; Decorated Motor Cars or Side Cars.   (Competitors must reside in Cuckfield Parish). Judging at 7 p.m.

At 10.0 p.m.—Fireworks in the Vicarage Field.

At 11.0 p.m.—Flares and Bonfire of Tar Barrels in Courtmead Field.

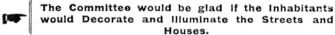

The Committee would be glad if the Inhabitants would Decorate and Illuminate the Streets and Houses.

Further information may be had from ARTHUR T. RAPLEY, Hon. Secretary.

Charles Clarke (Haywards Heath) Ltd.

Mid-Sussex Times - July 1919

CUCKFIELD PEACE CELEBRATION

July 19th 1919

An exciting day of celebrations was held in which everyone in the town could participate. When the costs and expenses were given in a Balance Sheet, the balance was £21.00. It was decided that this money should go towards the cost of inscribing on wooden panels the name of every Cuckfield man who had served in the Great War. It is hoped that this may be placed in the Queen's Hall.

The long programme which had been arranged for the Peace Celebration was carried through very satisfactorily, and that in spite of the rain everyone enjoyed themselves.

The town was bright with decorations, the church bells rang out merrily during the morning, the children had an excellent tea, which was arranged by the ladies of the Tea Committee, and the old people were entertained to a substantial tea, which they much appreciated and which was kindly given by Mr and Mrs A. Avery. The Boy Scouts were not forgotten, and Mr and Mrs Denman entertained them to tea, which they enjoyed.

The procession was the prettiest that has ever been seen in Cuckfield, the sports and other amusements in the Park gave great satisfaction, and the deck flares, fireworks and bonfire formed a fitting and splendid conclusion. A word of commendation is due to the Brass Band and to the Scout's Band and also to the many willing workers on the different committees, who accomplished so much in such a short time, being ably assisted by the Hon. Secretary Mr A. T. Rapley and his assistant Mr W. Gasson.

ARMISTICE SUNDAY 1919

The Service of Thanksgiving and Remembrance which we held on the evening of the Sunday preceding the anniversary of the signing of the Armistice was a great success, and in spite of the unfavourable weather there was a very large congregation. We are grateful to those who gave us their help so that everything passed off so well. We hope to have a similar service every year, for certainly it is right that we should remember with thankfulness the ending of the terrible war, and also that the roll of those Cuckfield men who gave their lives should be read at least once a year in the old Parish Church, so as to keep their memory green.

CUCKFIELD PARISH CHURCH.

A

Service of Thanksgiving

IN COMMEMORATION OF THE

SIGNING OF THE ARMISTICE IN 1918,

AND A

MEMORIAL OF THE FALLEN,

WILL BE HELD

ON SUNDAY, NOV. 9TH, 1919,

AT 6.30 P.M.

All Men who served in His Majesty's Forces are specially invited to attend, and Seats will be reserved for them.

The Offerings at this Service will be given to Lord Roberts' Memorial Workshops for Disabled Sailors, Soldiers and Airmen.

CHAPTER 10

1920

CELEBRATIONS CONTINUE

CELEBRATIONS CONTINUE

PEACE
WITH
HONOUR

QUEEN'S HALL, CUCKFIELD.

Welcome Home Dinner

to

THE CUCKFIELD MEN WHO HAVE
SERVED IN H.M. FORCES DURING
THE GREAT WAR.

14th JANUARY, 1920.

The Inhabitants of Cuckfield
request the honour of the company

of _____

at

A Dinner and Entertainment

to be given at Queen's Hall

on Wednesday, 14th January, at 6.30 p.m.,

to welcome home the Cuckfield Men who have

served in H.M. Forces during the Great War.

Menu.

ROAST BEEF.
Horse Radish Sauce.

ROAST MUTTON.
Onion Sauce.

BOILED MUTTON.
Caper Sauce.

ROAST PORK.
Sage and Onion Stuffing.

Roast and Boiled Potatoes.

Greens, Parsnips, &c.

YORKSHIRE & PLAIN SUET PUDDINGS.

CHRISTMAS PUDDINGS.
Sweet Sauce.

APPLE PIES.

CUSTARD.   BLANCMANGE.   JELLIES.

Cheese and Biscuits.

Coffee.

Ale, Lemonade and Ginger Beer.

Toasts.

" The King."

" Our Fallen Comrades."

" The Boys—God bless 'em."

By Canon WILSON.

ENTERTAINMENT,

Sustained by

Miss N. MOTION,

Miss COURTENAY,

Mr. THOMAS SYDNEY.

EX-SERVICE MEN ENTERTAINED AT CUCKFIELD

WELCOME HOME DINNER IN THE QUEEN'S HALL

A Happy Gathering on Wednesday 14th January 1920

When Cuckfield entertained 160 of its returned soldiers and sailors to a dinner and entertainment last April, it was recognised that another would have to be arranged later on for the large number who were then still on active service. The function came off on Wednesday evening, and like its predecessor, was a memorable gathering, over a hundred sitting down.

The Rev. Canon Wilson presided over the company, supported by Second Lieutenant H. E. Stewart, Mr F. Hoadley, Mr E. E. Napper, Mr J. B. Whitmore and others.

Those who accepted invitations to the dinner were -

Messrs H. Askew Jun	F. Attwater
C. J. Baker	H. Barnett
E. Barnett	C. Bell
G. Blackstone	D. Blackstone
G. E. Billingsley	C. Brigden
W. A. Brigden	C. Berry
C. Betts	N. E. Brown
F. R. Bourne	E. S. Butler
F. H. Botting	A. Carter
T. G. Carter	H. J. Chapman
T. Cook	T. Crouch
E. N. Cartwright	E. E. Dancy
W. Dance	G. Draper
S. A. Ede	G. Ede
F. Frost	A. Funnell Jun
J. Faulkener	C. Foulger
E. W. Fasrncombe	H. C. Franklin

A. Garner Jun.
H. S. Gasson
H. Garrod
F. Godsmark
G. Harvey
G. Henley
A. Hobbs
C. Howard
A. Jones
A. J. Jupp
W. S. Knight
H. Knight
A. E. Lingley
A. Marchant
F. E. Mitchell
W. A. Mitchell
E. Mc. G. Mitchell
M. Myram
T. C. Newman
F. H. Pelling
G. Perry
R. C. Pinder
W. J. Quickenden
L. S. Rowland
E. Sayers
G. E. Smith
H. Smith
A. J. Stevens
C. A. Tester
A. M. Tree
L. Upton
G. E. Wilson
J. J. Winterbottom

W. J. Gasson
G. Gasson
A. Godsmark Jun
F. Greere
F. Harvey
A. Hillman
F. R. Hounsell
F. Humphrey
W. A. Jennings
J. W. Jeffery
E. Knight
Weldon Knight
T. B. Malins
E. G. Markwick
T. Mitchell
W. E. Mitchell Jun
J. Murrell
R. Myram
A. Nye
J. Pennifold
W. Perry
A. Page
A. Randall
A. Sayers
F. W. Sissons
A. R. Smith
H. Starley
A. Stewart
T. R. Tester
Horace Upton
Harry Upton
S. Willsman
J. G. Wynter

The hall presented a charming appearance with its artistic decorations of flags and evergreens, whilst the long tables were gaily bedecked with vases of flowers, holly, ferns etc. this work having been accomplished by various ladies.

At a quarter to seven the Vicar said grace, and for some time afterwards the lady waitresses were kept busy supplying the wants of the guests.

At the conclusion of the feast several ladies and gentlemen joined the company for the several toasts. An envelope containing a cigar and cigarettes was served to each guest.

The Chairman first proposed the loyal toast praising the work and untiring energy of the King and the inspiration he gave all through the war.

The second toast was to 'Our Fallen Comrades'. In feeling words he said the toast would be received with sympathetic interest by them all. Eighty two men of Cuckfield had given up their lives in the most noble cause and grandest crusade that the world had ever seen. Some gave up their lives before seeing active service and their graves were in their own churchyard. Some were resting beneath the waves of the ocean and some were in graves in foreign lands. He said foreign lands, but where those men rested would be for ever English soil - consecrated by the remains of those dear men. They in that hall had been spared to return home, and they thanked God for that, but those who were at rest would never be forgotten and he hoped soon there would be a memorial erected in Cuckfield, which as far as they could make it, would be worthy of those brave men. He proposed also to inscribe their names on velum and keep in the Parish Church, so that their memory would be kept sacred, and as long as he was in Cuckfield that roll should be read out once a year. In that way they at least would remember them. The company rose and honoured the toast in silence.

The final toast was 'The Boys - God bless 'em'. Thanks was a small word but it meant a great deal for all they had done. They left their homes and all that was dear to them and their work and they had had many strange and wonderful experiences. Now they were back and each one had done his bit. It sounded very little but it meant a lot.

After talking about the courage, endurance and heroism of the men of all ranks who held their own in the field of battle, his attention turned to those who stayed at home but also played an important role. The V.T.C. had to stay at home but they undertook disciplinary training in order to make the shores of England safe and he (Canon Wilson) was afraid their services were not always estimated at their real value.

He coupled with the toast the names of -

Captain Ralph Wells. M.C.
Captain Newman
Lieutenant Drake R.H.A
Lieutenant T. H. Hounsell
Second Lieutenant B. Y. Bevan
Mr Ede
Chief Motor Mechanic N. E. Brown
Sergant W. J. Gasson
Air Mechanic A. Tree
Second Lieutenant H. E. Stewart
as representing the Navy, Army, Royal Air Force andVolunteer
Training Corps (3rd Volunteer Battalion of the Sussex Regiment)

So ended the second welcome home dinner.

A glass of hot punch was supplied to each guest as he left the hall.

CHAPTER 11

DECORATIONS AWARDED TO
RESIDENTS OF CUCKFIELD

DECORATIONS AWARDED TO RESIDENTS OF CUCKFIELD AS REPORTED IN THE CUCKFIELD PARISH MAGAZINES AND/OR THE MID-SUSSEX TIMES

A

Cuckfield Parish Magazine - April 1916
CORPORAL MICHAEL ANSCOMBE

Corporal Michael Anscombe (Sussex Pioneers) has been promoted to the rank of Sergeant. He has been acting Sergeant for some time and we have no doubt that he has well earned his promotion.

Mid-Sussex Times - 25th July 1916
PRESENTATION TO SERGEANT L. ASKEW

The Cuckfield Platoon of the Sussex Volunteer Regiment will shortly be losing the services of Platoon Sergeant Leslie Askew. He was one of the original members of the V.T.C. and has been the life and soul of the local Platoon.

On parade on Wednesday he was the recipient of a presentation from the members. The gift consisted of a luminous wrist watch and a mounted photo of the Platoon.

Major Lister, in addressing the men, expressed his great regret at losing Sergeant Askew and stated that he had set a fine example, not only to the Platoon but to the Company. He hoped that his merits would meet their due reward in the Army.

Platoon Commander C. H. Waugh then handed the gift to Sergeant Askew, emphasising the fact that it was entirely due to him that the Platoon existed today. On behalf of his old comrades he wished him every success.

Sergeant Askew responded in a few well chosen words. He had always had, he said, one object in view, that in justice to the men at the front, who were sacrificing everything, it was up to the old 'uns' at home to make themselves efficient to defend the homes in case of need.

Major Lister made an earnest appeal for more Volunteer recruits. In the old days Cuckfield was the second place in the county to establish a volunteer Force, Brighton being the first, and he should very much like to see the present generation exhibit the same high standard of patriotic fervour and respond as readily to Duty's call.

B

Cuckfield Parish Magazine - November 1918
HENRY LOWTHIAN BARGE
A promising career has been cut short by the death of Mr Henry Lowthian Barge, who has done very good work in devising means to combat the ruthless submarine policy of the enemy, and for his valuable services the Order of the British Empire was bestowed upon him. His family was well known in Cuckfield and great sympathy is felt for his widow and little children as well as for the other members of the family.

Mid-Sussex Times - 31st October 1916
PETTY OFFICER W. J. BARROW - NAVAL HONOURS
Petty Officer W. J. Barrow, whose name appeared in a recent list of navel men has been awarded the D.S.M. in connection with the Horns Reef Battle, in which he took part on board H.M.S Southampton. He is the third son of Mr and Mrs Spencer Barrow of Percy Cottages. Petty Officer Barrow was slightly wounded in the battle in which he gained his distinction. He was born at Cuckfield and joined the navy at the age of 17. He is now about 30 years of age and is married. Mr and Mrs Spencer Barrow have two sons in the navy and two in the army also two sons-in-law in the Army.

Mid-Sussex Times 9th May 1916
CORPORAL F. G. BEARD, 4th Battalion Royal Sussex Regiment
has been promoted to Sergeant.

Mid-Sussex Times - 9th May 1916
The son of Mr and Mrs John Bennett of Brainsmead has been appointed Brigade Sergeant Major of the 22nd Manchester Regiment.

Mid-Sussex Times - 2nd October 1916
BRIGADE SERGEANT MAJOR BENNETT MILITARY HONOURS
Brigade Sergeant-Major Bennett, 22nd Manchester Regiment, nephew of Mrs Constable of Churchyard Cottages and son of Mr and Mrs J. Bennett of Brainsmead, has been awarded the Military Medal 'for extremely able and gallant performances of his duty under very heavy shell fire for five successive days. He continued to issue ammunition in a front trench until his store was blown up'.

Mid-Sussex Times - 10th September 1918
WILLIAM BENNETT - AWARDED THE MILITARY MEDAL
Mr and Mrs John Bennett, of Brainsmead, have received the following pleasing letter from Lieutenant Colonel P. H. Hainson -

4th September 1918.
I am writing to congratulate you on the award to your son, Sergeant William Bennett, M.G.C. of the Military Medal for gallantry and devotion to duty during the recent fighting. Your son has thoroughly deserved the decoration and is a credit to the Battalion and to the Machine Gun Corps. Attached you will see the action for which the medal was awarded.

Here is a copy:-
'5828 Sergeant William Bennett, Machine Gun Corps.
At _____ between 20th and 29th July 1918.
For conspicuous gallantry and devotion to duty. During the period of operations this Sergeant was acting as Sergeant of a Section which was constantly under heavy shell and machine gun fire. Despite heavy casualties, Sergeant Bennett, by his coolness, indifference to danger, initiative and resource in command, materially helped to maintain the

efficient working of the Section. His example and leadership were of a high order and deserving of the greatest praise.'

Sergeant Bennett is 26 years of age, and before joining up worked for Mr Frank Webber of London Lane. He is an old boy of Cuckfield Church School.

Cuckfield Parish Magazine - June 1916

We wish to offer our hearty congratulations to **MAJOR A. H. BERLY,** R.F.A on his promotion to the rank of Lieutenant Colonel.

Cuckfield Parish Magazine - July 1919
CONGRATULATIONS

We wish to offer our hearty congratulations to **Miss Enid Bevan**, who received from the King, at an investiture held on June 26th, the Royal Red Cross, in recognition of her work as a nurse during the war.

Cuckfield Parish Magazine - February 1919
GUNNER SIDNEY BOURNE

We are pleased to see that Sidney has quite recovered from his serious attack of pneumonia and we congratulate him heartily on having been awarded the Belgian 'Croix de Guerre' for meritorious services on the lines of communication.

Mid-Sussex Times - 4th January 1916
MAJOR SERGISON-BROOKES

The name of Major B. N. Sergison-Brooke, D.S.O. appears in Sir John French's lengthy list of those whom he recommends for gallant and distinguished service in the field.

C

Mid-Sussex Times -15th September 1914
SECOND LIEUTENANT RALPH S. CLARKE

Ralph Clarke from the Surrey (Queen Mary's Regiment) Yeomanry has been appointed a Second Lieutenant in the Sussex Yeomanry.

Mid-Sussex Times - 3rd October 1916
SECOND LIEUTENANT R. S. CLARKE

Second Lieutenant R. S. Clarke, Sussex Yeomanry, son of Colonel Stephenson R. Clarke, C.B. of Borde Hill was on Thursday gazetted Lieutenant.

Cuckfield Parish Magazine - May 1920
CUCKFIELD V. A. D.

We are pleased to hear that **Miss Cooper** has been made a Member of the Order of the British Empire. We congratulate her on the honour and we are very glad of the recognition of the good work done by her and the Cuckfield Voluntary Aid Detachment.

We are also glad to hear that the good work which was done at the Hospital during the war has been further recognised, as **Miss Hope Lister**, **Miss Olive Turner** and **Miss Helen Wilson** have been mentioned in dispatches.

D

Mid-Sussex Times - 17th October 1916
GILBERT DENMAN

There are many in Cuckfield who will be interested to learn that the only son of Mr and Mrs J. Denman of Broad Street, was gazetted last week as Assistant Equipment Officer in the Royal Flying Corps. He is stationed at Farnborough. In September 1914, he joined the 1/6 Royal Sussex (Cyclist) Regiment, and was promoted a month later to the motor cycle section as a dispatch rider, with the rank of Lance-Corporal and Artificer to the section, which had a complement of sixteen motor cycles. This, together with the severe test he had to undergo prior to securing his commission, speaks well for his abilities and training at the works, at Cuckfield, of Messrs. J. Denman and Co.

Although he has not yet been overseas, his Regiment has been on active service since he joined, and he put in about nine months on the East Coast and later did duty on the South Coast. The position of

Assistant Equipment Officer is an appointment only open to men of considerable experience of motors and general knowledge of their management.

Second Lieutenant Denman is an old Belvedere boy, and his advancement, we are sure, will give pleasure to the Principal of the School (Mr C. J. D. Gregory, B.A.) and also to his school chums.

F

Cuckfield Parish Magazine February 1919
GUNNER FRED FULLER
Gunner Fred Fuller has been home on leave and took the opportunity to get married. We wish to congratulate him on this and also on the fact that he has brought home with him an embossed card, on which is a statement, signed by the Captain and Adjutant, to the effect that 'The name of Gunner F. Fuller has been inscribed on the Roll of Honour of the 15th Brigade R. H. A for acts of gallantry performed, September 1917 - March 1918.

Mid-Sussex Times - 9th May 1916
Second Lieutenant **WILFRED H. FURLONGER,** Royal Flying Corps, has been appointed Captain in the same Corps.

G

Cuckfield Parish Magazine - September 1918
HENRY GARROD
The Military Medal has been awarded to Private Henry Garrod, Sherwood Foresters, who is well known in Cuckfield as he lived for some time with his aunt, Mrs Tom Mitchell in London Lane, but he was severely wounded and gassed and for a time his life was in danger.

H

Mid-Sussex Times - 19th November 1918
AWARDED THE MILITARY MEDAL
PRIVATE A. J. HILLMAN

Mr and Mrs J. Hillman of 'The Highlands', have reason to be proud of their son, Private A. J. Hillman. He has been awarded the Military Medal for working with his Lewis gun against an enemy tank during an enemy counter-attack. He writes -

'Thank God for saving my life and for making me a good soldier. I am sure that many prayers have been raised for me in my dear old home and elsewhere'. Private Hillman was 19 years of age at the end of October last. Previous to joining the colours he was employed on the railway at Kingscote Station.

K

Mid-Sussex Times - 6th October 1914
MAJOR ARTHUR H. C .KENNY-HERBERT

Major Arthur Kenny-Herbert of 'Hillbrow', Cuckfield has been appointed Assistant Commandant of the Prisoners of War Camp at Shrewsbury

Cuckfield Parish Magazine - July 1919
DR COLIN KING has been awarded the Order of the British Empire for his valuable services in France as a doctor.

Cuckfield Parish Magazine January 1917
CORPORAL ALFRED C. KNIGHT

has recently been awarded the Military Medal for conspicuous bravery in taking ammunition up to the firing line amid heavy bombardment.

Cuckfield Parish Magazine - January 1918
CORPORAL CHARLES KNIGHT - PROMOTION
We have received the gratifying news that Corporal A. C. Knight has been promoted to Sergeant. At the outbreak of the war he went to France and remained there two years and four months and was awarded the Military Medal.

Mid-Sussex Times - 17th July 1917
FRANK KNIGHT - Gratifying Promotion
Mr and Mrs Knight of 'St Omer', Cuckfield were pleased to receive the news from their son Frank of his promotion to a chief motor mechanic in the Royal Naval Motor Boat reserve. Before joining the service in February 1916 he was with Messrs J. Denman and Company Ltd, Broad Street, Cuckfield.

Mid-Sussex Times - 19th December 1916
MAJOR STEPHEN KNIGHT - PERSEVERANCE REWARDED
Mr and Mrs Stephen Knight, of Cuckfield, have received the gratifying news that their eldest son, Sergeant Major S. H. Knight, has been given a commission in the Royal Sussex Regiment. Prior to the war he was a Sergeant in the local Volunteers, and retired, but when war broke out he rejoined as a Private. He went with the Royal Sussex to Gallipoli, and gradually worked his way up to Sergeant-Major.

Arriving at Egypt he attended the instruction school at Cairo for Officers, and headed the list of candidates at the examination. Hence his commission.

He is 27 years of age, and when at Cuckfield was very keen on football, and for a time held the position of captain of the Cuckfield Club for a season. His future will be watched with interest.

Mr and Mrs Knight have another son on active service in the East, he being in the Royal Engineers.

M

Mid-Sussex Times - 9th May 1916
HENRY C. S. MAINE has received a Second Lieutenancy in the Grenadier Guards.

Cuckfield Parish Magazine - November 1918
SERGEANT F. MARKWICK
We offer hearty congratulations to Sergeant F. Markwick who has been awarded the Military Medal for services rendered to his country at Wulverghem on 6th September 1918 and he has received a congratulatory card, signed by the Major-General Commanding the 30th British Division.

Cuckfield Parish Magazine - February 1918
CAPTAIN JAMES K. McCONNEL
Captain James Mc Connel, D.S.O., 20th Hussars is now acting as Brigade Major to an Infantry Division. He has been slightly wounded, but we are glad to hear that he is going on alright.

Mid-Sussex Times - 6th June 1916
SECOND LIEUTENANT R.H.C. MERTENS
Second Lieutenant R.H.C Mertens of the Cranleigh School Contingent, Junior Division, Officers' Training Corps, has been gazetted Lieutenant.

Cuckfield Parish Magazine - May 1919
MENTIONED IN DISPATCHES -
CHARGE SISTER ALICE M. MITCHELL
Charge Sister Alice M. Mitchell daughter of Mr Mitchell of 'Percy Cottages', has been mentioned in Sir Douglas Haigh's despatches published in the London Gazette for her good work at the Duchess of Westminster's Hospital in Northern France where she has been nursing for over three years. We offer her our congratulations.

Cuckfield Parish Magazine - February 1918
HARRY MURRELL
Lance-Corporal Harry Murrell, Royal Fusiliers, whose parents live at Brook Street, has been commended for distinguished bravery in the field on December 6th.

N

Mid-Sussex Times - 11th May 1915
A COMMISSION FOR PRIVATE NEWMAN
News was received last week that Private H. K. Newman of the Royal Army Medical Corps, had been given a commission as Second Lieutenant in the East Kent Regiment (The Buffs). He is the only son of Mr and Mrs Newman of Hanlye Farm, and a nephew of Mr A. Beeching J.P

O

Mid-Sussex Times - 27th October 1914
CAPTAIN FRANK OWEN - MILITARY APPOINTMENT
The London Gazette under the date of 17th October announces the following appointment - Captain Frank Owen to be Major (temporarily) in the 8th (City of London) Battalion London Regiment, (Post Office Rifles)

R

Mid-Sussex Times -12th January 1915
MILITARY PROMOTION
A supplement to the London Gazette of January 8th published on Saturday contained the following military appointment:

'Irish Guards, **CAPTAIN PERCY L. REID** to be Major'

CORPORAL L. ROWLAND

This well known local soldier the son of Mr and Mrs Rowland formerly of Mill Green Road, has been awarded the Military Medal. He is in the Royal Sussex Regiment and twenty six years of age. In civil life he was a gardener at 'Ockenden', Cuckfield.

Cuckfield Parish Magazine - September 1917
SERGEANT MAJOR RHODES R.E. has received the Serbian decoration for gallant service in that country.

S

Cuckfield Parish Magazine May 1918
MAJOR CHARLES GREATLY SAUNDERS

We offer hearty congratulations to Major Charles Greatly Saunders, who having been previously mentioned three times in dispatches, has now been awarded the D.S.O. for meritorious services with the Canadian Army at Paschendale.

Cuckfield Parish Magazine - November 1918
MAJOR CHARLES SAUNDERS

At the investiture held on October 19th, Major Charles G. Saunders received from the King the D.S.O. which was awarded to him some time ago.

Cuckfield Parish Magazine - September 1917
SERGEANT A. E. SELBY

- was awarded the Military Medal for gallantry at Pozieres.

Mid-Sussex Times - 10th October 1916
PRIVATE FRANK BENTHAM STEVENS - GRANTED A COMMISSION

It was announced in the 'London Gazette' on Wednesday evening, that

Private Frank Bentham Stevens, 1st Sussex Yeomanry, T. F., had been appointed Second Lieutenant for duty with the Royal Flying Corps, Balloon Commander. He is the son of Mr and Mrs W. Stevens of 'Garnalds'.

Mid-Sussex Times - 22nd September 1914
MILITARY APPOINTMENT
It was officially announced last week that Mr **EDMUND STEPHENSON CLARKE**, of Borde Hill, has been appointed to a Second Lieutenancy in the 4th Battalion Royal Sussex Regiment.

Mid-Sussex Times - 12th January 1915
IN THE SCOTS GUARDS
Second Lieutenant **EDMUND STEPHENSON CLARKE** from the 4th Battalion of the Royal Sussex Regiment has been appointed Second Lieutenant (on probation) in the Scots Guards.

T

Cuckfield Parish Magazine - October 1917
MILITARY MEDAL
SERGEANT TANNER, Rifle Brigade who was married in our Church in 1915 to Miss Mabel Ede is now home on leave, having just come out of hospital after being twice wounded in action. We wish to congratulate him on having won the Military Medal which was awarded to him for bravery at Ypres.

Mid-Sussex Times - 9th March 1915
LIONEL TURNER
A Commission in the army has been given to Mr Lionel F. Turner

Cuckfield Parish Magazine - November 1918
MAJOR LIONEL TURNER
We wish to congratulate Major Lionel Turner on his promotion to the rank of Lieutenant Colonel.

Mid-Sussex Times - 1st June 1915
LIEUTENANT MONTAGUE T. TURNER

Lieutenant Montague Turner of the 3rd Battalion Royal Sussex Regiment has been gazetted to the rank of Captain. The promotion dates from February 2nd.

Mid-Sussex Times - 24th August 1915
CAPTAIN MONTAGU T. TURNER

Captain Turner of the 3rd (reserve) Royal Sussex Regiment, has been appointed an Assistant Provost Marshall (graded for pay as a Staff Captain. The announcement, which appeared in Friday's 'London Gazette', is dated August 6th.

Mid-Sussex Times - 8th Jan 1918
CAPTAIN M. T. TURNER - MILITARY CROSS

Captain M. Turner of the Royal Sussex Regiment has been given the rank of temporary Major whilst employed as Assistant Provost-Marshal and also awarded the Military Cross.

V

Cuckfield Parish Magazine - February 1918
We are glad to hear that **PERCY VICKERS** has been promoted 1st Air Mechanic, R.F.C.

W

Mid-Sussex Times - 6th June 1916
CAPTAIN T. R. WELLS - MILITARY CROSS

The Military Cross has been awarded to Captain T. R. Wells of the 33rd Punjabis, attached to the Royal Flying Corps, for distinguished services in the Mesopotamia campaign. The gallant officer is unfortunately one of the prisoners of war from Kut. We are sure that heartiest congratulations have gone, and will go, to Dr and Mrs Wells in this great honour to one of their soldier sons.

Mid-Sussex Times - 4th September 1917
SECOND LEIUTENANT WOOLAN - AWARDED THE MILITARY CROSS

Many friends in Cuckfield as well as Haywards Heath, of Second Lieutenant E. B. Woolan, will be pleased to learn that he has received from the hands of the King at Buckingham Palace, the Military Cross. The gallant officer who has had fourteen months in France, has once been wounded and had six weeks in hospital. He has now returned to France.

Mid-Sussex Times - 4th May 1915
PROMOTION

CORPORAL STANLEY WOOD of the 1st Home Counties' Brigade Royal Field Artillery (T) has been promoted to Second Lieutenant. He is the third son of Mr James Wood of Broad Street and the second son to receive a commission during the present war.

Mid-Sussex Times - 27th October 1914
ROBERT WRIGHTSON - MILITARY APPOINTMENT

The London Gazette under the date of 17th October announces the following appointment - Robert G. Wrightson (late Second Lieutenant 1st City of London R.G.A.V. to be Captain in the 8th (City of London) Battalion London Regiment (Post Office Rifles)

Y

Cuckfield Parish Magazine - February 1918
FRANKLIN YOUNG

Mr Franklin Young, son of Mrs Young of 'The Studio', is to be congratulated on his promotion to 1st Air Mechanic in the R.F.C., a promotion which is all the more meritorious considering his youth.

Cuckfield Parish Magazine - November 1922
AN ECHO OF THE WAR -
AWARDS TO CUCKFIELD NURSES

On November 1st, a large number of V. A. D Nurses attended at the Pavilion, Brighton, to receive at the hands of the Duchess of Norfolk, medals which have been specially struck and were presented to them in recognition of their valuable services to the sick and wounded during the Great War.

In order to receive a medal it was necessary to have put in at least 1,000 hours and the members of the Cuckfield Detachment who received medals were as follows -

Mrs Bannister
Miss Enid Bevan
Miss Ethel Britten
Miss Campbell
Miss Cooper
Mrs Dalton
Mrs H.C.Franklin
Mrs H. Hills
Miss Huckett
Miss Knight
Miss Neate
Miss Reid
Miss Olive Turner
Miss Helen W. Wilson

CHAPTER 12

CUCKFIELD WAR MEMORIALS

CUCKFIELD WAR MEMORIALS

There are several memorials in Cuckfield in memory of those who served and gave their lives for their country in World War 1.

The stone 'Cross of Sacrifice' in the churchyard of Holy Trinity Church to the south of the Parish Church facing the South Downs.

The white marble memorial placed inside the church on the south wall.

Wooden panels inside the entrance to the Queen's Hall in the High Street.

The 'Richard Worsley Recreation Ground' behind the Queen's Hall.

The Kennedy Memorial. A private memorial erected by the Kennedy family in the bell tower of the Parish Church.

It was the relatives who decided where they felt was the appropriate place where each of their loved ones should be remembered. Some men are on all three memorials, others on just one.

A few of those who died had moved away to work, but their families chose to have them remembered at the place they still called home. A few came from other places to work in Cuckfield and they too wished to be remembered within the community. Some who lived in the town at the time but who had their origins elsewhere are not included here, if their relatives decided to commemorate them in another place.

Throughout the war the men were remembered in Memorial Services but the first time their names were listed anywhere was in August 1917.

Mid-Sussex Times - 14th August 1917

AN ACCOUNT OF AN EARLY WAR MEMORIAL PLACED INSIDE CUCKFIELD CHURCH

On August 4th 1917, there was fixed on the South Wall of Cuckfield

Church a memorial of the Cuckfield men who have fallen in the war. The names of the dead soldiers with the date and place of death have been engrossed on three specially printed cards which have been mounted and placed in a dark oak frame measuring three foot by two foot. The whole is surrounded by a block to which are fixed little sticks bearing the flags of Great Britain, her Colonies and the Allies.

Cuckfield Parish Magazine - November 1920

THE ROLL OF HONOUR

It will be noticed that the list of Fallen Soldiers has been revised and completed. For this we are indebted to Mr Sidney Bourne, who very kindly typed the lists on fresh cards. The names are now placed, not in alphabetical order but according to the date of death. It is a memorial which will always be preserved, but it will, we hope, be replaced before long by something more worthy of those whom we commemorate. A memorial inside the Church was unveiled in 1922.

THE 'CROSS OF SACRIFICE' WAR MEMORIAL IN THE CHURCHYARD

Cuckfield Parish Magazine - February - 1919
It will doubtless be the wish of Cuckfield people to have a memorial to those who have given their lives for us, and we shall naturally wish that it may be, as far as we can make it, worthy of them and worthy of Cuckfield. The Vicar would suggest that a public meeting should shortly be called, and that meanwhile people should consider the matter so as to have some practical suggestions as to the form which the memorial shall take. We shall also wish to have some permanent record of the names of all those men of Cuckfield who have served during the war.

THE GREAT WAR.

A PUBLIC MEETING

WILL BE HELD IN

The Queen's Hall,

CUCKFIELD,

ON

MONDAY, FEBRUARY 17th, 1919,

AT 7 P.M.,

To consider the provision of a suitable and worthy Memorial of the Brave Cuckfield Men who have given their Lives for their King and Country.

CHAIRMAN :

COLONEL STEPHENSON R. CLARKE, C.B.

All Parishioners are cordially invited to be present.

(Signed)   C. W. G. WILSON,
Vicar of Cuckfield.

CHARLES CLARKE (HAYWARDS HEATH) LTD., PRINTERS

Shirley Bond

Cuckfield Parish Magazine - March 1919

A well attended meeting was held at the Queen's Hall on Monday, February 17th to consider what form the Cuckfield War Memorial shall take. Colonel Stephenson R. Clarke, C.B., was in the chair, and it was decided that the Memorial to the Fallen should take the form of a Recreation ground and also a tablet or brass on which it shall be inscribed the names of all the men of Cuckfield who have given their lives for their country. A Committee was appointed to take steps to carry out this decision, and it will report in due time to another public meeting.

Note - Plans were changed, as can be seen in the notice below, the final decision was that the War Memorial should take the form of an octagonal stone base on which the names of those who gave their lives would be carved and above that would be a tall white column with a 'cross of sacrifice' on top. It would stand in the church yard to the south side of the church.

CUCKFIELD WAR MEMORIAL.

COMMITTEE:

Mr. WM. STEVENS *(Chairman)*,

Mr. B. Y. BEVAN *(Treasurer)*.   Mr. L. ASKEW *(Hon. Secretary)*,

Mr. J. DENMAN,   Mr. W. E. MITCHELL,

Miss K. GRAY,   Mr. D. C. MONRO,

Mr. S. KNIGHT,   Mr. A. T. RAPLEY,

Rev. Canon C. W. G. WILSON.

THE COMMITTEE appointed at a Public Meeting, held at the Queen's Hall, to arrange for the erection of a suitable Memorial to the Cuckfield Men who fell in the great War, have now brought their work to a successful conclusion.

A "Cross of Sacrifice," designed by Sir Reginald Blomfield, R.A., has been erected on the south side of the Parish Church and facing the South Downs. The main portion of the work was well carried out by Dove Brothers Ltd., of Islington, but the inscription and the names on the Cross were entrusted locally to Messrs. F. Hounsell & Son, and the path and surroundings of the Memorial were executed by Stephen Knight & Co., Ltd.

The Memorial was unveiled, after a Service in the Parish Church, by Mrs. Fisher (the wife of the Rev. Prebendary Fisher) and Mrs. Wm. Stevens, on Sunday afternoon, January 23rd, in the presence of a great number of Cuckfield people, and others from a distance. The Bishop of Lewes, the Right Rev. H. K. Southwell, C.F., C.M.G., D.D., dedicated the Memorial, while the Rev. Canon Wilson and the Rev. J. E. Dean took part in the open-air Service.

Contributions came in so freely from all classes that the Committee find themselves in the happy position of having in their Treasurer's hands a balance of £65, which it is proposed to hand over to the Parochial Church Council for the Parish of Cuckfield, in order that the income may be applied in maintaining the Memorial and the ground surrounding it in good order.

A Copy of the Inscription with a List of the Names inscribed on the base of the Cross accompanies this Report, and a Balance Sheet and a List of Subscribers are appended.

The Committee, in conclusion, desire to recognise heartily the energy and time which Mr. L. Askew, the Hon. Secretary, spent in carrying out his responsible duties.

CUCKFIELD.

November, 1921.

Mr. Leslie Askew, the Secretary to the War Memorial Committee, is to be commended on the way he carried out his duties.

LIST OF SUBSCRIBERS.

Mr. and Mrs. R. Anscombe
Mr. and Mrs. A. Anscombe
Mr. M. Anscombe
Mrs. Armitage
Mr. and Mrs. H. Askew
Miss M. Askew
Miss Atkinson
Mr. A. Avery
Mrs. A. Avery
Miss Avery
Mr. H. Bates
Miss Bennett
Lieut.-Col. and Mrs. A. H. Berly
Miss Best
Mr. B. Y. Bevan
Miss and Miss E. Birkinshaw
Mr. and Mrs. W. Bone
Miss Mary Bone
Mrs. Botting
Mr. and Mrs. Bourne and Sons
Mr. and Mrs. Bowley
Major H. M. W. Bridgman
Mrs. Britten and family
Miss Britton
Col. Sergison Brooke
Mr. A. Burtenshaw
Mr. S. Caffyn
Mr. and Mrs. H. Caffyn
Mrs. Maxwell Campbell
Miss Canaway
Mr. J. Cartner
Sir W. Chance, Bart.
Colonel and Mrs. S. R. Clarke
Miss S. Clements
Mr. and Mrs. Cole
Mr. and Mrs. Montague Colman
Mrs. Cooper
Mrs. Dance, William, James and Frank
Mr. J. Denman
Mrs. Denman
Mr. G. W. Denman
Mr. B. M. Drake
Mrs. A. J. Druce
Lady Fleetwood Edwards
A.E.
Mrs. Farquharson
Prebendary and Mrs. R. Fisher

Mr. Charles Fox
Mr. and Mrs. W. Garlick
Mr. and Mrs. H. Garlick
Mr. Gardner
The Misses Gibb
Miss K. Gray
The Misses Gray
Mr. and Mrs. Goodwin Green
Mr. A. J. Green
Mr. and Mrs. Herrington
Mr. H. S. Hotblack
Miss Huckett
Mr. and Mrs. F. Humphrey
Mrs. Jeffery, Jim, Tom and Steve
Mrs. Keep and family
Mr. A. Keyser
Sir A. Kleinwort, Bart.
Mr. S. Knight
Mr. A. W. Knight
The Misses L. A. & M. E. Knowles
Mr. A. C. Lampson
Mrs. Whitaker Lowndes
Miss Lowndes
Miss Maberly
Mr. and Mrs. Markwick and family
Mrs. Mertens
The Misses Mertens
Rev. R. H. C. Mertens
Mr. B. de M. Mertens
Mr. F. Meyer
Mrs. F. Meyer
Mr. W. E. Mitchell
Mr. J. and Miss E. Mitchell
Mr. and Mrs. D.C. and Miss Monro
Mrs. Morfee and family
Mr. J. S. Motion
Mr., Mrs. and Alfred Murrell
Mr. and Mrs. C. H. Neate
Miss Newboult
Miss M. A. Newman
Mr. and Mrs. G. Norris
Miss Oldcross
Miss Pattenden
Mrs. Pinder
Mr. R. C. Pinder
Mr. W. A. Pinder
Miss E. L. Plumb

Mr. H. J. Preston
Miss Priestman
Mrs. Reid
Miss Reid
A Resident
Mrs. M. Rhodes
Rev. Dr. Richards
Mr. and Mrs. H. Rowland
Mr. and Mrs. J. Rowland
Mrs. Henry Selby
Miss E. Shepherd
Mrs. Smith
Miss Smith
Mrs. Henry Schlesinger
Mr. H. E. Stewart
Mrs. H. E. Stewart
Miss D. J. Stewart
Mr. and Mrs. W. Stevens
Mr. F. Bentham Stevens
Mr. W. G. Stevens
Mr. T. I. Symons
Mr. and Mrs. J. Tester
Mr. G. Tester
Mr. C. Tester
Mrs. C. Tester
Mr. A. Tester
Mr. R. Tester
Mr. L. Tester
Mr. Stanley Towse
Miss L. Tidy
Miss M. Treagus
Mrs. Montagu Turner
Miss A. I. Turner
Mr. G. Vaughan
Mr. and Mrs. C. H. Waugh
Dr. A. E. and Mrs. Wells
Miss E. Whitford
Mr. W. P. White
Rev. Canon C. W. G. Wilson
Mr. and Mrs. Winder
Mrs. James Wood
Mrs. Worsley
Mr. R. S. L. Worsley
Mr. A. Young
Mrs. Young
Miss K. Young

BALANCE SHEET.

RECEIPTS.	£	s.	d.	EXPENDITURE.	£	s.	d.	£	s.	d.
To Subscriptions	737	8	0	ERECTION OF MEMORIAL—						
				Messrs. Dove Bros.	482	0	0			
				Messrs. W. Bainbridge Reynolds (Sword)	13	12	6			
				Messrs. F. Hounsell & Son (Inscriptions)	36	8	0			
								532	0	6
				SIR REGINALD BLOMFIELD, R.A.—						
				Architect's Fees				53	16	0
				S. KNIGHT & CO., LTD.—						
				Site Plan for Memorial, covering up Memorial prior to Unveiling	6	17	0			
				Steps to Memorial and Irregular Paving Surround and Turfing	32	8	0			
								39	5	0
				FACULTY—						
				Fees for Grant of				2	2	0
				MESSRS. CHARLES CLARKE LTD.—						
				Printing Appeal, Receipt Books, Announcements of Meetings, &c.	3	19	6			
				Printing Circulars and Tickets and Forms of Service for Dedication Ceremony	3	0	0			
				Report and Balance Sheets, List of Names Inscribed on Memorial and Envelopes for same ...	5	0	0			
								11	19	6
				MISCELLANEOUS ACCOUNTS—						
				H. Stevens & Sons				2	1	0
				H. Askew & Sons				1	2	0
				Postage, Writing Materials, &c., Cheque Book and Cheques ...				3	1	6
								645	7	6
				EARLIER DESIGN—						
				Mr. W. E. Tower — Architect's Fees	26	5	0			
				Messrs. Charles Clarke Ltd— Printing, &c.	15		6			
								27	0	6
								672	8	0
				Balance in Bank				65	0	0
	£737	8	0					£737	8	0

I have examined the Books and Vouchers relating to the above Account and compared the Balance with the Bank Pass Book and am of opinion that same appears to be correct.

November 15th, 1921.

W. T. C. RUST.

INSCRIPTION ON CUCKFIELD WAR MEMORIAL CROSS.

1914 - 1918.

Let us hold in grateful remembrance those whose names are here
recorded, who having left their homes at the call of King and
Country to fight for God and the Right, gave up their own lives
that others might live in freedom.

Frederick C. Anscombe	George Gibson	Ernest S. Pateman
John M. Ansell	Edward J. Hayward	Jesse Pelling
James Attree	Albert J. Henley	Alfred U. Pennifold
Ernest Attwater	Ambrose Henley	Charles W. Randell
Arthur James Ballard	Ernest Henley	Stuart K. Reid
Frank Bates	Frank Henley	William Rhodes
Jack Bates	Thomas Henley	James F. Ridley
George E. Bennett	Arthur Holden	Arthur Robinson
George E. Botting	Arnold W. Huckett	Frank S. Rowland
Thomas C. Bourne	Oliver S. Huckett	James Rowland
Alfred R. Burness	George Izzard	Sidney Scott
Cecil A. Bowell	Albert Keep	Albert E. Selby
William Bowley	Henry T. Knapp	Charles Selby
Joseph Card	Ernest Lander	Percy H. Selby
Hubert Cartner	William R. Lelliott	William G. Selby
Frank Chatfield	Mark Longhurst	Alfred E. Smith
Albert Chinnery	E. Whitaker Lowndes	Cyril R. Smith
Albert Croucher	Edward L. Lyon	Harry Smith
Thomas H. Dance	Joseph W. Markwick	G. Eric Stevens
Ellis A. Dancy	James Matthews	Harcourt C. Turner
William H. Dancy	Hugh G. Mertens	Horace Upton
Charles F. Doick	Thomas Mitchell	Nathan Upton
Harry Etherton	W. Holford Mitchell	Lawrence Upton
Wilfrid F. Fisher	William W. Mitchell	George W. Vickers
George Franks	David H. C. Monro	Charles H. Webber
Leonard Funnell	Percy E. Morfee	Edward Williams
Jesse Gander	George H. Murrell	A. Franklin Young

CUCKFIELD WAR MEMORIAL.

Unveiling & Dedication Ceremony,

Sunday, January 23rd, 1921.

ADMIT TO CHURCH.

*Please be seated by 2.45 p.m.—after this vacant seats
will be filled up as required.*

Invitation to the Unveiling and Dedication Ceremony

A Guard of Honour of ex-Service men, under the Command of
Major Ralph Stephenson Clarke was in position round the
Memorial & it was about 90 strong.

The Guard of Honour included with others: —

Will. Sisson	Charles Webber	Alfred Hillman
Walt. Angus	Albert Hawley	Reg. Hillman
H. C. Franklin	John Youngs	Herbert Vidler
C. A. Tyrrell	Will. Nye	Ernest Vidler
Cecil Cook	Ernest Lingley	Norman Bow..
Tom Cook	Albert Weber	Tom Newnham
Jack Bennett	Claude Selby	Tom Malins
Ern... Mays	Amos Turner	Reg. Chinnery
Stephen H. Knight	James Bruce	George Perry
William Knight	Frank Knight	Bert Avery
.. ..	Eric Hillman	Will. Robinson
Ed. McB. Mitchell	Robert Tester	Leon. Riches
Charles Randell	Walter Whitton	Chas. Riches
Arthur Hobbs	Percy Rist	F. Pelling
W. Slater	Jas Woodland	Charles Brigden
Harry Scurley	A. Tree	J. W. Scurr...
Horace Upton	Will. Jones	George Vidler
A. Beesley	O Baker	E. Billingsby
Chas. Marchant	Arthur Harding	Eli Rowland
Albert Marchant	Sidney Bruce	Will. Mewett
Herard Bennett	Frank Bolting	Tom Batchelor
Frank Pattenden	John Webb	Charles Slater.
Wm Hazelgrove jun.	W. S. Brookshaw	Thomas A. Avery

(Taken from the Church Log Book)

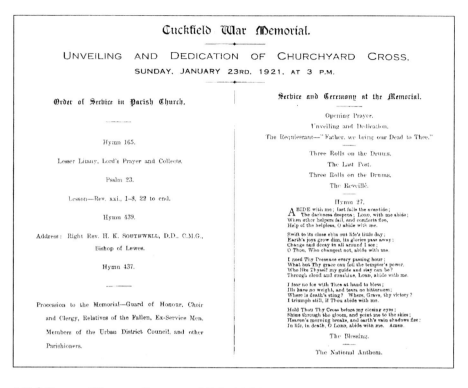

Cuckfield War Memorial.

UNVEILING AND DEDICATION OF CHURCHYARD CROSS.

SUNDAY, JANUARY 23RD, 1921, AT 3 P.M.

Order of Service in Parish Church.

Hymn 165.

Lesser Litany, Lord's Prayer and Collects.

Psalm 23.

Lesson—Rev. xxi., 1–8, 22 to end.

Hymn 439.

Address: Right Rev. H. K. SOUTHWELL, D.D., C.M.G.,
Bishop of Lewes.

Hymn 437.

Procession to the Memorial—Guard of Honour, Choir
and Clergy, Relatives of the Fallen, Ex-Service Men,
Members of the Urban District Council, and other
Parishioners.

Service and Ceremony at the Memorial.

Opening Prayer.

Unveiling and Dedication.

The Requiescant—"Father, we bring our Dead to Thee."

Three Rolls on the Drums.

The Last Post.

Three Rolls on the Drums.

The Reveillé.

Hymn 27.

ABIDE with me; fast falls the eventide;
The darkness deepens; Lord, with me abide;
When other helpers fail, and comforts flee,
Help of the helpless, O abide with me.

Swift to its close ebbs out life's little day;
Earth's joys grow dim, its glories pass away;
Change and decay in all around I see;
O Thou, Who changest not, abide with me.

I need Thy Presence every passing hour;
What but Thy grace can foil the tempter's power?
Who like Thyself my guide and stay can be?
Through cloud and sunshine, Lord, abide with me.

I fear no foe with Thee at hand to bless;
Ills have no weight, and tears no bitterness;
Where is death's sting? Where, Grave, thy victory?
I triumph still, if Thou abide with me.

Hold Thou Thy Cross before my closing eyes;
Shine through the gloom, and point me to the skies;
Heaven's morning breaks, and earth's vain shadows flee;
In life, in death, O Lord, abide with me. Amen.

The Blessing.

The National Anthem.

Mid-Sussex Times - January 27th 1921

CUCKFIELD WAR MEMORIAL

SUNDAY'S IMPRESSIVE DEDICATION CEREMONY
THROUGH SERVICE AND SACRIFICE TO VICTORY

In a few short months the glorious days of summer will return again and with them many visitors to Cuckfield to admire the beautiful old church and quaint tombstones of its ancient graveyard.

Every year this pilgrimage takes place, but this summer their gaze will fall on something new - a tall white column rising above the eighteenth century altar tombs and facing the South Downs - those immortal hills which have provided a subject for many a poet and prose writer.

They will know what this column - or Cross of Sacrifice - stands for before they read its inscription. It stands above the dust of bygone generations of Cuckfield, a white witness to future generations of the sacrifice made by local men in the Great War.

The octagonal portion of this 'stone of memorial' immediately below the column is filled on seven panels with the names of 81 men of Cuckfield who made the supreme sacrifice, and on the southernmost panel is this inscription-

1914 - 1918
Let us hold in grateful remembrance those whose names are here recorded, who having left their homes at the call of King and Country to fight for God and the Right, gave up their own lives that others might live in freedom.'

And what memories are stirred by a perusal of the names listed.

The task of unveiling the striking monument - a Cross of Sacrifice - was fittingly entrusted to Mrs Stevens and Mrs Fisher.

The former is the wife of Mr William Stevens, and the latter the wife of a former Vicar and a sister of the late Major Maberly. Each lost a son in the war - a son whose memory is dear and holy. The eyes of hundreds of people were upon them as they exposed the memorial to view, and it pleases us to think that just as these hundreds of people were thrilled by what they beheld and heard, so an 'unseen cloud of witnesses' was likewise moved and rejoiced because the men who had 'crossed over' had not been forgotten. As the service concluded a golden light shone in the sky, reminding one of the glory above the clouds and of the eternal happiness of those who, having borne their cross, had won their crown.

Cuckfield Parish Magazine - February 1921
THE WAR MEMORIAL

The most notable event of the month was the unveiling and dedication of the Cuckfield War Memorial on the afternoon of Sunday January 23rd, and it will long be remembered by us all. We were very fortunate in having such fine weather, and the service and ceremony were carried out in a way which was worthy of the occasion. We are much indebted to the Bishop of Lewes for his inspiring and helpful address and the Committee will doubtless wish to express their appreciation of the services of all who helped to make the proceedings both reverent and dignified. It was a matter of great satisfaction that so many of the ex-servicemen joined the Guard of Honour and so shewed their respect and esteem for their Fallen Comrades.

The Memorial is much admired, and when the inscription and the names have been blacked up, which will be done as soon as the stone is sufficiently dry, and the ground round the Memorial has been levelled and turfed, its beauty will be much increased.

Cuckfield Parish Magazine - March 1921
The War Memorial has been much improved by the levelling and turfing of the ground round it and by the laying down of a 'crazy paving'. While engaged in this work Mr Leonard Rhodes discovered a silver penny, which is probably of the reign of Henry 111 (1216 - 1272). It is an interesting relic of the past and it was possibly dropped by a workman engaged in building the south side of the Church, nearly 700 years ago.

MARBLE MEMORIAL INSIDE THE CHURCH

Cuckfield Parish Magazine - November 1920
Inside the Church are the cards bearing the names and other details of those who fell and it is known that it is the wish of many that this should be replaced by a memorial more worthy of them. This memorial will be placed inside the actual building where many of the men were baptised and confirmed and where they worshipped and where they were so often remembered in our prayers. The Vicar has already received a generous offer with regard to this memorial, and we hope that before long the work may be put in hand.

Cuckfield Parish Magazine - November 1921

ROLL OF HONOUR ON MEMORIAL
INSIDE THE CHURCH

On November 4th a Vestry Meeting was held at which formal approval was given to the design of a memorial tablet, of white Sicilian marble, to take the place of the Roll of Honour now on the south wall of the Church. The tablet will be the gift of an anonymous donor, (later named as Mrs Reid) and on it will be inscribed all the names of our Fallen that are on the big Memorial. We hope that the Faculty will soon be issued and then the work will be put in hand.

UNVEILING AND DEDICATION OF THE MEMORIAL INSIDE THE CHURCH

On St George's Day 1922, the Dean of Chichester unveiled and dedicated the inside war memorial. The memorial is the work of Messrs Hounsell and Sons and takes the place of the framed lists of names surmounted by the trophy of flags which has been on the wall for the past five years. The memorial is the gift of Mrs Reid of 'Mill Hall' and has been beautifully executed and much admired.

The names are the same as those on the public memorial in the Churchyard, but they are arranged according to the year in which the men died.

There are 81 names -

1914	6 men died
1915	18 men died
1916	3 men died
1917	25 men died and
1918	19 men died

Above the list of names is the inscription -

'Let us remember with gratitude and affection those who fell in the service of their country, 1914 - 1918'

and below the names are written the beautiful lines of Mr. L. Binyon:-

'They shall not grow old as we that are left grow old:
Age shall not weary them, nor the years condemn.
At the going down of the sun and in the morning,
We will remember them.'

MEMORIAL PANELS IN THE QUEEN'S HALL, CUCKFIELD

The inscription on the central section of the memorial tablets reads -

ON THESE TABLETS ARE RECORDED THE NAMES OF ALL THOSE MEN OF CUCKFIELD WHO AT THE CALL OF THEIR KING AND COUNTRY LEFT THEIR HOMES TO FIGHT FOR JUSTICE AND FREEDOM IN THE GREAT WAR 1914 - 1919

Four hundred and sixty men from Cuckfield went to war. Following some of the home-coming celebrations held in Cuckfield Park on 19th July 1919 by Mr Preston, there was a balance of £21.00. This money was spent on inscribing the name, on the wooden panels shown above, of every man who served. (source - 'A Chronicle of Cuckfield' by Maisie Wright)

Mid-Sussex Times - 22nd July 1920

RICHARD WORSLEY RECREATION GROUND CUCKFIELD OBTAINS ITS HEART'S DESIRE - A PICTURESQUE RECREATION GROUND

MRS. WORSLEY'S MUNIFICENT GIFT

Mrs Worsley of Broxmead, bought the field behind the Queen's Hall from Sir Merrick Burrell and presented it to the inhabitants of Cuckfield as a recreation ground. She wished it to be known as the 'Richard Worsley Recreation Ground' in order that the memory of her late husband might be kept alive and respected. She also wished it to be in remembrance of the men who went from Cuckfield to serve in the Great War. She also donated £400.00 to partly defray the cost of laying out the ground.

THE KENNEDY MEMORIAL

In the Bell Tower of Holy Trinity Church, on the South wall, is the Kennedy Memorial erected privately by Lady Kennedy in memory of her three sons. The family lived at 'Burnt House', Cuckfield. It consists of a large marble colonnaded memorial depicting three figures in military uniform and containing three plaques.

The first is dedicated to Paul Adrian Kennedy

The second plaque is dedicated to Archibald Edward Kennedy

The third plaque is dedicated to John Patrick Francis Kennedy

Across the bottom is written 'In thankful remembrance of their lives and proud remembrance of their death, their loving mother.'

APPENDIX

CHURCHES IN CUCKFIELD DURING THE WAR

There were four places of worship in Cuckfield between 1914 and 1918.

HOLY TRINITY CHURCH

Holy Trinity Church is the large Parish Church founded over 900 years ago. In the foreground is the war memorial, The Cross of Sacrifice. Any soldier who died at home is buried in this cemetery.

CONGREGATIONAL CHAPEL

The Congregational Chapel was established in Broad Street near the High Street in 1821. It ceased to be a church in the mid 20th century and is now offices, although the exterior remains very similar.

Mid-Sussex Times - 5th June 1917
Honours Roll
The Congregational Church Honours Roll is being revised and through the kindness of a friend is to be framed and placed in the church porch. An Honours Roll of all the old Sunday School Scholars now serving with

the Army and Navy has been placed in the schoolroom and is an object of interest to all visitors.

Note - I have been unable to establish whether this record still exists.

There were two small chapels at opposite ends of the town to serve local residents but which were still a part of the Parish and Ministered by Holy Trinity Church.

THE MISSION CHURCH ANSTY, LATER CALLED ST JOHN'S CHAPEL

The main part of the first building, made of iron, was opened on 29th November 1883. It was not licensed by the Bishop until 1885 from when it was named St John's Chapel.

A new brick built Mission Church of St John's, Ansty, seen above, was dedicated on Friday 10th December 1909 by the Bishop of Lewes. It was erected by Miss Best in memory of her father who lived at Harvest Hill. It closed on 25th December 2000.

BROOK STREET MISSION ROOMS

The Mission Room in Brook Street opened on Advent Sunday 1879 and continued serving the population at that end of the town until the 1960's. Following the rebuilding of the Mission Church at Ansty in 1909, part of that building was taken to Brook Street and set up there as a Class Room adjoining the little Mission Church there.

MAIN SOURCES OF REFERENCE

COMMONWEALTH WARGRAVES COMMISSION

This organisation holds the records of those who died serving their country and much more interesting information besides, such as the location and descriptions of cemeteries.

Their address is 2, Marlow Road, Maidenhead, Berkshire, SL6 7DX U.K.or go to **www.cwgc.co.uk**

CUCKFIELD MAGAZINES AND LOG BOOKS

The Parish magazines provided me with an insight into many aspects of life in the town and its people at that time. **The log books** were compiled over the years by Cannon Cooper 1888 to 1909, by Canon Robert Fisher from 1909 to 1915 and from 1915 on, by Canon Charles William Goodall Wilson, all Vicars of Holy Trinity Church. In addition to his own words, Canon Wilson added posters, pamphlets, letters, prints, programmes, photographs, wartime church services, welcome home events and other memorabilia of Cuckfield and its residents at that time. I am extremely grateful to the present Vicar of Cuckfield, the Reverend Nicholas Wetherall, for giving me permission to use this information.

CUCKFIELD MUSEUM

Situated upstairs in the Queen's Hall, Cuckfield, the musem contains many interesting artefacts concerning the history of the town. It also holds the original photographs of the soldiers, and I am grateful for permission to include copies of these in the book.

THE MID-SUSSEX TIMES NEWSPAPER

The Mid-Sussex Times was published weekly throughout the First World War and continues to the present day. Copies of the newspaper from the war years include excellent accounts of the people from Cuckfield who were serving their country both at home and abroad, letters the men sent home to their families and records of their activities. Full accounts of the church services held, other events in Cuckfield during the war, and the subsequent celebrations, are all covered in detail. I am very grateful to the present editor, Grahame Campbell for giving me permission to include this material which is of such local and national interest.

Copies of the newspaper can be read on film at some local libraries, one year (52 editions) per film. Telephone the library to check they have just what you need and to book a time to use the film reader. The films may also be purchased from the British Newspaper Library, Colindale Avenue, London, NW9 5HE Tel. 020 7412 7351

www.ancestry.co.uk
To discover more about anyone who lived between 1841 and 1901 look at the relevant census. They are taken every ten years. Some local libraries stock censuses for their area; telephone to enquire. I used the **www.ancestry.co.uk** web site to trace the soldiers and their families and I am grateful for their help.

INDEX

Ballard, George 75
Ballard, Jane 75
Ballard, Rose Florence 75
Bannister (Mrs) 29, 321
Barge, Henry Lowthian 308
Barnes, E. 283
Barnett, E. 301
Barnett, H. 301
Barnett, H. A. 245
Barracks Cottages 106, 250
Barrow, Albert 4
Barrow H. 283
Barrow, Walter 5
Barrow, William 4, 308
Bartlett (Mrs) 236
Bartlett, Lewis Frederick 20
Barton, F. C. 69
Batchelor, Thomas 24, 283, 334
Bates, Bessie 77, 78
Bates, E 80
Bates, Edward 80
Bates, Frank 18, 77, 78, 80, 332
Bates, H. 330
Bates, Jack 55, 56, 77, 78, 80, 332
Bates, Maggie 77
Bates, Marguerite Ethel 80,
Bates Norman 77
Bates, Sarah E 77, 80
Bates, William James 77, 78, 80
Beale (Major) 11
Beale (Miss) 164
Beard, Frederick George 5, 245, 246, 284, 308,
Beech Farm 87
Beeching, A. 7, 10, 316
Beeny, F. H. 208
Beesley, A. 334
Bell, C. 301
Bennett, Alfred 82
Bennett, Anne 82
Bennett, Ellen 82

Bennett, George Ernest 5, 18, 82, 332
Bennett, Harold 334
Bennett, Jack 245, 334
Bennett, John 83, 309
Bennett, M (Miss) 83, 330
Bennett, William 245, 309
Berly, (Miss) 117
Berly, A. H. (Lieutenant Colonel) 246, 310, 330
Berry, C 301
Berry, Frank 5, 283
Best (Miss) 117, 137, 330, 345
Betts, C. 301
Bevan, B.Y. 7, 19, 46, 50, 57, 61, 82, 223, 249, 280, 288, 304, 329, 330
Bevan, Enid 273 310, 321, 367
Bevan, Richard. A. xi, 7, 223
Bigg, Rosina 90, 138
Biggs (Mrs) 236
Billingsley, G. E. 301, 334
Binyon, L. 339
Birkinshaw, E. 330
Bishop of Stepney 20, 50
Bist, P. 285
Black , Douglas 237
Black, Leslie 237
Blackburn, H. 284
Black Prince HMS 113
Blackshall, F. 283
Blackstone, D 301
Blackstone, G 301
Blake, E.H. (Rev) 50
Blake, Walter 246
Bleach E. H 284.
Bleach, F 79, 285
Blowers, Charlotte 101
Bocquet, F. H. 235
Bone, Jack 118, 246, 247
Bone, Mary 118, 330
Bone, Norman 334

Ockenden Lane 75, 77
Old Beech Farm, Henmead 71
Oldcross (Miss) 330
Old Mill High Bridge 72
Old Thatch Cottage 230
Osbourne, G. 283
Osbourne (Miss) 117
Owen, Frank 316

P

Packham, May 367
Page, A. 302
Page, J. 284
Palmer, Leonard Adolphus 262, 283
Palmer, Leonard 5, 262
Parker, F. 284
Pateman, Alice 178
Pateman, Arthur 178
Pateman, Eliza 178
Pateman, Samuel Lewis 178
Pateman, Samuel Ernest 178, 332
Pattenden, F. (Miss) 83, 330
Pattenden, Henry Frank 262, 285, 334
Payne (Miss) 164
Peace Celebrations 291, 292, 293
Peace Treaty 286
Peacheys Nurseries 232
Peacock, Mrs 117
Pearce, Ellen. M. 179
Pearce, E. H. (Rev) 13
Pearce, Flora 179
Pearce, Frederick 179, 246
Pearce, Frederick James 179
Pearce, Jane Annie 179
Peel, Charles Lennox (Sir) 218
Pelling, Flora 180
Pelling, Frederick 180, 302, 334
Pelling, George 180
Pelling, Hannah 180
Pelling, Harry 180

Pelling, Jesse 55, 56, 180, 332
Pennifold (Mrs) 117
Pennifold, Alfred Unwins 41, 181, 332
Pennifold, Emily 181
Pennifold, Hannah 117, 181
Pennifold, John 117, 181, 302
Pennifold, L. (Miss) 117
Pennifold, Rhoda 181
Pennifold, William 181
Percy Cottage 275
Perry George 247, 302, 334
Perry, W. 302
Philpot, C. 47
Pickwell Lane 99
Pierce, A. R. 262
Pinder, R. C. 237, 302, 330
Pinder, W. A. 237, 330
Pix, A. 60, 283
Plumb, E. L. (Miss) 330
Portway, Ivy 49, 60
Portway, J. T. 263
Post Office Rifles 12, 78, 79, 83, 163, 181, 275, 316, 320
Pratt (Mr) 157
Preston, Arthur 117, 340
Preston, Emily 117
Preston, H. J. 330
Preston, Harry (Mrs) 117
Priestman, (Miss) 330
Pulley, (Mr) 13
Purkiss, (Mrs) 236
Purvey (Lance-Sergeant) 236

Q

Quaife, Ada R. 183
Quaife, Alfred 183
Quaife, Harold 183
Quaife, James 183
Quaife, Mary R. 183
Quaife, Stanley 28, 183

ABOUT THE AUTHOR

Shirley Bond moved to Cuckfield at the age of four and attended Cuckfield Church School until the age of eleven having been taught by Miss Lilian Gibb, Miss Tidy, Miss May Packham, Mr Arthur Rapley and Miss Stevens.

She was a member of the 1st Cuckfield Brownie pack led by Miss Enid Bevan and later the 1st Cuckfield Girl Guide Company when the leader was Mrs Gillian Mitchell. She was also a member of the church choir, the tennis club and the thriving amateur dramatic society.

With her parents, Basil and Edith Sangster who lived in Broad Street, she was a keen member of the Cuckfield Society, and her father produced a film strip presentation with numerous pictures and text describing the history of the town. He worked with Maisie Wright on her book, 'Cuckfield - An Old Sussex Town', and provided the original photographs for that.

After marrying in Holy Trinity Church, Cuckfield, Shirley moved away, but still enjoys visiting the town as often as possible.

She may be contacted on info@woodlandspublishing.co.uk